Why France?

Why France?

American Historians Reflect on an Enduring Fascination

With an Afterword by Roger Chartier

EDITED BY LAURA LEE DOWNS
AND STÉPHANE GERSON

CORNELL UNIVERSITY PRESS
ITHACA AND LONDON

The editors wish to thank John Ackerman, Alain Boureau, Alison Block Gerson, Fabrice Rozié, and Frédéric Viguier for their encouragement and support.

This work, published as part of the program of aid for publication, received support from the French Ministry of Foreign Affairs and the Cultural Service of the French Embassy in the United States.

Cet ouvrage publié dans le cadre du programme d'aide à la publication bénéficie du soutien du Ministère des Affaires Etrangères et du Service Culturel de l'Ambassade de France représenté aux Etats-Unis.

Copyright © 2007 by Cornell University

First published 2007 by Cornell University Press

Printed in the United States of America

Design by Scott Levine

Library of Congress Cataloging-in-Publication Data

Why France? : American historians reflect on an enduring
    fascination / with an afterword by Roger Chartier ; edited by
    Laura Lee Downs and Stéphane Gerson.
        p. cm.
    Includes bibliographical references.
    ISBN-13: 978-0-8014-4414-2 (cloth : alk. paper)
    ISBN-10: 0-8014-4414-4 (cloth : alk. paper)
    1. Historians—United States. 2. Americans—France.
3. France—History—Study and teaching (Higher)—United
States. 4. France—Historiography. I. Downs, Laura Lee,
1955– . II. Gerson, Stéphane.
    DC36.985.U5W49 2006
    944.0072'02—dc22
                                                    2006026587

Cloth printing   10 9 8 7 6 5 4 3 2 1

Contents

Why France?

Introduction

Laura Lee Downs and Stéphane Gerson

Why France? Answers will come, but first the question. It forced itself upon us in the spring of 2004, in Paris. To celebrate its fiftieth anniversary, the leading association of American historians of France was holding its annual meeting on the banks of the Seine—far from the college towns in which it usually convenes. Hundreds of American historians descended on the French capital. In the National Library of France, they gave papers and attended roundtables; they rekindled friendships with American and European colleagues; they milled about, discussing their research and France and other things, too. Their voices echoed in the cavernous halls of the Library, an austere structure of glass and metal that rarely inspires such exuberance. All of this lasted for four days and then, as suddenly as they had arrived, these historians scattered. They returned to their campuses or headed for archives and reading rooms where they continued the serious work of writing French history.

The meeting was impressive in its size, its intellectual heft, and its level of energy.[1] It made tangible France's longstanding resonance within the American historical profession. The United States may not have furnished France with an observer of Tocqueville's repute, but over the past half-century thousands of Americans have devoted their careers to the country—and oftentimes more than that. They have spent months and years there, written thousands of books and articles on French history, created journals, associations, and conferences. When other summer visitors head for Riviera beaches or Alpine trails, these historians scour dusty archives and obscure libraries. They have both made signal contributions to this scholarship and turned French history into a leading field of study in American universities. American history, by contrast, remains a minor field in France.

One understands why most French historians study their own past and why French publishers release countless books on French history and identity. But Americans? France, it is true, now ranks fifth among foreign investors in the American stock market. French is also the third most common foreign language in the United States (after Spanish and Chinese). Still, Paris has not constituted a leading strategic partner for Washington in decades. Nor has the country furnished the United States with a significant immigrant population. American historians of Germany long had names like Stern and Krieger, but Dupuis and Legrands are hard to find among their colleagues in French history.[2]

All of this intrigued us. We wanted to know who these historians were, what paths—intellectual and professional, personal and political—had led them toward France, and what later sustained them there (aside from the food). We wanted to find out whether these paths had crossed and redirected one another. We wondered whether initial questions faded or changed, and new ones emerged, as their relationships with France grew thicker and both France and the United States underwent historical mutations. "Why France?" thus led to "What France?": the country that these historians imagined, encountered, and depicted; the meanings and values they attached to France and its past; the ties they forged with the country and its residents—French, American, and other. We were especially interested in the changing stakes that have surrounded France in American intellectual life and society since World War II. Two kinds of evolution come together: the evolution of individual relationships to France over the course of lives and careers and the evolution of collective relationships over a half-century of American and French history.

These relationships—both positive and critical—provide a distinctive perspective on twentieth-century France. These historians saw it all, from the inside and from a patently American perspective: Charles de Gaulle and the country's postwar reconstruction, the end of the French colonial empire, May 1968, electoral victories by the Socialists and by the extreme right, anxieties about America and globalization, the rise and fall of French theory. Working and living in France, they have also experienced firsthand the forces of immobility and change that run through French society: its class structures, its understandings of sexual difference, its prevailing attitudes toward Jewish or Muslim residents.

‡

This book is thus about France. But it is also about the social, intellectual, and cultural contours of the United States from the Cold War to the present day. The profiles of those Americans who chose to study France illuminate a facet of our country's social and intellectual history and track the transformation of a profession. Likewise, the moments at which France resonated for these scholars reveal inherently American concerns and aspirations. As Emerson famously put it, "a foreign country is a point of comparison, wherefrom to judge [one's] own. . . . We go to Europe to be Americanized."[3] *Why France?* also adds a chapter to the long history of America's interactions with what was once called "the Old World."

Similar questions could be asked about England or Germany, but America's relationship with its "sister republic" across the Atlantic has a flavor all its own. "France occupies a place apart in the United States," the essayist André Siegfried commented in 1927. "No other country . . . is more passionately loved," and none "is more disparaged or more harshly condemned. It seems that there is always an excess in either direction, that either illusion or deep disappointment is alternately dominant." Let us add frustration with a country that, more than any other in Europe, has challenged its transatlantic ally over the past sixty years by charting an autonomous foreign policy. Exasperation with France has led again and again to its denigration as effeminate and frivolous, irrational and unbending.[4]

These charges and stereotypes have resurfaced with rare ferocity since the end of the Cold War. First came disputes over tariffs, imports of bananas, exports of Hollywood films. Then followed accusations that France had "betrayed" America over the Iraq War and abetted its enemies. French fries were renamed, Bordeaux poured into gutters. Finally, there were American denunciations of an inherently anti-Semitic country and post-Katrina schadenfreude in the face of riots in French suburbs—proof that holier-than-thou France, too, struggled with its own ethnic and social strife. Such language is over the top, no doubt, and it should not mask the less visible cooperation between Washington and Paris. Still, it would be easier to dismiss were it less pervasive in mainstream American culture and foreign policy: while the first knows little about France nowadays, the second derides the "Old Europe."[5] No one blinks when, to advertise a special about the French Revolution, the History Channel declares: "For two hours, it won't kill you to love the French."

This is the most visible facet of the Franco-American relationship these days, but not the only one. Cyclist Lance Armstrong recently told journalists that "I have always defended France and its ideas and, believe me, I must be one of the only people in the United States to do so." Maybe so, but other Americans have grappled with the country's complexities, none more so than these historians of France. Indeed, there was a striking disconnect during that Paris conference between their quiet efforts to explain France and the shrill anti-French invective emanating from other quarters. Three decades ago, a French observer presented the "sympathetic curiosity with regard to French affairs" typical of the historians collected here as a source of renewed Franco-American understanding.[6] One need not go that far to observe that, from Philip Augustus to the Vichy regime, from gender to postcolonialism, American scholarship has shaped France's understandings of its own past.[7] For this reason, these historians provide a unique window into a Franco-American connection that, frayed as it is, requires thoughtful and measured scrutiny. They help us understand the two-way relationship between intellectual milieus and fractious international relations.[8]

✣

There are many ways to write about this phenomenon. Analytical articles are one, and scholars have written several, typically from a high conceptual ground and with particular attention to political and intellectual trends.[9] We have opted for a different but complementary course: autobiographical essays that blend personal reminiscence, intellectual memoir, and critical analysis. While some American historians of France have written about their encounters with France, their reflections remain scattered.[10] The sixteen essays in this collection, in contrast, make up a sustained inquiry that is both idiosyncratic and collective.

It is idiosyncratic because each essay showcases individual motivations and opens a discrete window onto the place of France within the American imagination. The contributors were not given a template or asked for exhaustive accounts of their career or told to ponder the state of their field (although some chose to do so). Instead, they were invited to explain how and why they became historians of France, to reflect on the ways in which they have interacted with and represented France, and to probe their fluctuating relationships with the country. This book thus revolves around stories that, by virtue of being anchored in specific places and times, capture this phenomenon in its diversity and human dimensions. Illustrative rather than representative, these stories relate the experiences of historians from three generations, men and women who differ in their geographical and social origins, their approach to history, and their eminence.[11] The authors rarely generalize from their personal experiences or speak on behalf of this or that school or generation. Instead, they present singular itineraries in which rational decisions and intellectual arcs figure alongside serendipitous encounters and emotional responses. At the same time, the authors contribute to a collective inquiry. The whole may yield insights, however suggestive, that the parts cannot. This collection of essays, presented chronologically (according to date of Ph.D.), links individual motivations to larger trends and developments as it moves between the past and the present, the personal and the collective.

But this volume is equally about these men and women themselves. If the writing of history is always a form of autobiography (as some claim), then it behooves historians to reflect on the intellectual, political, and affective facets of their scholarship. Often neglected in the name of objectivity, the personal dimension surfaces in these essays as one ingredient among many in the alchemy of scholarship, neither autonomous nor marginal.[12] "History thrives in measure as the experiences of each historian differ from that of his fellows," the historian J. H. Hexter proposed a half-century ago. Countless historians have written memoirs since the eighteenth century, yet such introspection— all the more essential for people who study countries other than their own— has not come easily. At the risk of generalizing, one could say that historians view their craft as a shared rather than an individual endeavor and that, more than literary critics or anthropologists, they are reticent to speak about themselves, theorize about what they do, and draw broad conclusions from their particular experiences. When Lewis P. Curtis invited fifty-two American historians to pen autobiographical essays on their craft in 1970, thirty-seven turned him down. One replied that "this kind of self-consciousness . . . [is] rather offensive, from both the scholarly and the aesthetic point of view." Another explained that "one somehow recoils from looking too deeply into one's own soul. Who knows what one would find?"[13]

If only four historians declined to participate in *Why France?*, it is partly because, while the unease persists, the profession has grown more comfortable with self-revelation during the intervening decades. Historians now live in a society that is obsessed with the self and operate in an intellectual world that values individual "subjects" as much as collective or impersonal forces. Questions about the impact of one's vantage point and subjectivity on one's craft and depictions of the past have become legitimate. It is increasingly difficult to hide under a veneer of pure detachment what happens behind the scenes, in the kitchen of history.[14] Memoirs and interviews with historians are increasingly numerous, as are autobiographical collections. There are now volumes by historians from the working class and by historians of refugee origin, volumes by Jewish historians, by women, and by African Americans. Besides recounting vocations and careers, they typically portray shared journeys, document struggles for recognition or justice, and "make public what had heretofore been private" or silenced by academic norms.[15] Identity politics are often part of the equation.

Why France? focuses, however, on an object of study—a place that is both real and imagined—and on individuals who made it their own in different ways.[16] Its recourse to critical autobiography also responds to a persisting divide between the academic and non-academic worlds. American historians of France seldom speak publicly about issues of broader cultural or political relevance.[17] This includes the Franco-American relationship. And yet, as Herrick Chapman puts it in his essay, France is "too implicated in our common future to leave to pundits and politicians the job of defining 'the French' for the rest of us." Shunning footnotes and jargon, the contributors to this collection thus intervene in a public conversation regarding America's relationship with France and, hence, the world beyond its borders.

Our focus on a country and autobiography is not without risks: romantic images of France or oneself, a vision of historical research that revolves around nation-states alone, and naïve confidence in the ability of memory to recover personal and collective experiences. Autobiography may also end up fashioning coherence and unified selves out of selected threads of the past. Several contributors confess that they were tempted to write stories of pure happenstance or overdetermination.[18] Still, after-the-fact narratives are instructive in themselves, especially in what they keep in and what they leave out (in this case, sustained reflection on how an affiliation with France might play into class relations and impart social status in the United States). Such narratives can also reveal patterns, thematic lines, or motivations that had previously escaped attention. Without pining for an idealized France or untangling a relationship woven in myths alone, the essays that follow offer rich if fleeting glimpses into a "France" that is experienced at the confluence of work and life. Some contributors define themselves as European or comparative historians; some believe that national histories are bound to fade away in a globalized world.[19] But they also agree that, for more than half a century, American historical writing has entailed deep knowledge of specific places. In cases such as ours, it has also involved—and still involves, at least for now—distinctive forms of cross-pollination and new incarnations of a familiar type: the American abroad.

✠

Until the advent of mass tourism in the mid–twentieth century, interest in France—let alone admiration for the country—concerned but a minority of

Americans: upper-crust East Coast residents, southern gentry, and, by the late nineteenth century, members of the upper middle class.[20] New immigrants were too busy fleeing the social strictures that Europe represented and integrating into the New World to devote much attention to the Old. Still, some Americans made their way to France.

The diplomats Franklin and Jefferson, Adams and Morris arrived in the late eighteenth century, and they were soon joined by other travelers. Scientists and persons of independent means encountered doctors and art students perfecting their training; businessmen came in search of new opportunities; journalists filed dispatches for American newspapers. Thirty-thousand Americans traveled to Paris between 1814 and 1848, mostly men at first, later women too. That number went up as trains and steamships made travel easier, as leisure time became more plentiful and new destinations such as spas grew more inviting. Students, too, made the journey. By the 1930s, there were "home study courses for European travel" on American campuses, guided school trips to France, undergraduate study-abroad programs, and a course in French civilization for foreigners at the Sorbonne (with tuition but no exams or assignments). The Wilsonian spirit of American internationalism and intellectual exchange met an official French campaign to create Francophile elites in the United States—and lessen German intellectual supremacy—by bringing French culture to campuses and *alliances françaises*.[21] Artists and writers likewise flocked to France throughout the nineteenth century, all the more so after the Civil War—and Gilded Age collectors followed in their wake. They returned to Paris after each world war to create mythic expatriate communities—abodes of the modern—in Montmartre and on the Left Bank. Saul Bellow once recalled that by 1948, writers, artists, and students mixed with "cathedral lovers, refugees from the South and the midwest, ex-soldiers on the G.I. Bill, sentimental pilgrims" and also "adventurers, black marketeers, smugglers, would-be bon vivants, bargain hunters, bubbleheads." Julia Child arrived the same year.[22]

Some Americans ended up in France, while others chose to go there. Bellow suggests some reasons why, but key elements of this relationship were in place already with Thomas Jefferson, that upholder of rugged agrarian democracy who nonetheless thrived in the lively cultural mingle of Paris. There was practical curiosity and a quest for individual and collective self-improvement, which led the envoy to seek innovative techniques for himself and the young American republic. There was the Francophilia of gentlemen and ladies who, having learned French at home and at school, could rhapsodize about France's historical and artistic riches, its esteem for intellectual pursuits, its culinary pleasures, and its "politeness of the general manners," all of which would benefit provincial America. But there was also offended republican virtue, dismayed by an unjust monarchy and endemic poverty, skeptical of France's ability to generate true freedom, appalled by aristocratic decadence and women hunting "pleasure in the streets" of a depraved capital.[23] Ultimately, Jefferson captures the ambivalence—a "happy inconsistency," as one scholar put it—of Americans who conjured up positive and negative images of France and the French to outline the needs, simple domestic virtues, and social opportunities of their own exceptional democracy.[24]

Innumerable books have examined the ways in which American visions of France evolved between Jefferson and Vincente Minnelli's *An American in Paris* in the 1950s. Some show how elite and later middle-class Americans came to France to acquire the patina of taste and fashion their femininity or virility. Others emphasize the emergence, in the late nineteenth century, of a picture of quaint, organic France—a nostalgia-fueled respite from the noise and dust of American modernity. Still others trace the turn from self-improvement to recreation and Parisian pleasure and freedom as alternatives to American conformity, standardization, or racism. The poet Hart Crane's 1929 postcard from Paris rivals Bellow's list in its powers of evocation: "Dinners, soirées, poets, erratic millionaires, painters, translations, lobsters, absinthe, music, promenades, oysters, sherry, aspirin, pictures, Sapphic heiresses, editors, books, sailors. *And how!*"[25]

Few of these Americans escaped, however, Jefferson's happy inconsistency and idealized visions of France. Few failed to find France—at once familiar and alien—a good place to be a foreigner and think about Americanness. And few achieved, or even sought, what Edith Wharton called a true "exchange of experience" with France and French "ways" in all their contradictions.[26]

It is against this backdrop that, around 1950, American historians began to travel en masse to France. Crossing the Atlantic on a liner to sift through old documents—this was a new notion. But an American field of European history had been taking form during the preceding decades. For much of the nineteenth century, history mattered little to a country that looked toward a shared future rather than the past.[27] The individuals who did write history— Puritan clergymen, lay officials, and amateurish patricians—produced literary and romantic works infused with religious language and visions of American destiny. Curiosity for distant countries was slim. This changed between the 1870s and 1920s. To meet the needs of an increasingly urban and industrial country, higher education was transformed into a center of undergraduate teaching, professional graduate training, and specialized research. European history benefited from this surge in liberal arts courses and German-style research seminars.

It also benefited from a growing, though by no means universal, sense of common origin or connection between the United States and Western Europe: European history as an early chapter in a story of American freedom or—following World War I—a story of shared interests and destiny. "It is the historian's business to tie Europe and America together in the popular mind," declared the president of the American Historical Association in 1922. Nearly ten percent of the Association's 2,800 members studied European history, and, after 1914, they gravitated toward Great Britain and France rather than bellicose Germany. As German science gave way to French culture, French became the leading language taught in American high schools. Likewise, the French Enlightenment and Revolution were bedrocks of the new Western Civilization college courses that, from 1919 on, would assimilate new immigrants and prove the superiority of Western rationality, progress, and freedom over barbarism—Bolshevik and other.[28]

Only after World War II, however, did French history become an independent scholarly field and a career. Earlier trends intensified. University enrollments and faculty sizes skyrocketed, and so did funding for programs in Western (and American) civilization. The country needed to understand the Cold War world and build collective security around the "Atlantic Community," understood as a political alliance, a democratic dike against totalitarianism, and a framework for historical study.[29] Area studies programs and European history both took off, the latter breaking into nation-based associations that created their own journals and conferences. British history was in front, followed by Russia, France, and Germany. "Much of the solid work of research and of synthesis on European history, literature, art is being accomplished in the universities of the United States," declared the Yale-based president of the new French History Society, founded in New York in 1950.[30] The president's confidence in American scholarship matters more here than his overemphatic assessment, but growing numbers of Americans were indeed launching careers as professional historians of France. They made up between five and seven percent of the profession's ranks during the following decades. While male Wasps continued to dominate, there was a significant influx of women, Jews (some of refugee origin), and other minorities in the 1960s. These historians embarked on ambitious and highly specialized research projects— on the Middle Ages and the French Revolution, French socialism and paths of modernization. Regardless of the topic, they now made their way to France for yearlong or summer stays. The country and its archives beckoned. Thanks to a strong dollar, Fulbright grants, generous sabbatical policies, and jet service (launched in 1958), both grew ever more accessible in the 1960s and 1970s.[31]

By then, claimed Bellow, France was no longer the scene on which "the greatest problems of existence might be represented." American artists and writers were finding other destinations, leaving but tourists and terrorists in Paris. Well, not only. Alongside advertising executives and department store wholesale buyers, scholars were now a fixture.[32] Willingly or not, historians had taken on the mantle of Jefferson and Wharton. During the decades that followed, they would both walk in their footsteps and chart their own singular relationships with France and the French.

✢

> "The big ocean liner, snow white, with two red and black slanting funnels, lay at anchor, attracting seagulls. The sea was calm, the lens of the sky was set at infinity. The coastline—low green hills and the dim outlines of stone houses lying in pockets of mist—was three pale French colors, a brocade borrowed from some museum. . . . He studied the stone houses. They were more distinct now. The mist was rising. . . . The light splintered and the hills and houses were rainbow-edged, as though a prism had been placed in front of his eyes. The prism was tears. Some anonymous ancestor, preserved in his bloodstream or assigned to cramped quarters somewhere in the accumulation of inherited identities that went by his name, had suddenly taken over; somebody looking out of the porthole of a ship on a July morning and recognizing certain characteristic features of his homeland, of a place that is Europe and not America, wept at all he did not know he remembered."

> —WILLIAM MAXWELL, *The Château* (1961)

In the summer of 1948, when Harold Rhodes peered from his porthole at the Norman coastline around Cherbourg, traces of the recent war were everywhere to be seen and felt—in the streets filled with hollow, bombed-out buildings; in the train stations lying half in ruins; in the faces of children, thin and pale in their black school smocks; in the eyes of the adults who had lived through it all. All across France, the American visitor came face to face with a kind of penury that would make Europe stand in stark contrast to the ease and comfort of American plenty for at least another decade.

Yet within and around the gnawing poverty lay a particular kind of good that the violence of war had not destroyed, a good that the sixteen contributors to this volume might recognize in Harold Rhodes's sudden awareness of "all he did not know he remembered." For not long after the fictional

Mr. Rhodes set off on his voyage of discovery, the first of our authors, John Baldwin, left a world that Rhodes's creator, Illinois-born writer William Maxwell, knew very well, that of the midwestern American middle class at mid–twentieth century. Coming of age at the end of a war that had brought the United States out of its worst economic crisis and to new heights of prosperity, John Baldwin confronted the "otherness" of Europe at a time when European dependence on American largess had never been so great, at a time when the standard contrast between the two continents, captured by the well-worn binary opposition "European sophistication/American naïveté," was cast in dramatic, almost paradoxical relief by the stunning contrast between European poverty and American abundance. For despite its ruins and hunger; its threadbare clothing and cold, comfortless houses and apartments; its scratchy refusal of American occupation in the aftermath of war in favor of a rapid reassertion of national autonomy, France and its cultural riches continued to fascinate, drawing young Americans away from the New World and back toward the Old.

While rarely evoked in detail by our contributors, the particular forms that Europe's postwar penury took in France until well into the 1960s constitutes a key aspect in the mise-en-scène of the young American scholar's arrival in France, a part of the unbridgeable gulf of difference that yawned between the comfortable world left behind and the difficult one that loomed ahead. Comfortable because known, comfortable because there is no language problem— these two aspects of the comforts of home receive explicit treatment in the essays that follow. But one essential element in the evolution of those Franco-American relationships is the extraordinary movement of France (and, indeed, of all Western Europe) from the grinding poverty of the 1940s and early 1950s to the remarkable prosperity of the late 1960s and beyond.[33] In reading chronologically, from John Baldwin to our youngest contributor, Todd Shepard, one cannot help but notice that the element of struggle with a materially poorer way of life gradually falls away from these essays, first fading with those contributors who spent their formative research years in France in the 1970s and finally disappearing altogether with those who first went in the 1980s. Difference still abounds, but it is no longer defined by a notable gap in material well-being.

The tale of American "innocents" abroad is, as we have seen, as old as the first encounters between citizens of the New World and the Old in the late eighteenth century. What, then, is specific to the tale of American historians of France? What lends this tale its particular shape and interest? Literary critic Alice Kaplan's marvelous memoir *French Lessons* describes the process of falling in love with another language, a process that, in turn, gives access to another culture and to the possibility of reinventing oneself in the new language (and culture): "The first day of class. I look out over my classroom. Most of the students are just back from their junior year. They have that look—the way they wear their clothes and part their hair. I see it in their eyes, they're transformed, they want me to help them keep it all going."[34] For the student of French studies, the language is prior. Hooked by the challenge of mastering French, students then discover bit by bit the culture that learning a new language has "let them in on."[35] For historians, it would seem, the process is reversed as the scholar moves from choosing history to choosing *French* history, and from there to an interest in polishing their language skills. For many of our contributors, French was, quite simply, the foreign language they knew best at the moment they first landed in graduate school. Choosing France seems to have constituted what Leonard Smith aptly calls "the path of least linguistic resistance."

In the case of historians, then, a fascination with the culture, with specific elements of French history, and with the particular historical problems that are best pondered through studying France obliges young scholars to acquire the language or brush up on their rocky high-school French so that they may extract new secrets from the archives. In some cases, this process then gives birth to the desire (however temporary) for self-reinvention in the new language. British historian Richard Cobb famously spoke of the "second identity" he acquired while living and working in France: "to speak and to write in French is to acquire a second personality." Nothing made Cobb prouder than hearing a French colleague tell him that he "wrote, spoke, and thought *comme un titi parisien*."[36]

There is some of this in the essays that follow. More common, however, is an account of how the need to master both language and culture gradually gave rise to an awareness of a distinct "self" that is inhabited by French, that expresses itself in words and bodily gestures that are not those of one's native tongue and culture, words and gestures that are more or less self-consciously acquired and deployed. This consciousness of a specifically French, or Franco-American "self" often manifests itself in the sense expressed by many of our authors that they occupy an intermediate terrain, one that Robert Paxton characterizes as "an imaginary mid-Atlantic space," neither American nor French but deeply involved in the two while at the same time standing at a critical distance from each. This distance, which calls to mind Edith Wharton's "exchange of experience," is gradually achieved through knowledge of and involvement in the other culture. But as Robert Paxton's essay illustrates, some measure of that desire to inhabit the other cultural identity, to master (or at least achieve competence in) its language, its gestures, its local customs is the necessary passage by which the American historian of France comes to occupy the "mid-Atlantic space." This desire must be known and experienced at some point, even if the desire to "pass" as "French" is then set aside in favor of more realistic and ultimately more productive encounters with France as an "other" that, if not fully knowable, can nonetheless be partially grasped through the exercise of the historian's craft.

✢

If the specific forms of enchantment with France and things French that animate the world of French Studies (and of American Francophilia more generally) are not unknown to historians, that enchantment is by no means constitutive of the approaches our contributors have adopted. Indeed, all stress in one way or another the importance of gaining access to France while remaining American. Each essay reveals how sustained contact with France has enabled its author to deepen his or her understanding of American society and culture and to gain a critical vantage point from which to explore in a new light the unexamined familiarity of ways of being that one has known and inhabited since birth. The class relations of present-day America were thus laid bare for a number of our contributors by the simple experience of living in a society where the language of class informs social policy, political discourse, and everyday discussion. One might say the same for questions of political choice, which take on a different coloration once one has spent time in a country where genuine left alternatives exist on the spectrum of ordinary politics.

This was especially so in post-'68 America, when France loomed large as the promised land of *genuine* revolution—as opposed to America's ersatz "revolution" that threw off the yoke of colonial domination without overturning social and class relations. France fairly shimmers on the horizon of many (though not all) of the later essays in this volume as a nation that boasts (or once boasted) a truly radical and leftist political alternative—both a socialist *and* a communist party, with the latter flourishing from 1945 through the mid-1980s. How exciting, how different, how refreshing for those of us raised on the non-alternative of Republican versus Democratic dominance of the House, Senate, or presidency. If the comparative poverty of France marked the adventures of those who did their research during the 1950s and 1960s, political envy often marks the experience of those who embarked upon that adventure during the 1970s and 1980s. Only with the generation working in France during and since the 1990s does the Franco-American encounter look less one-sided, as France passes from an economically impoverished but culturally rich destination to a politically desirable model to emulate to a country whose different solutions to a common set of problems around inequality, poverty, race, and gender remain, as Todd Shepard puts it, "compelling to think about as well as resistant to easy answers."

It is interesting that the search for personal "roots" plays no role in the attraction these scholars feel for France. Indeed, only one of our authors evokes anything that remotely resembles a French ancestor (Barbara Diefendorf and her mythic uncle). So in what guise did France beckon? And why France? Why not Germany or Britain, Russia or Poland, Italy or Spain, Belgium or the Netherlands? Some of these historians made it to France via another European country (Germany, most commonly). But Jan Goldstein perceptively notes that in the melting pot that is famously the United States of America, the categories of "cultural ancestors" and "personal ancestors" do not always overlap. We would venture to guess that in the period following World War II, France offered access to America's European heritage that seemed at once less problematic than that offered by Germany and more "exotic" and "continental" than that offered by a (deceptively) familiar Britain. As long as Franco ruled, Spain was unlikely to attract—much less welcome—foreign scholars, while European languages other than French, Spanish, and German were rarely, if ever, to be found on the menu at most American high schools.

Yet the complex encounters with France and the French that are recounted in these pages lead one to wonder whether the very lack of direct ancestors might not have made exploration of that part of America's cultural heritage that is bound up with France less fraught for American scholars, less laden with familial baggage. Are the feelings of freedom that so many of our contributors avow having experienced as foreign participants in French culture and scholarly life enabled precisely because France is *not* the land of one's own ancestors? As the one major European country that sent pretty much no one to what would become the United States, France has a peculiarly free-floating status in the immigrant bouquet that makes up the United States. Hence, substantial working-class populations from all other European nations washed up on American shores between 1620 and the present, each leaving visible traces and concrete images of their particular ethnic and popular cultures on urban and rural America; traces that are often organized around food and drink but also around religious festivals: German beer gardens, Irish bars, St. Patrick's Day, or the Festival of San Gennaro. Only France has planted no outposts of French popular culture in the United States (with the partial exception of the Cajuns, who do not seem very linked to France in the popular imagination). One consequence of this absence has been a tendency for "France" to represent elite and bourgeois culture in American discourse, as if the entire French nation consisted of well-dressed people who dined at Maxim's every night. France thus floats more freely in the American imagination, a movie screen onto which fantasies both positive and negative are often and easily projected.

For American historians of France, the lack of familial or memorial links to France has had very specific consequences, for, as Jan Goldstein notes, "American historians' relation to French history has always been more abstract, more conceptual or, if one is partial to Freudian vocabulary, sublimated than their relation to the history of other European countries." For this reason, she adds, political philosophy has constituted the "major tie" between the two countries. It is the "myth of origins" shared by these two revolutionary nations "that draws American historians to France, that makes France function for many of us as a second, surrogate homeland, even if, as is most often the case, we have no flesh-and-blood ancestors there."[37] The ties that bind American historians of France to their "surrogate" homeland thus contain a uniquely ideological element and turn on the play of similarity and difference between the political, social, and economic structures of these sister republics.

The constant passage between France and the United States, the sense of living with a foot inside two homelands, has created in each of our contributors a kind of transnational identity forged out of conflict and hardship, of enchantment and exasperation, of admiration for and rejection of particular aspects of French society and institutions as they are discovered during his or her initiation into France and things French. Among the qualities admired are the sense of solidarity and the generous welfare state that both embodies and reinforces that solidarity. Other contributors—like many American travelers before them—point to a refreshing lack of prudery and Puritanism, to the immediacy of various sensual pleasures that are curiously curtailed in the United States (the pleasures of the table, the fine clothing and artfully dressed shop windows, the wine). Still others revel in a Parisian cosmopolitanism that is generated, in part, through the French Republic's definition of a *laïc* public space (that is, neutral and secular) in which one can exist as "a citizen of the world" rather than as the mere sum of one's identities. Interestingly enough, the French Republic's conception of public neutrality is also at the heart of what is most criticized in these essays, namely, the "don't ask, don't tell" attitude toward racial, religious, and other forms of identification and the rampant racism that can flourish beneath such official neutrality.

These essays thus reflect the simultaneous pull of attraction and rejection as our protagonists struggle to master the language and negotiate a socio-cultural system that seems to welcome them at one moment only to freeze them out at the next. Nothing better illustrates the simultaneous tugs of attraction and rejection than the rites of passage through which American historians of

France first encounter the culture and begin to forge their transnational identities.

These rites are generally concentrated in a single year of research, more or less adequately funded, during which one gathers all that is needed for one's dissertation while navigating the tooth-gnashing frustrations of French bureaucracy. Electing to make of necessity a virtue, some contributors chose to see the multiple (and often seemingly pointless) hoops to be jumped through in order to acquire one's residency papers and library passes as sources of insight into the larger, long-term structures of the French state. Others sought— impatiently—to cool their heels, complaining mightily as the paperwork moved ever so slowly, awaiting the day they might finally enter the archives and libraries to begin full-time research. Finally, the great day arrived, and our ardent young scholars crossed the threshold of the National Library or Archives only to meet new layers of bureaucracy and encrusted, long-accumulated and apparently irrational ways of doing things—from the byzantine cataloguing systems to the two-hour lunchtime closures in all but the largest libraries. Once again, our scholars had to cool their jets and patiently, slowly learn the ways and means of each research institution. For by this point it had become clear to each one of them that France was not about to adapt to them. If they were to survive and prosper during their research year, they would have to find ways to adapt to France.

Meanwhile, on the home front, there were new kinds of food to be cooked (blood sausage, *topinambours*—we call them "Jerusalem artichokes"—and chicken, sold complete with head, feet, pin feathers, and innards), the mysteries of the *chaudière* to be unlocked (vital if one is to enjoy heat and hot water), the particular delights of one's neighborhood to be unwrapped and experienced. Throughout these months of struggle with the language, with archivists reluctant to hand over the goods, with the feelings of loneliness and unrecognition that come from dwelling in a society that seems to have precious little time and indulgence for the awkward, tongue-tied Americans in their midst, many of our contributors felt that, as Lynn Hunt wryly put it, "I loved so much about France, but I didn't feel loved back."

But if these historians' transnational identities first took shape over the course of that crucial initiatory year, they acquired flesh and depth through ongoing critical engagement with France and the French, an engagement that was progressively structured over the course of an academic career, repeated visits and sabbaticals, and the ties that develop with particular persons and institutions. From Todd Shepard's relationship of open, mutual hatred with his extreme right-wing host family in the early weeks of his junior year abroad to Steve Kaplan's verbal fisticuffs with the keepers of the flame of French Revolutionary history at the time of the bicentennial celebration in 1989, passing by more "polite" or implicit, if no less deeply felt, forms of struggle over questions such as whether and to what extent one should adapt one's way of being to French ways of life, these essays bristle with moments of conflict and struggle, anger and rejection, moments that seem deeply formative of the engagement that all sixteen ultimately formed with France.[38]

One vital source of this engagement is, clearly, the simultaneous experience of France in two temporalities. For even as our scholars wrestle daily with the culture as it exists now, warts and all, each of them is at the same time plunged deep in the study of another France at another epoch, when religious hatreds prospered, when colonial domination, slave-trading, or rampant antifeminism formed a part of the common currency of the day. As those who earn their daily bread by peeling back the layers of the present to reveal the sometimes ugly faces of the past, these historians are in fact ill-placed to indulge in mindless Francophilia precisely because the mythological space required to nurture an ideal, *museumified* France is incompatible with the kinds of critical and reflective spaces necessary to accomplish their intellectual work. Moreover, awareness of difficulties past seems to aid these scholars to both acknowledge and reflect upon the problems that dog France in the early twenty-first century, from high unemployment and uneven social integration to uncertain economic growth and the expansion of the extreme right. Among other things, this awareness incites our historians to feel deeply involved in current debates over the Muslim headscarf or the PACS (civil unions for both homosexual and heterosexual couples) or the efforts to redress the male-female imbalance in politics (*la parité*).

Each of our authors thus ends by embracing, in one way or another, the particular transnational identity he or she has fashioned in the archives, on city streets, in whatever bits of the countryside lay near to hand, from ties of friendship and intellectual exchange that have been nourished across years of constant movement back and forth across the Atlantic. Neither tourists nor expatriates (only one of the sixteen expresses the wish to live in France full-time), historians of France have created and nourished a very specific kind of Franco-American relationship in which France and the United States are apprehended as evolving organisms rather than as static, idealized entities. Even in their most dithyrambic moments, these historians resist the romanticized visions of the "French way of life" that surfaced in the writings of American visitors to Europe at the end of the nineteenth century, many of whom longed for escape from American modernity by connecting with the notionally more "organic" society of France. Such longings now find expression in the works of Peter Mayle and company, writers who turn a willfully blind eye to the high-speed trains, sprawling *hypermarchés,* and grim suburban projects that mark France's present-day landscape so that they may seek a refuge from modernity in an "eternal France" ruled by unchanging values and quaint, grumpy peasants.

By contrast, our contributors' commitment to history and their acute sense of the forces of change lead them to write against the notion of this "eternal" France in favor of more nuanced accounts that mix the positive and negative features that have gone into making up a distinctively French modernity. If the transnational identities forged by American historians of France over the course of their careers allow them to understand the United States in a new light, they also enable the development of critical perspectives on contemporary France. Hence, no sooner does one of our authors let slip a moment of rapture experienced in contemplating the beauties of Paris or the splendors of the table than we are reminded of France's darker side: its ferocious and bloody wars of religion in the sixteenth century, its recurrent anti-Semitism, the increasing alienation of the people from their governing elite, the ugly glow of cars and public buildings set afire by angry French youths in France's poorest suburbs who despair of ever finding a place in the allegedly color- and religion-blind Republic.

✢

And what of the future? Can one peer ahead five decades and imagine a comparable book being written by a future generation of French historians? While the current Francophobia is unlikely to have any lasting impact on the future of French history in the United States, broader political and cultural factors are at work that make this future uncertain: globalization, concern with colonial and postcolonial studies, the trend toward comparative and transnational history, the declining geopolitical importance of Europe. "Neither as scholars nor as human beings can my generation remain in the world into which we were born," concluded Caroline Walker Bynum, then president of the American Historical Association, as she reflected, in 1996, on the impact of such factors on the future of the historical profession and her own primarily Eurocentric generation.[39]

The contributors to this volume register an awareness of those changes, musing near the end of their essays on the possible future of French history in a global world. Some feel that national histories will continue to be relevant for the simple reason that the nation-state remains the context for governance, military power, and economic regulation. As such, it remains a key constituent of cultural identity. Others see in the decline of French language teaching in

America the portent of French history's decline—along with other nationally bounded histories—in the cursus of higher education.[40] The interest in colonial and postcolonial studies, with its emphasis on transnational interaction and multiple, shifting loci of identity, has taken French history by storm over the past ten years, relocating metropolitan France in the larger context of its imperial holdings and demonstrating the extent to which French history has in part been "made" on its imperial frontiers. Highlighting two-way relationships of cultural transfer rather than one-way relations of imperial dominance, this new work has enriched our understanding of France even as it has altered our sense of what constitutes national history. But it has not yet succeeded in tossing France out of the arena altogether. Nor is it clear that this might even be a goal of colonial and postcolonial history.

More unsettling is the sense, expressed by many of our contributors, that France itself has lost intellectual and political vitality. While France continues to appeal to them all on a personal level, a number of essays end on a note of concern, uncertainty, even criticism. Unsure that France can—or should—maintain its different political model. Critical of the rigidities of the bureaucracy and of the growing alienation between the French people and their governing elite. Since the 1980s, events such as the rise of the extreme right-wing National Front Party, enduring unemployment, the government's ineffectual response to the 2003 summer heat wave, the rejection of the European constitution, and most recently the suburban riots and massive student demonstrations of 2005 and 2006 suggest that France is no more capable of solving its social problems than the United States. We are a far cry from the wistful yearnings of young scholars of France for the kind of left alternative that they found lacking in America. As one American historian of France wrote on an Internet forum on French history: "Many American academics looked to the French model [of integration] for an alternative and are now finding that it isn't working very well. That leaves the question of where we go from here."[41]

In the end, the sustainability of French history and the resonance of France in America may well lie as much in the ability of France to sort out its contemporary problems as it does in current rethinking of global (as opposed to national) points of reference or in trends in language instruction. For the answer to the question "Why France?" lies, quite simply, in the capacity of our sister republic to stir the imagination, curiosity, delight, indignation, and admiration of Americans across the generations, a capacity that only France itself can really put at risk.

CHAPTER 1

☙ A Medievalist and Francophile Despite Himself

John W. Baldwin

On October 1, 1953, a twenty-four-year-old Fulbright student disembarked from the French liner *Flandre* at Le Havre in Normandy. Of the thirty-odd fellow Fulbrights on board, no one could have been less prepared for the future. He was a teetotaler and nonsmoker who did not know how to pronounce the French word for the ticket he held in his hand. Like the 70,000 young Americans who had preceded him to the Norman beaches a little less than a decade earlier, all his expenses were covered by the United States government, but unlike these predecessors, his prospects for returning were not at risk. Thus began an adventure that has lasted for more than a half-century. To the often-posed question of "Why France?," why did he become a French medieval historian, the short response is equally banal: he did not choose France; France chose him. Joining a long line of Americans since Thomas Jefferson, he was seduced.

The narrator of this story writes in the third person, not out of any pretension of objectivity—certainly not in this postmodernist age—but in an effort to create distance and to reduce the temptation, as much as it is humanly possible, of self-fashioning or of *nombrilisme* (navel-gazing) as it is so aptly designated in French. Being a medievalist, he is not only acutely conscious of the alterity of the age he studies (the Middle Ages has always played the "other" to modernity) but of his own alterity in contemporary society. By recounting his story at the end of his career, however, he has the advantage of hindsight. What was an incoherent maze of choices en route becomes an intelligible roadmap when looking back. The false turns and dead ends can be ignored; the paths leading to the future are now clear.

Born in Chicago in July 1929, John W. Baldwin passed his infancy in a city burdened by the Depression and the reign of gangsters. In the alleys of the middle-class North Side the childhood game was not cowboys and Indians or even cops and robbers but cops and Dillinger, after the celebrated gangster, whom every kid wanted to play. His toys of preference were tin pistols and rubber-band guns, which packed a smarting wallop. Red-haired, freckled, asthmatic, and skinny, he stuttered badly, for which he was sent to the speech clinic of Northwestern University every Saturday morning, but the quiet, pure air and sunshine of a summer with his grandmother in the Pennsylvania mountains cured him. (It nonetheless returns whenever he speaks a foreign language.) His father was a manufacturing engineer who worked for the Westinghouse Corporation. Since any salaried position was sufficient to live on during the Depression, job security, not to speak of promotion, depended on one's willingness to "transfer." After eight years in Chicago, John's family moved every three to four years, to New Jersey, to Maryland, back to New Jersey, and then to Pennsylvania.

Although his parents were college graduates, they had both attended public schools in the midwest and had no hesitation entrusting their children to the public school system. As a result, most of John's primary and secondary education was mediocre. In New Jersey the system followed the fad of "progressive education," inspired by the philosopher John Dewey, that emphasized personal development and social integration over the basic skills of handwriting, spelling, and grammar. The fourth grade offered the usual session on the Middle Ages that included recreations of castles and tournaments, but John's specialty was the Apache Indians, to which subject he devoted a "research project." To save money, the school system in Catonsville, Maryland, reduced the foreign languages taught in high school to Latin and French. Being conscientious, John selected the former because it was offered for four years, whereas only two were proposed for the latter. France was on the distant horizon, and its language was deemed useful only for cooking and high fashion. One exception, however, intruded upon these restricted horizons. At Catonsville High School the mandatory course on modern European history was taught by a certain Miss Bell, who was a passionate devotée of the Enlightenment and the French Revolution. Scribbling the names of revolutionary heroes on the blackboard, she set her students to write essays on the meaning of liberty, equality, and fraternity. In her grand scheme the true dividing line in history came at the end of the eighteenth century when France passed from the "believing mind" of the Middle Ages to the "inquiring mind" of the Enlightenment. Because of his recently formed religious convictions, John did not find the "believing mind" to be a stigma, but at the same time, he received a glimpse of the significance of France and its revolution. With (secular) missionary zeal, Miss Bell left Catonsville to preach the blessings of the Enlightenment to the believing minds of South America.

During the early 1940s, John's mother and father underwent a religious transformation that affected the entire family. Although both had been raised conventional Presbyterians, John's mother's intensive study of the Bible convinced her of the evangelical position on faith and the scriptures. Although never rejecting Presbyterianism, she led her family through a conversion from "nominal" to "born again, believing" Christianity. The evangelical ethos of total "commitment to Christ and his will" transformed the household. Since commitment required separation from the contemporary world, John was persuaded that a college of like-minded students was preferable to Rutgers, the local state university in New Jersey. (Elite and Ivy League universities were out of the question, on financial as well as ideological grounds.) The leading evangelical institution of the day was Wheaton College in Illinois. Although John was schoolworthy and had obtained good grades, the competition for admissions in 1946 was fierce (one out every ten applicants was accepted), exacerbated by returning veterans applying on the G.I. Bill. His letter of acceptance was a joyous occasion.

Wheaton College's distinction lay in Biblical Studies. Despite what other biblical scholars thought about its hermeneutics, the school enrolled more students in Greek courses (including Classical Greek) than any other institution of higher learning in America. Because of the dominance of theology, John elected to study Greek and German starting his first year in college. These languages were essential for research in Protestant theology. (Marginalized once again, French was considered useful for those who had received a missionary vocation to Africa.) But the professors who succeeded in winning his admiration were two historians who specialized in modern English and American history and awoke him to the high calling of scholarship. After two years (and perhaps still under Miss Bell's spell), John abandoned theology and gave himself over to history. The course in the Middle Ages, however, was a disappointment. The professor had had no training in the subject and merely repeated the lectures he had heard from his own undergraduate work. By his senior year, John's religious concerns directed his attention toward the medieval period. Whatever the pitfalls of medieval obscurantism, this was the age of western civilization in which religion was central to society and to which the "believing mind" provided the dynamic. The summer after graduation in 1950, John acquired two books that reinforced this emerging preoccupation.

Henry Adams's *Mont-Saint-Michel and Chartres* offered an imaginative and comprehensive vision of the eleventh to thirteenth centuries that embodied their achievements in two architectural triumphs, the Romanesque abbey and the Gothic cathedral. Henry Osborn Taylor's two-volume work *The Medieval Mind* revealed the thought and emotions of the entire era, which became all the more real because Taylor succeeded in evoking them directly from the Latin sources. Needing no more persuasion, John decided to wager a year of graduate work on the Middle Ages. Fortunately his father had recently accepted a position at the engineering school of the Pennsylvania State College that allowed free tuition and board and room at home. Although John's Master's thesis, entitled "Medieval Symbolistic Thought in the *De Sacramentis* of Hugh of Saint-Victor," was little more than a paraphrase of Hugh's treatise, it nonetheless provided needed exercise of John's high school Latin and confirmed his wager.

Since Wheaton had little standing among its peers and Penn State offered only a Master's degree, John's applications to the graduate universities that offered medieval work were not competitive. When Johns Hopkins in Baltimore, Maryland, was alone in offering a tuition scholarship, he decided that it was his best bet. In 1951 the medieval chair at Hopkins was held by Sidney Painter, who was distinguished in English history, particularly the reign of King John (1199–1216), but his interests extended into French history as well. The first challenge facing John, therefore, was to accommodate his own preferences for intellectual history with those of Painter's on institutions. After realizing that Painter had little interest in intellectual history, John's best recourse was to shift his examination fields to the institutional histories of England and France. The second challenge was the French language itself, requisite both for the degree and, of course, for work on France. John set about teaching himself French by reading historical texts with a dictionary. He succeeded sufficiently to pass the history field exams, but a specific language exam was also required. Painter administered it orally by handing John a text written by Robert Fawtier, to be translated on sight. After five excruciating minutes of listening to English words inserted into French sentences, Painter finally interrupted: "John, you can stop now. Don't worry, I shall pass you, but someday you will succeed."

For the dissertation, John found a compromise between Painter's interests and his own in the concept of justice. After producing a first-year paper on the subject in the twelfth and thirteenth centuries, John turned to the economic notion of the just price. In a visiting lecture, the Cambridge economic historian Michael Postan argued that the medieval concept was essentially based on the cost of production and the labor theory of value. John envisaged an eventual dissertation entitled "Catholicism and the Rise of Socialism" echoing the celebrated titles of Max Weber, *The Protestant Ethic and the Spirit of Capitalism*, and R. H. Tawney, *Religion and the Rise of Capitalism*. As it turned out, John's research demonstrated that the just price was actually the current price on the market, thus suggesting that "Medieval Catholicism and the Rise of Capitalism" would have been more appropriate. The just price, however, was a legal theory and required competence in canon law. Painter put John in contact with Stephan Kuttner, the distinguished historian of medieval canon law at the Catholic University in Washington, who offered help not only in legal science but also in paleography, an essential skill since the relevant texts were not yet edited. A prospective dissertation, therefore, required access to manuscript collections in Italy, France, Germany, or England, and the available source of funding was the Fulbright scholarship for graduate research. Because Germany was still recovering from the war and England too competitive, John chose France over Italy and was accepted. On the eve of departure, he faced the prospect of leaving the States for the first time to a country for which he was scarcely ready. His Latin and thesis preparation were adequate, but his minimal reading knowledge of French was innocent of grammar and pronunciation. To anticipate a new life in France, he imposed on a fellow graduate student to accompany him to a bar in Baltimore, where he imbibed his first beer. Thus initiated, he set out to learn what the new country would teach him.

Even when pronounced in English, *éblouissement* best articulates John's first impression of the night of October 1, when he arrived in France: the shrill whistle of the boat train as it passed through the Norman tunnels, the lights strung as pearls along the vast boulevards as the bus proceeded from the Gare Saint-Lazare to the Cité Universitaire, the first spotting of a *pissoir* (public urinal) and the discovery of what a baguette and butter can do for ham when accompanied by a *demi*. . . . Paris of 1953 was luminous, vibrant, and welcoming by comparison to the darkened, ravaged, and rationed London, not to speak of devastated Munich. John was fortunate to find lodgings quickly at the Cité with Maurice Jeanjean, a candidate for the School of Colonial Administration who was seeking an Anglophone roommate. This resulted in a friendship between two families that has lasted the decades. Not too surprisingly, within two months John also met a young woman who was to become his companion for life. A medieval historian herself, Jenny Jochens was not French but Danish. In those days bourgeois French girls did not usually associate with foreign students, and, as always, foreign students in great metropolitan cities socialize more readily with other foreign students. Holding a French government fellowship to study canon law, Jenny attended the same seminar on medieval canon law. Their mutual interests and their common enthusiasm to explore France bonded them quickly. (Of course, Jenny's superior French was an additional boon.) Together they have shared the adventure of France for the past half-century.

Student life began in Paris by standing in lines: at the university for matriculation, in front of the libraries to find seats, at the center of student services at 15 rue Soufflot for restaurant cards and tickets (where the line extended down the street), and in front of student restaurants (where the line decomposed into crowds). Food in the student restaurants was good and remarkably cheap (about thirty-five cents a meal) if one was willing to wait and to endure the cacophony that erupted when anyone entered wearing a hat (a custom peculiar to student restaurants at the time). The queue at 15 rue Soufflot also offered cheap theater tickets. Movies in which the current language was enunciated realistically were not intelligible to John's incipient French, but the theater provided a better medium for learning. Not only did the actors pronounce their lines clearly, but John could read a text before hearing it on stage. John and Jenny must have seen at least twenty plays that year. The Comédie Française at the rue de Richelieu and the Théâtre Marigny were their most frequented halls, Molière and Claudel their preferred authors. Student freedom also permitted romantic escapades such as a midnight promenade across Paris starting from the Porte d'Orléans, dining on soup in Les Halles, and watching the sunrise from Montmartre before taking the first Métro home. After exhausting the monuments and museums of Paris, the two medievalists began to attack the Gothic churches outside. The excursion fare of a *billet de bon dimanche* permitted them to visit a new cathedral every Sunday. When they exhausted the supply of cathedrals, they took advantage of the winter vacation to hitchhike into Burgundy as far as Auxerre and the spring break to explore Normandy as far as Mont-Saint-Michel. The generosity of truck drivers made this mode of transportation not only cheaper than trains or buses but faster as well.

The weekly daytime routine revolved around the Sorbonne and the Bibliothèque nationale. Once a week, Gabriel Le Bras, the eminent canonist and future dean of the law faculty, offered his seminar, where he worked on his current research before a class of assistants and advanced students. Jenny and John were the only foreigners, the only non-Catholics, and (almost) the only non-clerics. (Their common destiny appeared inevitable.) Le Bras was cordial and receptive, but John always remained at the end of the line of those waiting to see him because he couldn't bear to have anyone overhear his French. Although Le Bras agreed to read his dissertation chapters, the professor never found the time. His greatest service was to introduce his assistant Pierre Legendre, who guided John through the labyrinth of libraries, bibliography, and legal technicalities. The real work of the week, however, took place in the Salle des manuscrits on the second floor of the Bibliothèque nationale. From nine to five John struggled to make sense of the medieval handwriting on the parchment of the Latin codices of canon law and to reconstruct the medieval theories of the just price, but it would have taken much longer were it not for the interest and expertise of two *conservateurs,* Jacqueline Rambaud, a student of Le Bras, and the incomparable Marie-Thérèse d'Alverny. Their unfailing help, coupled with the exemplary policy of unrestricted access to all manuscripts for qualified students, made the Salle des manuscrits an unparalleled place in which to work. Below was the larger and more bustling Salle des imprimés, where printed books could be read in the winter gloom of half-lighted tables surrounded by shabby and odorous men who scribbled notes on the margins of newspapers.

Jenny returned to Denmark in July 1954; John remained in France another year to finish his research. They were married at Christmas in 1954 and proceeded to Baltimore that summer. John defended his dissertation in 1956, and he obtained an instructorship at the University of Michigan in Ann Arbor, where three children were born in rapid succession. *The Medieval Theories of the Just Price: Romanists, Canonists and Theologians in the Twelfth and Thirteenth Centuries* was published in 1959. Highest among John and Jenny's priorities, however, was another stay in Paris. The catalyst was Pierre the Chanter, a prominent theologian at Paris at the end of the twelfth century whose unedited *questiones* and biblical commentaries John had come across while working on the just price. Awarded a Guggenheim fellowship to finance the project, he and the family returned to France in 1960.

By 1955 John and Jenny's conversion to France was complete—a process for which their years as students had set the pattern. With three children under five and a fourth on the way, the major family requirement in 1960 was space. They rented a house in the suburbs of Issy-les-Moulineaux, where Jenny could better care for the children while John took the Métro to the Bibliothèque nationale each day. This displacement did not hinder them from attending the theater in town, if at a reduced frequency. The weekly excursions outside Paris were transferred to Thursday, the school holiday, when the family left the infant Birgit with a neighbor and took Peter and Ian in a rented car to explore the Île-de-France. The successful formula was to choose a church for the parents and a *château* for the boys. When they discovered the charming fortified village of Gerberoy in the Beauvaisis where Pierre the Chanter had lived, they also acquired the habit of preceding all sightseeing with a lunch in a local restaurant. During the week John returned to the daily routine of uninterrupted hours at the Salle des manuscrits with unfettered freedom to decipher, log, and transcribe hundreds of unedited folios from the school of the Chanter that furnished the texts for his next book, entitled *Masters, Princes, and Merchants: The Social Views of Peter the Chanter and his Circle* (1970). Productive as that year was for the parents (Christopher was born immediately upon their return in 1961), it was also a year of isolation, Jenny with the children in Issy, John with his manuscripts in Paris. Reflecting on his first decade as a medievalist, John concluded that he had spent a third of the time in France and yet did not know a single French historian of his generation. This situation is unimaginable today, when scores of foreign scholars are sponsored by the École des Hautes Études en Sciences Sociales and are welcomed each year by the numerous universities that succeeded the old Sorbonne. At the time the Sorbonne remained rigidly hierarchic, and the impact of the Sixième Section (now the École des Hautes Études) was only beginning to be felt. There was, however, an important exception. In February 1961 John was introduced to Jacques Le Goff, a graduate of the École Normale Supérieure, who was also a neighbor in Issy. Le Goff invited him for a prodigious lunch; that was one of the hallmarks of his generosity. Although very different in their approaches to history, Le Goff and John shared common interests in economic theory and the schools, all of which contributed to a friendship that has remained strong to this day.

While in Issy, John received a call to return to Johns Hopkins occasioned by the unexpected death of Sidney Painter. The invitation was too enticing to resist, and the family returned to Baltimore. After John's courses were established and the dissertations of Painter's orphaned doctoral students were shepherded, he finished a first draft of his book on the Chanter. When a sabbatical leave became available for the 1965–1966 academic year, the couple naturally made plans to spend it in Paris. The project was the penetration into government of masters trained in France at the turn of the twelfth and thirteenth centuries. Since schooling was now a problem for the family, the two older boys spent the year with friends in Denmark, made feasible by their fluency in Danish and English. To avoid isolation this time John and Jenny moved into Paris to an apartment on rue de Vaugirard; Birgit and Christopher attended the École maternelle on rue Madame. Residing within walking distance of the Bibliothèque nationale, John acquired the habit of lunch at home with the family. Rue de Vaugirard was also next door to the state theater of the Odeon under the dynamic direction of Jean-Louis Barrault. During that year they saw every play on the program, occasionally entertaining friends for supper after the performance. Furthermore, 1966 was the year that the barrier with the historical profession was breached. Again, the situation was not abnormal;

it only required a prompting occasion, one that was furnished by Jacques Le Goff when he invited John to speak on Pierre the Chanter to his seminar at the École des Hautes Études. John might wonder what the audience understood of the presentation when he insisted on calling his subject "Pierre le Chanteur" rather than "Chantre," but the session was well attended by medievalists. Following the seminar, Bernard Guenée and Pierre Toubert and their spouses were among the guests at Le Goff's legendary repast. Through a mutual acquaintance, Georges Duby likewise brought John down to Aix-en-Provence to speak to his seminar. By their departure that spring, John and Jenny had met and begun to form friendships with the French historians who were at the fore of medieval history.

The sentiment may be banal, but nevertheless: the process of maturation remains inexorable. While John advanced in his professional career in the States, his generation of friends in France achieved prominence as professors at the Sorbonne, the École des Chartes, and the Collège de France; as president of the École des Hautes Études en Sciences Sociales; as director of the Archives nationales and the Bibliothèque nationale de France; and as members of the Académies in the Institut de France. Their continued interest and encouragement naturally facilitated John's own work. In the 1970s medieval studies in France was centered on the seminar of Georges Duby at the Collège de France. Enlisting scholars from all facets of the Middle Ages, Duby assembled them on Thursday afternoons to discuss the major themes of his forthcoming book, *Les trois ordres ou l'imaginaire du féodalisme*. In 1972 John was invited to present a paper and lead a febrile discussion in a hot and smoky room on the notions of Parisian schoolmen on social hierarchy. Like much of the seminar's discussion, this one was incorporated into the book. By then, however, John had turned to a new project, the reign of Philip Augustus (1179–1223), the king contemporaneous with Pierre the Chanter whose approaching anniversary focused on one of France's most important monarchs. Philip had last been studied by the German Alexander Cartellieri a half century earlier, but what was more astounding, Philip's royal registers, the first of the French monarchy, although mined for centuries, had never been fully published or studied.

The National Endowment for the Humanities supported the new project by providing a fellowship in 1972–1973 that enabled the family to move to Copenhagen, where the children's Danish enabled them to continue their schooling while John commuted to Paris for a week every month. Thereafter the NEH continued to support the project through smaller grants every spring from 1975 to 1979. Although the organization possessed funds for publishing such documents, his French colleagues were persuaded that if France could afford an atomic bomb, it could also publish its own archives. Robert-Henri Bautier, member of the Académie des Inscriptions et Belles Lettres, agreed to direct the publication of the registers in the academy's series *Recueil des historiens de la France,* and the *chartistes* Michel Nortier, Françoise Gasparri, and Elisabeth Lalou generously contributed their expertise to the endeavor. Equally important, Jean Favier, director of the Archives nationales, and Lucie Favier, head of the Readers' Service, guaranteed full access to the necessary documents. When Philip Augustus's accession to the throne was commemorated by a weeklong international colloquium in September 1980, John presented the first paper after the introduction of Robert-Henri Bautier, the organizer of the program. In 1984, at the invitation of Georges Duby, he delivered four lectures on the reign at the Collège de France. A study of the reign appeared in *The Government of Philip Augustus: Foundations of French Royal Power in the Middle Ages* (1986) and *Les Registres de Philippe Auguste* (1992). Throughout the spring visits of the 1970s and 1980s, numerous opportunities opened to make informal presentations to the seminars of colleagues as well as formal lectures, all encouraged by the numerous Parisian universities and the emerging prominence of the École des Hautes Études en Sciences Sociales. From 1983 to 1987, with the children now on their own, the day excursions out of Paris were prolonged into bicycle trips lasting a fortnight to explore the medieval monuments of Normandy, the Loire valley (twice), and the departments of the Nord and Pas de Calais. The formula was irresistible: a leisurely ride of a little over thirty kilometers along superbly paved tertiary roads through unhilly, charming countryside, locating a hotel by mid-afternoon in the nearest town, visiting the sites, and culminating in an ample repast stimulated by a well-deserved appetite from the day's exertions. This idyll came to a brutal halt in June 1988 when their daughter Birgit was killed by a drunk driver outside of New Haven, Connecticut, while John was in Paris.

Jenny and John retreated to their house in Baltimore, pulled the blinds to their studies, and drowned their bereavement in work. Jenny wrote two volumes on women in medieval Iceland, and John oriented his studies away from the schools and government articulated in the Latin of clerics and sought to approach the lay classes of the aristocracy through their own idiom of vernacular literature. Once again lacking expertise in the skills of medieval French, he received indispensable help from David Hult, his colleague at Johns Hopkins, and encouragement from Michel Zink at the Collège de France. He centered his attention on the romances of Jean Renart and Gerbert de Montreuil and the *fabliaux* of Jean Bodel, all of whom were active during the reign of Philip Augustus. The endeavor resulted in two books, *The Language of Sex: Five Voices from Northern France around 1200* (1994), which focused on this defining function of the laity, and the more general *Aristocratic Life in Medieval France: The Romances of Jean Renart and Gerbert de Montreuil, 1190–1230* (2000). The latter work benefited from Pierre Toubert's invitation in 1995 to John to try out his ideas on an audience at the Collège de France. By 1997, approaching retirement and a high stock market encouraged Jenny and John to invest their savings in an apartment on rue Charlemagne, which enabled them to divide their time between Baltimore and Paris. (Not surprisingly, it is situated within the ancient walls of Philip Augustus, John's chosen monarch.) The inertia of seniority also brought unexpected pleasures. His books on Philip Augustus and medieval sexuality were published in French. Colleagues in the Académie des Inscriptions et Belles Lettres elected him to foreign membership, and the President of the Republic decorated him with the Légion d'Honneur. John could understand *how* the decoration might have happened because he knew the friend who had lobbied so persistently for it, but *why* was a mystery. Even the French ambassador in Washington was perplexed, refusing steadfastly to come to Baltimore to confer the decoration on a candidate of whom he had never heard. The greatest satisfaction of seniority, retirement, and residence in France, however, is the opportunity to engage with the next generation of scholars. The previous cohort had been overshadowed by the stellar names of Georges Duby and Jacques Le Goff, but it is not to their discredit that equally important work was done by the *conservateurs,* archivists, *chartistes,* and other scholars like those who have already been mentioned. As for the next generation who bear the future of medieval studies, it would be otiose to try to name all who have made themselves known and shared their work, but John would be remiss if he did not acknowledge historians like Jean-Claude Schmitt, Alain Boureau, Nicole Bériou, Dominique Barthélemy, and Martin Aurell and literary scholars like Michel Zink, Danielle Regnier, and Dominique Boutet.

✄

John Baldwin's metamorphosis into a historian of medieval France was due to a succession of personal choices, most of them contingent. As an age of faith, the Middle Ages doubtlessly responded to his religious convictions at the time, and after those convictions subsided, the initial commitment to the medieval period remained. The theory of the just price attracted him because of its moral dimension. Pierre the Chanter could not be resisted because of his biblical preoccupations, his ethical fervor, and his engaged scholarship. If Philip Augustus was chosen because of an approaching anniversary, the choice was doubtlessly prepared by Sidney Painter's comparable study of his contemporary, King John. The "linguistic turn" certainly facilitated John's shift to vernacular literature, but the move was principally motivated by growing doubts about approaching the laity through clerical Latin. Without a *baccalauréat* and the superb education offered to a *chartiste* or a *normalien* (graduates of the École des Chartes and the École Normale Supérieure), John was acutely conscious of his lack of a solid foundation in French language, culture, and history. His lifelong concentration on the decades surrounding 1200 was therefore a strategic decision to limit his investigations within a scope he could master and to add breadth through multiple facets rather than chronological extension. Despite longstanding friendships with Jacques Le Goff, Jean-Claude Schmitt, and Georges Duby, he has been relatively immune to the influence of contemporary medieval historiography articulated by the *Annales* school and Duby's signal traits. France's underlying contribution to John's historical endeavors was its receptivity. Thanks to republican equality, he was never refused access to the collections at any library or archive, national or local. His colleagues and friends accepted him as a peer. Whatever its fluency, his accented French will always reveal a lack of schooling; nonetheless he has never been made to feel excluded.

The Middle Ages made him a historian. Thanks to the fortuity of a Fulbright scholarship, it likewise brought him to France, but it was medieval France that made him a Francophile and introduced him to the values and amenities of contemporary French living. The stereotypical "young American in Paris" who frequents cafés, smokes Gauloises, sports berets, and writes the great American novel did not last long. Abetted by Jenny's Francophone skills, he found France an unexcelled place in which to live. Born in midwestern America but growing up during the war and its immediate aftermath, John, unlike the evangelicals of today, showed little susceptibility to politics. His earliest visual memories of France include the ubiquitous "Yankee Go Home" scribbled on walls right next to the unenforced "*Défense d'afficher.*" Throughout the 1970s the Gaullist radio droned its anti-American message in the background, but John paid it little attention because it never seemed to matter to his friends and acquaintances. The periodic strikes could be equally ignored. In 1968 he was in America and knew of the impact on France of the events of that year only secondhand, but in 1964 he had declined an offer from Berkeley because he feared the influence of the drug culture on his adolescent children. Because he had always voted Democratic in the American elections as a Marylander, he developed a fascination for the Left in France, since a socialist Left was of little consequence at home. He followed closely on television Mitterrand's unsuccessful presidential bid in 1966 (the candidate lived on rue Guynemer, around the corner from rue de Vaugirard); the defeat was as severe a disappointment as the many Democratic failures that he has since endured in America. Only in retirement did he start reading *Le Monde* on a daily basis, and only in these later years did he begin to experience doubts about the Jacobin state to which Philip Augustus had contributed. The inability to enact or even to enforce desirable policies, the increasing alienation between the electorate and the elite governing classes, the rigidity of the research institutions composed of functionaries defending their turf (this problem does not, however, concern historians), the arrogance and unreality of Gaullist foreign policy. . . . such issues began to trouble him, but these are the complaints of old men.

CHAPTER 2

🌿 A Mid-Atlantic Identity

Robert O. Paxton

A smallish town in the Virginia Appalachians might seem impossibly remote from France. Even so, France was actively present in my home town in the 1930s and 1940s. Lexington is a college town. Two professors of French were frequent dinner guests of my parents. My piano teacher and church choir director, another frequent dinner guest, had studied in Nadia Boulanger's famous summer course at Fontainebleau. A Catalan painter, Pierre Daura, had met a Virginia girl at the École des Beaux Arts in Paris and married her. Exiled from Franco's Spain, the Dauras made their home at St.-Cirque Lapopie in the *département* of the Lot. When war broke out in 1939, they resettled in the countryside near Lexington. My father, a lawyer, helped Pierre Daura with his citizenship papers. The Dauras were joined for a while by their brother-in-law, the better-known French painter Jean Hélion. I still have the copy of Hélion's memoirs that he inscribed to my mother.

The isolated local intelligentsia of my parents' generation in American small towns valued France as an indispensable link to the cultivated outside world. That is probably less true in today's multicultural climate.

The two world wars made France still more salient for my parents' generation and for my own as well. My father was just getting into uniform when World War I ended, but his first cousin reached France in 1918 as a volunteer in a decorated ambulance unit. It was the high point of this shy man's life. My parents were grieved by the defeat of France in 1940 and supported Roosevelt fervently in his struggle to overcome isolationism and contribute to the defeat of Hitler. My older brother was just getting into his uniform when World War II ended, but by then it was Japan that was on our minds.

The D-Day landings took place just a week before my twelfth birthday. I followed the liberation of France on maps at school and at home, in the evening around the radio with my parents. Listening to the news was a significant event in my household—the local weekly newspaper in Lexington was the family enterprise. Our interest in the Normandy landings became more personal when a cousin, John Paxton from Kansas City, stopped by on his way to board a troopship in New York. Almost everyone knew someone fighting in France. A small town near us, Bedford, Virginia, lost nineteen boys with the 29th Infantry Division on Omaha Beach on D-Day and the next day, the highest casualty rate in the United States in proportion to the size of the town.

Dissatisfied with the local high school, my parents sent me in 1948 to the Phillips Exeter Academy in New Hampshire for my last two years of secondary school. Exeter brought Europe decisively into my universe. My teachers at Exeter, like most in their profession, took it for granted that familiarity with European history and culture defined an educated person.

It was at Exeter that I began to study French. My older brother had studied Spanish, but he had come to feel that this choice had been a mistake. I recall quite clearly my mother's assertion that French was the language that opened up the greatest literary and cultural riches. So the decision was made. Fortunately I had two master teachers of French in secondary school and college—Paul Everett and Francis Drake. Both swept their classes along with an infectious enthusiasm for mastering the pronunciation of *u* and for La Fontaine. Even today I can recite "*Le renard et le corbeau.*" All my French teachers (none of them French) took for granted that France was the country where intellectuals were the most appreciated. That sounded good to me.

Other influences at Exeter were decisive. Henry Bragdon's history courses, including History 6 (modern Europe), made me want to become a historian. Then there was Harry Francis, who had come back to graduate from Exeter after a year at the University of Grenoble. Harry had done serious climbing in the French Alps and had an easy familiarity with classical music and painting (his father was on the staff of the Cleveland Museum). He seemed to me almost impossibly sophisticated, infinitely more interesting than my other, more provincial classmates. After homework at night we sometimes went out for a cup of cocoa, and I would try out my French on him. Shortly before graduation, we camped for a weekend on Mount Washington. I dreamed of someday acquiring as much European polish as Harry Francis.

The summer after my graduation from Exeter, in June 1950, my father took the whole family to Europe. London was the principal destination, as my parents wanted to commune with their English roots. It was unthinkable to miss Paris, however. We spent a week at the Hotel Lutetia without having the slightest idea about that hotel's sinister role as Gestapo headquarters during the occupation or about the dramatic scenes of reunion that took place at the Lutetia when the survivors of the Nazi camps returned in 1945.

I was so excited by my first landfall in Europe that I had been on deck for hours since dawn. Even as the *Queen Elizabeth* came alongside the pier at Southampton I could see that everything was strange. I was looking down at railroad wagons, trucks, cars, and houses, but none of them looked like the railroad wagons, trucks, cars, and houses that I was used to. The landscape was impossibly green. I had read Montesquieu's *Lettres persanes* at Exeter ("*Comment peut-on être persan?*"). Now I wondered how one could be English and live amid such total unfamiliarity.

Such radical otherness was not disagreeable. It was exhilarating. It gave me a lifelong taste for exploring distant places, experiencing unfamiliar landscapes, and living abroad. Although I have now visited every continent, only once—in Antarctica—could I recapture that full shock of discovery I felt on seeing the coast of Kent in 1950.

The trip also confirmed my fascination for the war I had followed from a safe distance as a schoolboy. World War II was still a palpable presence in Britain and France in the summer of 1950. Physical destruction was ubiquitous in London. Acres of the city around Saint Paul's Cathedral lay in ruins, and most of the Christopher Wren churches that we wanted to see had been burned out. Physically Paris seemed intact but shabby. I was quite unaware of the emotional ruins that lay hidden behind that façade of normality.

My decision to become a historian affirmed itself gradually through high school and college. I do not recall a single decisive moment of choosing. Many of my family's friends were professors; my parents did not share the general American condescension for that profession. As for history, I had grown up in a family for whom the past was a vivid presence. My parents were keenly interested in their English ancestors, even though they had left in the seventeenth century, and in the early history of Virginia. Their idea of a good time was a visit to Monticello, Carter's Grove Plantation, or Westover, the seventeenth-century estate of William Byrd.

It was the American Civil War that engaged my family's historical interests most actively. My father's grandfather, a brigadier general in the Confederate Army, was killed in the battle of Chancellorsville on May 3, 1863. From where we lived we could see his substantial house on a hilltop, occupied by another family since 1865. My father in the 1940s even chased down some of the furniture that had been dispersed in 1865, and we had to endure a cripplingly uncomfortable Empire sofa. Lexington contained the tombs of Lee and Jackson, and my grandmother was one of the local volunteers who showed tourists around the Lee Chapel. The town had been occupied and partly burned by Union troops under General David Hunter in 1864, after which a Confederate officer from Lexington led a raid that burned Chambersburg, Pennsylvania, to the ground. The Civil War was not a remote abstraction to the people of Lexington.

I did not want to become a historian of these familiar matters, however. It was not (as my French friends tend to think) that there was not enough history in Virginia; the trouble was that there was too much of it. I wanted to know about other pasts. Instead of studying history in order to reinforce my original identity, I thought that the study of another history might liberate me from the American South's provincialism and culture of victimhood and help me move out into a larger world. I wanted to be a historian of Europe, and since French was the first European language I had studied, France would inevitably be a central concern.

The France that attracted my attention existed largely in my mind, of course. I had been taught that France was preeminently the country where intellectuals are most prized. Everyone I knew who had spent time in France took this idea for granted. Beyond that, I had learned, France was a country of artistic and cultural riches. I imagined that in France it did not much matter if one were clumsy at sports (as I was). I had absorbed from parents and teachers the notion that Europe was at the center of the globe, the place where western civilization began and where it was most completely developed. Europe was the big time.

I must admit that my image of the Europe I wanted to study was not entirely favorable. Growing up during World War II and studying, with Henry Bragdon, World War I and the sad failure to follow it with a lasting peace (Bragdon had written a biography of Woodrow Wilson), I came to feel that Europe had betrayed its brilliant possibilities and succumbed to nationalism, dictatorship, and war. Europe's twentieth century seemed to me particularly disastrous. I wanted to find out what had gone wrong.

That interest ripened in college. I majored in modern European history at Washington and Lee University and at Oxford. My most impressive professors—James G. Leyburn, William A. Jenks, John M. Roberts, James Joll—became role models. I watched them closely to see what made a teacher succeed. My final decision to become a professor of contemporary European history was made following my military service, in fall 1958. My two years in the Navy included a summer in the Middle East. More shocks of discovery in Beirut,

Damascus, and Cairo developed even further my taste for *dépaysement*. Just before leaving the Navy, I took and passed the examination for the Foreign Service. The State Department would not wait while I got a doctorate, however, so I turned down the Foreign Service appointment and entered the doctoral program in European history at Harvard in September 1958.

My choice of Vichy France as the subject of my doctoral dissertation came about only later, at the end of a circuitous, accident-filled route. When I departed for a research year in Paris in September 1960, I had something else in mind. In 1960 the French Army was in a state of open revolt over the fate of French Algeria. After six years of inconclusive French military action against the Algerian independence movement, President Charles de Gaulle had opened negotiations with Algerian representatives. Much of the French colonial population in Algeria, supported by a substantial part of the officer corps, refused to accept any negotiated settlement. They threatened to overthrow the French Republic in order to keep Algeria French. I wanted to study historically how the professional culture of the French officer corps had been formed. It occurred to me that learning how French officers were socialized at the French military academy at Saint-Cyr (the French West Point) would help explain their solidarity as a professional corps and their sense of mission to save an abstract France from France's actually existing government and citizenry.

I was rebuffed, however, when I went to the French Army's archives in the *château* of Vincennes, in the Paris suburbs, to explain my project. All the archives of the military academy at Saint-Cyr, I was told, had been destroyed by American bombers in 1944. No serious research could be done on my subject.

Raoul Girardet, of the Institut d'Études Politiques de Paris (known as Sciences Po), the most thoughtful scholar of French military institutions and attitudes, had agreed to give me informal advice on my dissertation. I told him that my subject was impossible. Since French military society interests you, he told me, why not study the officer corps during the German occupation of 1940–1944, that most fascinating and painful moment when French officers were seeking their legitimate chief. Was he at Vichy, in the person of Marshal Pétain? Or was it General de Gaulle in London? Or General Giraud in Algiers? If I wanted to study the Armistice Army of Vichy France, M. Girardet said, he could put me in touch with General Weygand, French commander-in-chief in June 1940 and after that the Vichy government's minister of defense. That sounded like a good idea to me, and my supervisor at Harvard, H. Stuart Hughes, had no objection. By October 1960, I was launched on a doctoral dissertation on the Armistice Army of 1940–1944 and, without knowing it, on a lifetime's engagement with Vichy France.

So it was back to the French Army archives at Vincennes. But the reply was no more encouraging than before. All French archives were closed for fifty years. I could not see any official documents concerning the Armistice Army. "Read *Les Grandes Vacances* by Francis Ambrière," one archivist told me. "That novel contains everything you need to know about the Armistice Army."

A novel was not my idea of historical research. But even without access to the French archives, it turned out that in 1960 abundant sources were available in France for a study of the Armistice Army: the press, the stenographic transcripts of the public hearings of the postwar collaboration trials, personal testimonies and memoirs, the five volumes of documents of the French delegation to the Armistice Commission at Wiesbaden that the French government had published beginning in the 1950s. I decided to go ahead.

That year of research in Paris, from September 1960 to August 1961, constituted my first real immersion in French society. My Washington and Lee classmate Jean-Marie Grandpierre kindly took me under his wing and introduced me to his friends in Paris. My French improved under their merciless scrutiny. Over the Christmas break (graduate students couldn't fly home in those days), I drew on my ornithological hobby and joined a group of biology students who were going to spend two weeks banding birds on the island of Ouessant, off the Brittany coast. Subjected to a daily barrage of their friendly chatter, I finally crossed the linguistic threshold. I could chatter back. I watched immense seas crashing onto the cliffs at the foot of the lighthouse of Cré'ach, the first of many bewitching landscapes that compose my visual memory of France. I am still in touch with the friends from my Ouessant days.

At work, I interviewed about thirty retired colonels and generals, some of them several times. The conversations were invariably fascinating and sometimes tense. Not only were the defeat of 1940 and the German occupation extremely touchy subjects; the Algerian War was also devouring everyone's attention. Most of the officers thought that the United States was not helping France as much as it should. Senator John F. Kennedy had even given a speech in favor of the independence of Algeria that made him famous (and infamous) in France. One of the officers I interviewed, Colonel Charles Lacheroy, disappeared underground as a militant of "*l'Algérie française*" soon after our conversation in February 1961. At the other extreme, Air Force General Pierre Gallois understood that even to win such a war would do France more harm than good.

After I returned to the United States in August 1961, my undergraduate classmate Henry Turner, completing his doctorate in German history at Princeton, alerted me to the existence in the National Archives in Washington of thousands of microfilm reels of archives captured from the German Army in 1945. As Turner suspected, they contained fascinating documents concerning German officers' contacts with the Vichy French Armistice Army. The German archives gave my work an entirely new dimension. A further year immersed in them enabled me to present a much more complete and nuanced account of Vichy-German relations, of the role of the army in Vichy's National Revolution, and of Vichy's active pursuit of a foreign policy of armed neutrality.

My first book—*Parades and Politics at Vichy*—was published in 1966. I did not expect it to be translated into French, and it was not. Indeed, it was barely noticed in France. Its existence was noted in three lines in the *Revue française de science politique,* in a list of recently received books that would not be reviewed. Other than that, nothing.

My study of the Vichy officer corps, however, led imperatively on to a sequel. I had discovered that the common French understanding of the Vichy regime was not supported by what I had found in the German archives and other contemporary documents. Whereas the standard view since the 1954 publication of Robert Aron's classic *Histoire de Vichy* held that all initiatives during the occupation years came from the German side and that Vichy mainly reacted, the German archives showed that Vichy had enjoyed a certain autonomy during the first year. It had used this margin of maneuver to pursue vigorously its own dual project: the National Revolution at home and, abroad, a policy of neutrality upheld by an effort to keep both Axis and Allied armies out of the French empire ("*défense tous azimuts*"). Reports from Vichy by American diplomats, consulted in the National Archives in Washington, confirmed this interpretation. I embarked with mounting excitement on a general study of Vichy France.

My second book appeared in the United States in 1972 as *Vichy France: Old Guard and New Order, 1940–1944.* One of my Harvard mentors, the master analyst of French politics Stanley Hoffmann, generously offered to find me a French publisher. Gallimard turned me down, but Les Editions du Seuil decided to take the risk. My editors at Le Seuil were keenly aware that my book, since it was in such flagrant contradiction to received views, would be scrutinized minutely. Many of my assertions inspired incredulity. Le Seuil feared, quite legitimately, for its reputation. Therefore my editors assigned one of their younger colleagues, Michel Winock, along with the young historian Jean-Pierre Azéma (whose mother was doing the translation) to review my text. Winock and Azéma went over my manuscript line by line and sent me numerous queries. I was able to justify most of my assertions with documentary evidence.

I was grateful for their care, for a furor arose when *Vichy France* was published in French translation as *La France de Vichy* in 1973. While many of the newspaper reviews were favorable, *La Revue française de science politique* was quite negative, as were many former Vichy officials and supporters. Approval from newspapers and doubt from academia was the opposite of what I had expected. Nor had I expected the French public to seize on this book with such intensity. I found myself swept up in a violent debate. I had to defend my conclusions in many public appearances and in discussions on radio and television.

After 1973, therefore, my relationship with France changed. I was no longer an anonymous graduate student preparing a thesis or an unknown American assistant professor. I was now someone who had written a notorious book. For the French reading public, I had entered into the category of public intellectual. This meant that I was expected to state an opinion on practically anything. Was it possible that the French enthusiasm for intellectuals, which once had so attracted me, could verge on the uncritical?

As for me, I now had a mission. I had to defend my interpretation of Vichy France. In my office at Columbia I hung a copy of a well-known Vichy poster that I had found in a right-wing bookstore on the rue de Vaugirard. Marshal Pétain looked out regally under the legend, *"Comprenez-vous mieux que lui les problèmes de l'heure?"* (Do you understand the problems of our time better than he does?). I attached to it my reply on a slip of paper: *"oui."*

My French readers were divided. Whereas many of them—usually the older ones—found my book farcically wrong and profoundly wounding, others—especially younger people—were convinced by my interpretation. I even had fans. Over the years, I had the immense satisfaction of watching the first group diminish and the second expand. As serious research on Vichy got underway in France in the 1970s and swelled to a flood after a new law in 1979 began to open the French archives, an emerging school of French contemporary historians tended to confirm my views, at least in their main lines. Some particular points were criticized: John Sweets and Pierre Laborie, on opposite sides of the Atlantic, found in their studies of particular localities that popular enthusiasm for the Vichy regime was less broad and less enduring than I had said. By and large, however, the new French scholarship accepted the internal origins of the National Revolution and the autonomy and vigor of Vichy's initiatives.

I was not, contrary to the belief of many French people, the first person to undertake scholarly research on Vichy. The German historian Eberhard Jäckel and two French scholars, Yves Durand and Henri Michel, had preceded me. I had several advantages, however: a fresh point of view, distance that passed in France for objectivity (I was not truly objective, but at least I was not involved in any French clan), and the formidable heavy artillery of the German archives. Moreover, it was my good fortune, as historian Henry Rousso later pointed out, to appear on the scene just as the events of 1968 produced a generation of young readers who rejected their elders' comfortable fictions and who were eager for a fresh look at France during the German occupation. For whatever reason, after 1973 my professional life was indissolubly linked to the flood tide of French national debate about the occupation years, and this tide would carry me along up to retirement and beyond.

After 1973 I needed to be in France at least part of every year to work. The very concept of coming to France to work was quite outside the comprehension of my friends, both American and French. When I told my American friends that I was off to France for several months, they responded with knowing winks. No, I would say, I will not be in Saint-Tropez but in the Bibliothèque nationale six days a week. Sure, they said. When I arrived in France, my French friends all wished me "*bonnes vacances.*" No, I would say, I am spending six days a week in the Archives nationales. Well, anyway, they would say, "*bonnes vacances.*" There has always been a disconnect in my life between the tensions and pressures I experienced in France and everyone else's expectation that in France pleasure comes first.

My work experience in France was filled with contrasts. If any essentialism lingered in my image of France, it did not survive the research I carried out in the archives of fifteen rural departments for my 1996 book *French Peasant Fascism: Henry Dorgères' Greenshirts and the Crises of French Agriculture, 1929–1939.* Moving back into the 1930s, I thought, might liberate me from the passions surrounding Vichy and also from the remaining obstacles to research on the war years. I discovered that the 1930s aroused strong feelings, too, and that access to departmental archives for the prewar decade could still be difficult. I discovered that the *archives départementales,* which I had imagined as identical branches of a monolithic state in the Napoleonic mold, varied profoundly according to the personality and opinions of each director. Most *directeurs des archives départementales* received me with professionalism and courtesy, though with a surprising variety of procedures for obtaining clearance for consulting the archives. In a few departments, the director was visibly elated to welcome a foreign researcher and volunteered extra help. In one department, my very presence seemed to offend.

❧

I have now been visiting France for fifty-five years. In the last two decades I have spent between two and three months in France each year. My wife,

Sarah Plimpton, an unconditional Francophile, had bought a tiny garret apartment in the Marais years before we met, and we spent our summers there. I wrote in the salon, she painted in the bedroom. In 1992 we fixed up a small stone barn near Cluny where we could escape from the noise and heat of Paris to a more bucolic work setting. Our lives have thus become deeply involved in the delights and pains of a second home in France. We have struggled to persuade ferrets to leave and plumbers to come.

So why France? The reasons have evolved and expanded over the years. The ties are multiple. First I came to visit. Later I came to study. Still later I came to prepare myself to write and teach young Americans about the history of France and of Europe in the twentieth century. After 1973 I came to participate in debates about Vichy, to defend my interpretation, and to work on new books. Finally, after all, I came in order to enjoy the pleasures of the table, the artistic treasures, the landscapes, and the friendships to be found in France.

Now I have acquired a peculiar identity shaped simultaneously by deep Appalachian roots combined with active involvement, professional and personal, in France. In wanting to learn about Europe, I never meant to cease being American. I never meant to expatriate myself and become French. I wanted to appropriate France intellectually, without ceasing for a moment to be American.

After a time I no longer felt completely at home in either the United States or France. I came to inhabit a new continent of my own making, somewhere between the two, in an imaginary mid-Atlantic space. I did not consider my mid-Atlantic identity a liability. I thought of it more as a liberation than a constraint. I felt enlarged by it. It enabled me to move about freely in both the European space and the American space without ever becoming enclosed in either one.

Mastering the French space meant speaking good enough French to "pass." I wanted to become so fluent that I could step out of my American identity at will (carefully keeping the key to let myself back in) and move freely and surreptitiously within French society. It was an alluring test of prowess, and I clung for a long time to the illusion that I would succeed. Well beyond middle age I still spent at least a few minutes every day perfecting pronunciation, rehearsing complicated turns of phrase, and looking up new words. Once when I was mistaken for Danish I thought I was really getting somewhere. Finally, when someone commented, after what I considered a particularly dazzling flourish, "*Ah, Monsieur est belge,*" I had to admit to myself that I would never pass clandestinely among the French.

Just as the France that had caught my adolescent attention existed largely in my mind, I came to understand that I, too, existed partly in the French imagination. On bad days I felt that it was hard for me to be perceived in France as an individual, so strong is the assumption, even among some otherwise sophisticated French people, that all Americans conform to one simple type. I became something of a connoisseur of national stereotypes, on both sides. I encountered my first French stereotype of the United States in the fall of 1960. The little sister of one of my new friends asked me what floor I lived on. I was puzzled for a moment until I realized that she thought all Americans inhabit skyscrapers. Since then I have very often heard intelligent and cultivated French people express surprisingly essentialist and conspiratorial views of the United States.

I believe that French perceptions of the United States have improved since my first regular stays in the 1960s. I do not mean that they have become more favorable (why should they?) but that they are now based on more information and are more nuanced. A great many more French people, especially young people, have traveled or studied in the United States, where their presuppositions were tested against direct observation. One could hardly cling to the persistent nineteenth-century French perception of America as the apex of modernity, for example, after a bumpy bus ride from JFK airport along the seedy and paper-strewn Van Wyck Expressway. In my own professional life, the most significant improvement in French reactions to the United States has been the wide opening of French academic life to outsiders. When I was a young assistant professor in the 1960s, many French academics ignored American scholars. Today American scholars of France enjoy fruitful cooperation and warm friendship with French colleagues.

On the American side, the common stereotypes seem to me to have evolved less. The stereotypes on both sides have distant origins and astonishing longevity. American stereotypes of France go back at least to Jefferson and Adams. The theme of French decadence was reinforced when American soldiers encountered ubiquitous bars and legal bordellos in 1917. The newer theme of French ingratitude began over war debts in the 1920s and was solidly entrenched in the 1960s during the presidency of Charles de Gaulle: we saved them twice, the logic went, so they owe us subservience. The crudity of these stereotypes becomes particularly conspicuous when the president of the United States himself uses them for electoral advantage. The efforts of several thousand American scholars of France to impart a more nuanced and informed view have not weakened them.

I have lived through two periods of popular irritation between the two countries. Both times I tried to open American eyes. In the middle and late 1960s, I traveled around to campuses and civic associations in the United States with a lecture that tried to present General de Gaulle more sympathetically, as a European practitioner of *realpolitik* who supported the United States when American policy was supportable. Currently I find myself trying to counteract the effect of books with titles like *France: Our Oldest Enemy*. I have no desire to place either country on a pedestal, defend either one unconditionally. But the simplistic portrayal of one or the other in black or white as inherently evil or good makes a healthy relationship impossible.

Having devoted a large part of my professional career to studying France in its darkest moment since the Black Death, I am sometimes asked if this has given me negative feelings about the place. No, I say, there was always the other France, the France of the *Declaration of the Rights of Man* and of the Resistance. Similarly, although I object strenuously to current American policies, I know that nearly half of my fellow citizens share my opposition. From my mid-Atlantic vantage point, I can see things to deplore and reasons for hope on both sides.

CHAPTER 3

✄ Tough Love for France

Herman Lebovics

All of my historical work (and much of my life) has been dedicated to refusing, disassembling, and attacking laws and rules. Questioning the idols of authority has not made my personal life or my professional one easy. But it has
benefited my history writing by adding the passion of engagement to the scholarly work. When, in my late twenties, I had become emotionally and intellectually ready, France took a privileged place in my imagination as the
homeland of secularism, freedom, and equality—of rules not imposed from
above. But to discover this potential France, I soon learned, I first had to peel
back some layers of the really existing France.

Brought up in a refugee, unskilled, working-class, Orthodox Jewish family, I got a great dose of fear of the world outside. I was born in Czechoslova-
kia in 1935. My family lived in a small village in the extreme eastern part of
the country, where the Jews—many of them religious—spoke Yiddish and
Hungarian, and the peasants spoke various Slavic dialects. Soon after I was
born my parents decided to move to America to harvest the rich rewards of
life in the New World. In the classic immigrant pattern, my father left first, in
1938. But history—unexpected as usual—caught up with us. A year later, now
stateless, with no passports, just a travel document issued from Budapest (the
country had just been invaded and divided between Germany in the West and
Hungary in the East), my mother, sister, and I made a harrowing voyage to
the United States. We had planned to travel west from the United Kingdom,
but in 1939 that was no longer possible. Instead we were forced to go south. In

Genoa we found a boat that would take us to America. I can still recall the smell of third class, that mixture of sweat, diesel oil, and salami. Proust would not have liked it. Arriving in New York, my waiting father and his uncle loaded us in a car for the drive to Bridgeport in nearby Connecticut. During the ride, I remember finally feeling safe. As the car rolled to our new home, I sunk into a deep sleep in the precious feather bed my mother had brought with us to our new home.

Bridgeport was an ugly industrial town. Apparently it had always been so. But it had rubber and brass factories vital to what became, soon after our arrival, the war effort. There were plenty of jobs. My mother worked as a seamstress and my father held down two industrial jobs to make ends meet.

My neighborhood was ethnically very mixed. Bridgeport had a large Hungarian community. Along with the several Hungarian kids who gathered after school to play touch football in our little green park surrounded on all sides by factories, other families came (some fairly recently) from Norway, French Canada, Italy, and Ireland. And then there was Ricardo, our American Indian buddy.

Once I started public school, I integrated easily into my America-in-the-plural. I had learned English in a few months. At home we spoke a classic immigrant mélange of Yiddish, Hungarian, and English—often in the same sentence. Our hybridized language evidenced the archaeological strata of our lives. But whereas I embraced my variegated new world, my mother and father responded to the refugee experience and the murder of most of the family that had stayed behind by hewing even tighter to a sense of group loyalty. The survival strategy they followed in this strange new world—along with many of their condition and generation—was that, if we followed the rules of G–d and that of the sanctioned American public order, we would be safe. This was an old practice/strategy of East European Jews that, it must be said, seemed to have worked at certain conjunctures in the past.

Accordingly, in this fearful world, the explanations for why human situations played out in a certain way came down to me either as "it is natural" or else as citations of rules and obligations that G–d had imposed on us. From my first memories, I can recall that I was not an obedient believer. But only when I was much older could I put my "no" into words. I preferred to pass the long dreary Orthodox Sabbaths immersed in faraway worlds. Without a guide or mentor, I read whatever came to hand in our little local library, an elegantly white Greek-columned building surrounded by the noisy, ugly mills of our neighborhood. I began with the books with red covers. Then I tried the blue ones. But soon I decoded the promise of book titles. By my early teens, I made the discovery that if I chose books according to their authors, I would more likely be pleased with my finds. I read only fiction. I didn't much like the books our teachers made us read. Only in college did I voluntarily begin reading "true" books.

As a sophomore in college studying philosophy, I was assigned some Spinoza to read. I found him interesting but was not particularly drawn by his dry, mathlike mode of presentation. Home on vacation, I asked a fund-collector for a Yeshiva who had come to the house to solicit for his charity, what exactly the ceremony of *Cherem* (excommunication) was that Spinoza suffered in the Amsterdam Jewish community: "Sonny-boy, behave yourself and you will never need to know what happens in a *Cherem*." I was infuriated by that answer. I still feel rage now as I write about the experience. It propelled me faster along my road to rebellion. I became a Spinozian on the spot. By my graduation from the University of Connecticut, I had added a Voltairean fundamentalism whose bible was *Candide,* and I had begun to read Marx.

But none of my freelance adolescent and college reading should be understood in a "textual" sense. Like an athlete, I always challenged myself to ever harder reads, with the usual result that I didn't deeply understand much of it. The fiction of my teens, as well as Spinoza, Voltaire, Marx, and other authors I read during my college years, my "head-stuffing period," helped me build a sensibility, a stance in the world, which was different from the restriction and caution my parents urged upon me. That sensibility judged orthodox religion—all orthodox religions, including the periodic anti-Semitic words and acts on the part of some of our Hungarian Christian neighbors—not as community- or divinely ordained values, as some born-agains do today, but rather as darkness, suffocation, and bigotry. I majored in history and philosophy at UConn. I enjoyed talking philosophy, but history became my true love.

Although I had wanted to go to Wisconsin for graduate work, in the 1960s the most interesting history department in the country, I could not afford it. As in college, where I had worked in steel plants in the summers and campus jobs during the school year, I needed to pay my own way. I was forced to accept a good-sized fellowship at Yale—I could afford nothing else. Yale had a splendid library and a dear man, Hajo Holborn, a German émigré whose good will and intellectual generosity reinforced my resolve to do a thesis on Weimar and Nazi history. The Germans had been decisive in my life story: they were the principal cause of my coming to America and the indirect cause of my parents' re-ghettoization. I wanted to find out how come I had become an American.

At the end of my first year in graduate school, I married Victoria, a graduate student in the French department. In 1959, we went off to Berlin so that I could research and write a socio-intellectual history of the array of ideas worked out by those neo-conservative intellectuals who, though sympathetic to National Socialism, stood aloof from the street politics of fascism. Appropriately named *Edel-Nazis* (classy Nazis), they provided words and slogans that Hitler and the National Socialists could plug and play on their way to power. Berlin in 1959–1960—just before the wall—was the greatest school of my life. And the Freie Universität of (West) Berlin was intellectually and politically the most exciting place I had ever seen.

Not because of the professors, *überhaupt nicht*. In the late 1950s and early 1960s, most of them were still intellectually paralyzed by the horror of having to confront the Crimes of recent German history. Attending their lectures, I realized that they had not yet discovered a way to do so. I found rather that, perhaps because they were young and perhaps because they had clean hands but so much guilt, my fellow students were discussing the important questions of society and history. The year started with my frequenting the Socialist youth group that had just been expelled for wanting to hang on to the Marxist principles which the party had just jettisoned at its Bad Godesberg congress. Looking for new directions, my comrades of the Socialist student group would read anything, discuss anything, and write theses on any topic that might reinvigorate or reinvent what Perry Anderson would later call "Western Marxism." With glasses of cheap wine in our hands, and the *U-Bahn* stopped for the night, we would sit up all night listening in fascination to one of our comrades reading from their dissertations on Rosa Luxemburg, or Antonio Gramsci, or Herbert Marcuse, or fascism, or some key—if not always well-known—issue in the history of socialist struggles. These evening sessions and frequent participation in political demonstrations against the United States and the Adenauer (Christian Democratic) government deepened both my education and my commitment to changing American society toward great openness and freedom.

We decided to spend the spring break in France, Victoria's country. We left overcast, grey, tense Berlin for Paris and the light. I was immediately enchanted by the food. Of course the city's beauty seduced me, too. In 1958, Charles de Gaulle's new government had come to power by means of something very close to a military coup d'état. When we arrived in the spring of 1961, France was waging the last phase of the Algerian war. With the shock waves of colonial war buffeting French society—for the first time, draftees had been sent to fight for the empire—Paris was, if anything, even more politicized than Berlin. Machine gun–armed policemen were everywhere. The police stopped students all the time. We joined the many, mostly illicit, antiwar demonstrations.

But the political discourses of Paris and Berlin differed radically. In Berlin, politics, still tinged with guilt, were, finally, about the Nazi past and a *possible* democratic future. In Paris I met people who explained to me the dreadful ways in which the French leaders of the day were violating the *nation's traditions* of liberty and justice. Here was a people that had overthrown an archaic, clerical, monarchical order and then made those transvaluations its raison d'être. As a political animal, I was delighted by this historical achievement. In terms of my personal condition, I decided to learn more about this country that had made the revolution that first gave equal civic status to its Jews. Here was where I could learn more about how to live as a left-wing, secular Jew. In mid-August 1961, back in Berlin, as we packed to return home, we heard the shocking news that the government of the GDR had put up a wall between the eastern and the western sectors of our city.

I came back to America cured of German history. In my stay I had met very good young people both while doing politics and in my classes in the social sciences. *My* German generation felt deep remorse and sought to remodel German society. I returned home feeling that the country—at least West Germany—would be "safe" with them. I hurriedly turned my research into a thesis and then a book on the intellectual forebears of Nazism in Weimar Germany.

Finishing that work freed my soul of the obsessive "Why the Nazis?" question that still haunts contemporary history writing. Just as I turned my thesis into a book, a group of younger German historians at the University of Bielefeld, led by Hans-Ulrich Wehler and Jürgen Kocka, began their great project to master the recent German past. They identified the decisive negative turning point for Germany as having occurred in the years from Bismarck to Hitler. Their studies privileged the working class (why no socialism?) and the state (why authoritarian rule?). So although the Bielefeld School did work much more interesting than that of my Berlin professors, and even had good politics, I found that they left out too much German history. They gridlocked themselves in the years between 1870 and 1933. Moreover, they embraced the thesis of a particular German path. As a student I had been privileged to read and see great creations of *European* culture that were "Made in Germany." I felt that there was more to Germany than the Nazis, and the German *Sonderweg* (special path) appeared to me the path of many other countries of central and Eastern Europe, as well as Japan in Asia. In my German-comparative studies I had learned that, like one of those viruses that under certain conditions can turn virulent, even the most democratic societies risked fascist episodes. I wanted to know more about how some twentieth-century societies

had avoided barbarism. France seemed to me a likely case in point. And, besides, like so many German exiles and settlers before me, I wanted now to live,
as the Germans used to say, "like a king in France."

So in the 1970s began my great romance with France. But like many another great love, it worked initially because it was blind. As I learned more
about the country and its history, I realized that I had gotten "engaged" to a
rather naïve vision of the land that had given us liberty, equality, and fraternity. The slogans were inspiring, but the practice not always equal to them.
Still, with time and deeper understanding, I grew into a more mature and
richer relation with *La France*.

As my interest in France deepened, I began to appreciate how I had learned
to do French history in Germany: how sophisticated theory can inform historical writing; how in my analyses I always had to engage with questions of
social conflict over resources and instruments of power; how culture and ideas
mattered; and, finally, how there was no contradiction between *l'engagement*
and honest history writing. My French story started in Strasbourg, a wonderful crossing point to make my own move to the other side of the Rhine. I spent
several summers learning the language from the local, slowly spoken French
and reaching for my German only in cases of communications emergency.

Up to that point my own interests had run to the history of ideas. But social history was becoming the principal paradigm, both in Europe and at
home. Taking as my model Hans Rosenberg's political-economic study of the
second German empire, *Grosse Depression und Bismarckzeit,* I began a work on
the socioeconomic history of France in those same depression years (1873–
1896) that had struck everywhere in Western Europe. The study took me more
time than anything else I have written. For as I worked on the book, I also had
to learn more French language, more French history, and more economics.
*The Alliance of Iron and Wheat: Origins of the New Conservatism of the Third Re-
public, 1860–1914* finally came out in 1988. It was organized around a largely
implicit comparison of the German and French solutions to the problem of
containing revolution.

That work has stood up—if the evidence of people still citing it counts—
I think, not because it was comparative but because it was situated in a European field. I have never thought of France in isolation from neighbors and its
empire; I have never written solely national history. I have never taught a
course on the history of France, nor of any one nation. This, my first work on
French events, was not the liveliest piece of writing, with its columns of international trade statistics, discussions of tariff revisions, and graphs on XY axes.
But the book was, and is, important for me because its publication gave me
permission at last to turn to cultural history.

For by the late 1980s, I had decided that I could better understand economic, political, and social relations from the perspectives of cultural representation. Indeed, it was evident to me that we could best read the force vectors of the twentieth century from the languages, images, symbols, and rituals of the era. France lay at the epicenter of the study of the ways of cultural power. So by the 1980s, France for me meant not only a revolutionary tradition. It also was generating the most useable cultural theory for historical work.

The questions of power that my earlier focus on ideas and then economics had not satisfactorily answered, together with the key role of representation and symbol I learned doing movement politics, gradually led me to turn my attention to the force of culture in social, political, and economic life. In 1963, John Hope Franklin, the great historian of African-American history, who was then chair of history at Brooklyn College of CUNY, had given me my first job. Once settled in New York, I immediately took up the civil rights activities I had begun in New Haven by joining the Harlem chapter of the Congress for Racial Equality. But instead of advancing American social justice together, our chapter, and the others after ours, tore themselves apart in a destructive political struggle. In response to the split in our movement, the whites and blacks on the left invented a new rhetoric of pluralism: people should work to raise political consciousness in their own community. This temporary blowout patch to a harmful break in the freedom struggle has caused endless confusion, in later debates in the United States and France, between advocates of a misunderstood and conjuncturally induced "multiculturalism" and unitary republicanism.

In the wake of the feminist breakaway from the male-dominated student movement, the fragmentation of the civil rights movement, and the rise of other kinds of ethnic identity politics in the 1990s, we began to see emerge in the United States what the philosopher Jürgen Habermas soon labeled "the new social movements." I welcomed them, for each recognized in different realms that language and symbols, images, and ceremonies were, and had always been, forces for oppression or progress in history. I decided to make these new multi-faceted advocacies—to the degree I could—my own. But what could such a method mean in a France that was centralized, mono-cultural (or so the republican discourse had it), and bound with strong chains to the printed word? Surely the country in which I was spending most summers, the country I had come to enjoy and to find beautiful everywhere I traveled—the land and people with which I experienced a deepening love—could benefit by allowing the great diversity in its history and society to come into play.

I continued to think a lot about the apparent diversity that I saw when I was in France—its rich variety of regions, its varied ecologies, its several religions (including, as I then observed, *laïcité,* ex-Catholicism, and Islam), its complicated secular-religious demarcations—and all the delicate balances that permitted such social complexity and heterogeneity to stay in dynamic equilibrium. Except, of course, when it toppled over, as it did explosively in the summer of 1968.

The decade after May '68 had been especially marked by militant left regionalisms (Occitanie, Larzac, Brittany). Politicized differences in the regions were matched by a new sense of differences in the working class. Although the republican contract acknowledged only French citizens all legally equal to each other, I was seeing much more diversity. In the Jacobin tradition, republicans believed that all in France were or ought to be equal partners in the nation. But I also saw in the TV news and in the newspaper reports and opinion pieces suggestions that the "minorities," "Islam," or the "immigrants" represented a problem for France. How could an American, especially one sensitized all of his life to the politics of difference, miss these signs of a relatively new postcolonial France?

I was in Paris in the summer of 1973, for example, when the CFDT labor union took up the cause of the foreign or minority workers—mostly north and sub-Saharan African in origin—who could not get promoted out of the infernal Renault body shop to better jobs in the plant. Officially the company stratified the work force by skill level, but immigrant workers remained stuck in the worst and poorest paid jobs. We marched together that marvelous day—CFDT members, immigrant workers, and various *gauchistes* to protest the discrimination visited upon the newest members of the French working class. This was the first Paris demonstration—as far as I know—against racism in the workplace. But thinking a little about the racial prejudice against the people from the one-time colonies who had helped create the thirty glorious years of French economic growth soon led me to see the strong traces in metropolitan France of the former colonial empire. Engaged so recently with both the tragedies of German history and the scandal of racial prejudice at home, I have to admit I was shocked and a little disillusioned with my France.

A turning point for me was the great left victory in the elections of 1981. The jubilant socialists now began to celebrate the minorities, not—as in the 1970s—as just so many more candidates for the classic republican assimilation project but as members of a culturally pluralist nation. But I did not *learn* from these political experiences in Germany, France, and the United States. Already in college—having studied as much philosophy as history—I had been persuaded that Kant's and Ernst Cassirer's arguments that we fit new experiences into existing mental frames was right. And when later I read historian Joan Scott's denial that experience is the basis of our knowledge, it only confirmed what had become for me an epistemological certainty. Although not a *source* of coherent knowledge, my experiences nevertheless launched me into a series of new mental historical experiments that tested ideas of social pluralism versus unitary inclusion in contemporary French social debates. By a similar process, my march with the body shop workers at Renault had impelled me think about the importance of the colonial empire in creating modern-day France.

In Germany, in France, and back home in the United States, I learned how fictions such as race, nationalism, and cultural superiority could be powerful instruments of social hegemony and contestation. Reading Gramsci, the Frankfurt School, and Michel Foucault helped me turn my insights into research questions. We make the world in which we live. It is not "naturally given." Still, I have never been persuaded that the stuff of which we make it is language. Societies give languages their meaning and their power to produce action, not the other way around. But the study of culture, I realized, was the way into understanding the coding, symbolization, and aesthetics of power in a society.

In the late 1960s I was fortunate to take a position at Stony Brook, an exciting new New York state university in the making. Here we could create a place of research and teaching that would better suit our sense of the needs of American learning. Here, too, I could start again. And I have benefited greatly in spending most of my career at Stony Brook. I met Aldona Jonaitis, a colleague in the art history department who would teach me much about how to read images and a little something about her own interest in the cultures then called "primitive." Her subject was the art of the peoples of the northwest coast of Canada. Learning about Amerindian identity politics reinforced questions I had for my own field. Could a nation, a group, a person choose their own identities? Do all get but one identity? Oppressed people's intellectuals seemed to be arguing that. But so did the Nazis, among other fascists, and the ideologues of Vichy France. Clearly identity was not an answer—it was the problem. And a highly contested French identity offered me a rich field of investigation.

These meditations led me in 1992 to publish my *True France*. In it I argued that after its defeat in the Dreyfus Affair, the French right wing launched the claim that, although the republicans had gained control of the legal state, it was members of the right wing who spoke for the real France, the true France. Delving into French ethnological theory and literature, I spelled out the deleterious consequences of claiming that there was but one way to be French. The monistic racial and ethnic cultural program of the Vichy state was, of course, the best object lesson. I also sought to sketch an alternative vision present in

French history of a pluralist, more open France. American scholars received it well. The book was published in translation as *la "Vraie France."* The French edition was what I would call an underground classic, almost a *samizdat:* everyone told me they had read it, but few had bought it. Ah, the mighty photocopy machine! Except for some favorable reviews in French scholarly journals, the book fell flat among most of the Paris intelligentsia. I felt somewhat vindicated, and deeply touched, when a young African-French employee at the publisher's warehouse handed me some author's copies, with the words, "Monsieur, there are many true things in your book." But the fact remained that the exhilarating pluralist discourse of the left that had inspired my research had yielded to increasingly harsh new political realities. For the socialist government under Mitterrand had dealt with the increasingly bad economic conjuncture of the early 1980s by moving to the right, both economically and socially.

By the early 1990s, the extreme-right leader Jean-Marie Le Pen was using the social malaise to garner support among the discontented and the resentful. With unemployment growing, his "France for the French" found a strong resonance. The left responded by closing ranks, as it had done during the Dreyfus Affair and again at the moment of the Popular Front. To Le Pen's racist clash of civilizations, the left responded with a unitary republican discourse. Le Pen had successfully transformed the hope of a rich multiplicity into a discourse of racial division. Indeed, the North African immigrants were different, he claimed. They could never be real French. They should return to their own true homes. Just as *la "Vraie France"* appeared, the parties of the left put forth their own, admittedly republican, version of a True (inclusive) France.

I had chafed under my own re-ghettoized upbringing. I had experienced and studied the violence of National Socialist exclusionism. And I had witnessed the post–civil rights era swing to Black Nationalism in the United States. Could a culture of mutuality and solidarity ever be built? I asked myself. Many good and fair-minded French friends thought so. Cultural unity was the precondition to social solidarity, they proposed, and social solidarity was the fundament of economic, social, and political justice. I decided to test how a culturally unified France might look. This research led me to write *Mona Lisa's Escort,* about André Malraux's creation of France's ministry of cultural affairs. Aiming to re-unify a badly divided France after assuming the presidency of the new Fifth Republic in 1958, de Gaulle appointed Malraux minister of cultural affairs and asked him to revive, refurbish, and diffuse French culture to a broader swath of French society. My book's guiding questions were: did this strategy work and what did that renewed culture look like?

I found my answer in May 1968. Sociologist Pierre Bourdieu's 1968 inquiry into why workers and peasants do not visit art museums (*The Love of Art*) was important for me. Like the arts buyer that he had once been, Malraux was polishing and rearranging old treasures and then making them available to anyone with the means to appreciate them. But, Bourdieu showed, most of the population did not know the codes for art, the ways of understanding and (apparently) effortlessly assimilating art that bourgeois individuals had learned at home and had assimilated as a habitus of (apparently) effortless and instant appreciation of cultural production. So, for most of France the treasures were not seen, and when seen, not appreciated. They did not have the means to do so.

In 1968, the students and intellectuals who were destined to be its bearers rejected the house of culture that Malraux had restored. I realized that patching, refurbishing, and diffusing *a* heritage institutionalized for an earlier and different republican society was not the way out of France's ongoing cultural crisis, which was at the same time a social crisis. In other words, not only was France stagnating economically, with persistently elevated levels of unemployment since the economic downturn in the early 1980s, she was culturally immobilized as well.

After the publication of *Mona Lisa's Escort,* I, too, felt stuck. I had learned that neither American-style pluralism nor nineteenth-century Jacobin republicanism made sense for the modern, urban, high-tech society that France had become by the end of the twentieth century. But why was there so much talk about difference in intellectual life and otherness in social relations? Was there some special barrier blocking the road to a better France? My friends Gérard Noiriel and Patrick Weil had taught me that France was a nation deeply marked by its immigrants. I also knew that it was the European country with the greatest number of Muslims, mostly from the now dissolved colonial empire. Throughout the 1990s I heard more and more talk about the supposedly insoluble immigrant question. Le Pen's extreme right movement grew in tandem with the urgency of this "problem."

I let my historical unconscious guide me. Or was it just my bad memory? My socioeconomic study of how the Third Republic had been rooted had included a chapter on the colonies, for it was there—in the empire—that a patriotic concord had united clerical and republican France. *True France* contained a chapter on the Paris Colonial Exposition of 1931. It proposed that republican France had made the colonial empire a part of its identity. In writing the book on Malraux, I discovered that the ministry of cultural affairs had largely been built by old colonial hands.

Clearly, there was some theme for which I was not too systematically searching that linked France's colonial story to that of metropolitan France.

Upsetting many friends both in France and the United States—especially specialists in the Classical Age who wanted to continue to believe that the cultural
France they knew had come into being in the seventeenth century—I asked
myself out loud to what degree modern France had been created in the
colonial empire. I plotted the following thought experiment: what could we
say about contemporary France if we started from the premise that it was a
product of its colonial past, and that that past had not passed? So I began the
book in *la France profonde,* with a chapter on local farmers' resistance to the
government's desire to confiscate their land and use it to train troops for postcolonial wars. The narrative then moves between protestors and the conserva-
tive-dominated French state as each struggled to imprint its own vision of
what once-colonial and now postcolonial France was and should be.

My question put into perspective the so-called "immigrant question" or,
more elegantly, "multiculturalism" versus "republican inclusion." Worries,
conflicts, doubts about the future cohesion of French society, about the future
of the new French—especially those living in the poor neighborhoods of the
cities—fell into place as a part of the colonial past-present of the country. I
ended the book with a chapter on the cultural and political debates about the
colonial and regional past since, in the new millennium, officials had revealed
plans for new official places of memory: in this case, museums about people
(*musées de société*). That part of the story still needs telling. But we have to wait
for the creation and opening of these new places that will collect and try *to contain memories before we can* complete that inquiry.

✖

Writing *Bringing the Empire Back Home* led me toward a conclusion important for me both as an American and a historian of today's France: the United
States will not have democracy until the impediments of racism and empire
are removed from our society. Likewise, France will not become what, as a be-
ginner, I had thought it already was until it solves its domestic colonial question. The French people have it in their heritages and capacities to move their
democracy toward a more nuanced and tolerant inclusiveness. Meanwhile, in
my *Imperialism and the Corruption of Democracies* I have continued to offer my
contributions to the study of the empire at home, of how democracies have
been and are impeded by unmastered colonial pasts.

Since at least the Vietnam war, I have felt an intensifying dividedness about
the United States. It pains me almost every day. America gave me and my family shelter. I cannot ever forget this asylum. I am profoundly indebted to the
society that allowed me, the child of refugee parents whose schooling stopped

at elementary school, to pursue a university career in which I do work that I love. My sons live in the United States; so do my family in all its permutations, my friends, and my delights.

And yet since the start of the Iraq invasion I have felt as if I am living in something like a farcical remake, as Marx might have termed it, of the Roman empire. America has, I believe, changed since "the good war," the war against fascism and racial hatred. I wrote earlier that—to update Du Bois—race is the American question of the twenty-first century. But I now fear that the risks to democracy may be replacing it in urgency. We are living the growing intellectual and political debasement of the American people by our rulers and the media. There is always a new enemy to fight and a new terrorism to oppose. A capitalism that eclipses the ruthlessness and public-be-damned attitude of the nineteenth century robber barons dominates the economy. The modest safety net–welfare state started in the New Deal has been demolished. We are watched, investigated, contained. Elections are fixed. I do not yet see serious internal oppositional forces forming. Despite the many good reasons French voters had to vote "no" on the European constitution in 2005, the outcome saddened me. If we Americans have not found our way toward democracy, perhaps a stronger Europe might have served—a little bit—as the counterforce to overweening power.

So, despite errors, omissions, flaws, and the pressures of American-led globalization, I root for France. There, traditions and practices of democracy, justice, and equality—however unevenly practiced—are still alive. I study France to see how democracy grew, sometimes faltered, and yet grew some more. I have made the land my second homeland, as it has been the second homeland of humankind. It is my principle of hope.

CHAPTER 4

Fantasy Meets Reality:
A Midwesterner Goes to Paris

Lynn Hunt

F. Scott Fitzgerald opened the door to France for me when I was sixteen. Since he had grown up only a few blocks away from our house in St. Paul, Minnesota, curiosity prompted me to read *Tender is the Night,* set on the French Riviera. One novel quickly led to another and yet another, and soon I had devoured all of Fitzgerald, then all of Hemingway, Stein, and the rest of the "lost generation" of American expatriates in Paris. Without Fitzgerald, France would have meant to me what it meant to any other ordinary kid growing up in the midwest of the 1950s: nothing more than a faraway and vaguely glamorous spot on some other part of the earth.

Nothing else whispered things French in my ear: my father had not fought in World War II, my mother's German-speaking, immigrant father came from Ukraine, and my parents spoke excellent Spanish, having met and married in Panama during the war. For them, expatriate life meant the tropics, giant papayas, drinking martinis by the pitcher under a whirling fan, and making friends in engineering, business, or the army. The literary hijinks of Paris or the Riviera could not have been further away. Fitzgerald made them part of my dream world, transmuting adolescent sexual longing with its insistent future orientation into nostalgia for the past intensities of the left bank.

Still, Fitzgerald's France only lurked in the background while I took German in high school and started out as a German major at Carleton College. German stood for family connection and for the social mobility offered by the United States in the postwar period. My maternal grandfather had welded ties for the railroad, and my maternal grandmother was one of fourteen children from a family that farmed in western Minnesota. With no running water and no electricity, her family's farmhouse near the village of Odessa (population 204 in 1900, half that today) felt much further away from St. Paul than the measurable 170 miles. My grandfather said almost nothing about his early days in Ukraine, except that he had emigrated in order to avoid being drafted into the tsar's army. He and my grandmother attended German-language services at a nearby Lutheran church. German therefore represented a link, however tenuous, with those worlds, even then fast receding from both my own landscape and that of the country.

When I switched my major to history, the German influence carried over. As a college student in the 1960s I shared my generation's obsession with understanding the whys and hows of the Nazis. Would I have resisted the Nazi evil if I had been a student in the 1930s? The concern was personal as much as it was generational: my grandfather's first name was Adolf, after all, and he dropped an occasional anti-Semitic epithet. I remember wincing but saying nothing. My mother made it clear to us from an early age that references of that sort were unacceptable. We should never even call people "Jews"; they were "Jewish people." A world of difference apparently separated the noun from the adjective. The issue of personal versus collective responsibility could not have been etched in sharper relief, and so at Carleton I spent hours in the library arguing with classmates about Hannah Arendt's *Eichmann in Jerusalem*. Although I eventually came to disagree with Arendt's pejorative judgments about the French Revolution, she quickly became (and thereafter remained) my intellectual heroine. Her very existence proved that a woman could have a major impact on philosophical and political discussions.

Everything pointed me toward graduate school to study the Nazi phenomenon, so I did just that—for a month or two. By the beginning of my second quarter at Stanford, I had decided to focus instead on the French Revolution. Fitzgerald had by this time received significant reinforcements. I had learned French because it was required of a German major. Once signed up as a history major, I had taken a course on the French Revolution from Carleton's most charismatic professor, Carl Weiner. Although he emphasized interpretation and analysis as much as anyone, Carl also had a flair for storytelling, perhaps in part because his wife Ruth was the college theater director. Waving a sword borrowed from the wardrobe, stamping fiercely back and forth in front of the class, Carl recounted the fall of Robespierre in staccato detail. Would the sections rise in Robespierre's support one more time? Could the entire Revolution hang in the balance at 2 a.m. on a heavy summer night in July 1794? I was hooked, especially after writing my research paper on

Saint-Just, the youngest and most evangelical of the revolutionaries. Weiner had introduced us to two major lines of interpretation that would stick with me for a long time: J. L. Talmon's genealogy of "democratic totalitarianism," according to which Rousseau and the French Revolution were the ultimate sources of Soviet dictatorship, and the Marxist lineage that ran from Marx himself through Albert Mathiez and Georges Lefebvre up to Albert Soboul. Before long I had started reading the collected works of Marx and Engels and then Lenin and Mao. Fitzgerald and Marx no doubt made for a peculiar mixture, but whoever said that France was synonymous with consistency?

In some ways the Nazi seizure of power and the French Revolution posed the same question: How could an unexpected mass movement take shape almost overnight and change the course of history? Yet the French Revolution signaled creativity, optimism, and forward movement whereas the Nazi rise to power bespoke anti-Enlightenment irrationalism and reactionary politics. Genes probably explain my preference for optimism, though Minnesota's ethos of "hitch up your pants, get to it, and do good" certainly helped too. I had grown up with a stay-at-home mother who nonetheless found political activism irresistible; she believed that every single person could make a difference and that it was her duty to act accordingly. She worked with countless organizations and causes to put her beliefs into practice. As a teenager temporarily banished upstairs with my younger sisters, I could hear the low rumble of a nighttime political meeting in the living room, whether about integration, hot school lunches, or charter amendments to restructure city government. Nothing was too big or too small to escape my mother's purview. It fell to my sisters and me to pass out flyers in the neighborhood and hang around the edges of Democratic-Farmer-Labor party booyas. A "booya" was a giant collective meal prepared in big kettles. The term is thought to be a derivation of *bouillabaisse.* Whatever its provenance, all those booyas paid off, and my mother went on to hold elective office for twenty years. I came away with the sense that all social change is in the first instance local. Eugene McCarthy, standard-bearer of the antiwar movement, came from the land of ten thousand booyas.

For those of us in college in the mid-1960s, my mother's brand of step-by-step political melioration seemed insufficient. Revolution was in the air, even in Northfield, Minnesota. We were angry: at the dean of students for supporting the college's role *in loco parentis,* at the establishment for not dismantling segregation more rapidly, at the government for continuing to prosecute a war that made no sense. All of a sudden we discovered that we had been molded to accept things as they were, that the ideology of "liberalism" (meaning then "too moderate") had kept us from seeing, much less challenging, the injustices of the status quo. Many of my friends went to graduate or professional school; some went into the Peace Corps; no one confessed to an interest in business. The fury of feeling duped led a few into complete rejection. Although I was prepared to yell and to march, I was not headed underground. I hoped to make my contribution to changing the world in the classroom.

There were good political reasons for choosing the French Revolution, but they had not entirely overshadowed the more personal, Fitzgeraldian ones. Even though I had yet to set foot in Europe, my father had been to Paris once in his youth, and he spoke wistfully of Fouquet's on the Champs-Elysées. With only such bits and pieces of data at hand, a thought experiment still yielded quick results: "Would you prefer to spend the rest of your life going to Paris for research or going to Bonn or some other German city?" The question answered itself. The present entered into the equation as well. Rather than working with a senior eminence in the field of modern German history, I was opting to study with a relatively unknown assistant professor who wrote about lawyers in the French Revolution. I had signed up for Philip Dawson's research seminar on the Terror when I first arrived at Stanford, and it made my decision easy. Phil offered a perfect combination of direction, encouragement, concern, and laissez-faire. My research paper did not prove particularly memorable—I wrote on the radical Parisian politician Chaumette, like Saint-Just a victim of his own political successes—but I got my first taste of the two lasting satisfactions of French history: it led everywhere and you could share the journey.

Phil set the tone by keeping his basement office door open for frequent consultations about sources, interpretations, and everything from Wittgenstein to whether to boycott classes in opposition to the war. During the upheavals of late 1967 and early 1968, his office offered a steadying place of respite and renewal. Current events fed into our understanding of the Year II and vice versa. Everything seemed relevant: the protests against the war, the intensity of our social interactions as students at a time of crisis, and, yes, even my readings, which focused on Hegel, Jean Starobinski's fascinating intellectual biography of Rousseau, Thomas Kuhn's study of scientific revolutions, and Claude Lévi-Strauss's cultural anthropology. I had been led to these books by the sole woman on the history department faculty, Margot Drekmeier, who gave an intense ten-week reading seminar on Rousseau in 1968. Having written her dissertation on the salons of Enlightenment France, she appreciated as much as anyone the ways in which big ideas intersected, especially in times of turmoil. All of this reading led in one way or another back to the French Revolution and the question of social change. Many years later, after publishing my first books, I sometimes wondered if I should not change topics, going backward or forward in time, or broadening out to other countries. But I have yet to succeed in pulling myself away from the vortex of 1789.

Two of my classmates in the seminar on the Terror made unforgettable impressions on me: Tim Tackett and Jim Clifford. Tim had already seized hold of his interest in religion and revolution and demonstrated his indefatigable talent for research and writing, even at age twenty-two. He seemed to know just what he wanted to do, topic-wise and life-wise, which was far from being my case in either area. We would weave in and out of each other's lives for decades to come, only to end up as colleagues fifty miles apart in southern California. Jim had the most prescient topic in the seminar, it seems to me in retrospect, because he chose to work on the Revolution's Committee of Public Instruction, which played such an instrumental role in the cultural revolution of the Year II. After a year in sunny California, which he found altogether too sybaritic, he headed off to graduate study at Harvard and a remarkable career as a historian of anthropology. Since he began with French anthropology, our paths too continued to cross. My sense of the community of French historians is that people may come and go, but you never lose them, in part because they remain tied to France. You will run into them again in the Métro, an archive, or some restaurant you thought you had discovered for yourself.

Stanford is not exactly a household word for political excitement: known affectionately to insiders as "the farm," it is located in a town of the Silicon Valley called by some "Shallow Alto." The school I attended between 1967 and 1970 in hindsight seems almost hallucinatory: massive demonstrations, complete with tear gas and riots, against the Stanford Research Institute and Hewlett-Packard because they worked for the Defense Department; conflicts between graduate students over whether and how to protest; fisticuffs in faculty meetings. Add the sudden widespread availability of marijuana, the birth control pill, women's liberation, the first comings out of gays and lesbians, and the frantic efforts of male graduate students to get out of the draft, and you get an inkling of the atmosphere. Everything seemed up for grabs; no one knew what might happen next, either individually or to the nation collectively. We smoked (almost anything), drank, and stayed up to all hours. We argued, had affairs, felt confused, and somehow managed to complete our work. In the midst of the invasion of Cambodia and the killings at Kent State, I took my doctoral exams and prepared to go off to Europe for the first time and start my dissertation research. I would try to figure out why some towns experienced violent uprisings in 1789 and others did not. Revolution was far from an abstract concept, especially after May '68 brought France back directly into the revolutionary orbit.

Up to this point, I have told my story as if everything revolved around the decision to go into French history, and in fact, that is how it felt to me. Despite fancying myself an introspective person, I had no clear long-term goals and frankly not a very clear sense of who I was or wanted to be. My choices seemed limited: high school teacher, secretary, or, miracle of miracles, college professor. I had had one female professor in college and one at Stanford, and she held the lowly position of lecturer. Fitzgerald notwithstanding, I did not aspire to be a writer (and I certainly lacked the skill). I simply lurched forward, certain only that I wanted to do the next thing: go to France and write a dissertation. Somehow life would gather itself in the folds attached to this spine. And so it did—over the long term.

In September 1970 Fitzgeraldian fantasy met reality when my plane touched down at Orly. I knew not one person in Paris, did not have an apartment, and had no hotel reservation. What was I thinking? The welcome bureau at the airport sent me to the Grand Hôtel de Champagne in the first *arrondissement,* a hotel that was far from grand but propitious in name (a few months later, I would end up centering my dissertation on two towns in Champagne, Troyes and Reims). After being felt up in the ancient elevator by the bellboy, who had instantly sized up my Minnesota naïveté, I gulped, threw down my bags, and raced out to nearby Notre-Dame, where I fell into a kind of Wordsworthian swoon. I couldn't believe it. Even with all the pictures I had seen, it was so much grander and more soaring than I imagined. Two minutes from my hotel, and here was the Seine, Notre-Dame, the Sainte-Chapelle. The sky with those Poussinesque clouds. The booksellers on the quay. The vistas toward the statue of Henry IV and the Pont-Neuf. St. Paul and Stanford seemed pitiable.

Within a week, I lay in bed, in the same hotel, cramped up with food poisoning acquired at a cheap Greek restaurant on the rue Grégoire de Tours. Reading Henry James's novel *The Ambassadors,* about another American innocent in Paris, I felt on the verge of abject defeat. Running down the hall to the "Turkish" toilet did not help. Every time I spoke French, especially at the Bibliothèque nationale on the rue de Richelieu, my interlocutors looked at me with nearly total incomprehension. About the only thing I could order with confidence was a *croque monsieur.* I had no idea where to begin with my research; I only knew I was going to compare two towns at the beginning of the French Revolution. How would I pick them among scores or even hundreds of candidates? Should they be northern or southern towns, big or small, manufacturing centers or administrative hubs, as different as possible from one another or similar in most respects? If I picked the wrong ones, would my project be fatally wounded? When I went to seek advice from François Furet, professor at the École des Hautes Études en Sciences Sociales, I got the distinct sense that he found me slightly comical. He immediately shunted me off to someone else.

For many years thereafter, France presented to me these two very different faces: one minute, the electricity of discovery, to be followed not long after by the anxiety of rejection. On the one side, there was the glistening of the streets in the evening lights after a rainfall, the difference between a dry and a not so dry *chèvre,* Romanesque churches in Burgundy, and *Le Monde des livres;* on the flip side, there was the nagging fear of using the wrong word or phrase, never fitting into French clothes or shoes, never fitting in, period. I loved so much about France, but I didn't feel loved back. I have never been so thrilled, and never so depressed, as in France. But I decided that night reading *The Ambassadors* that I would just have to pick up the gauntlet. Now I did have a goal: to speak well enough to be understood by anyone and eventually to be taken seriously by French historians themselves (forget about fitting into the clothes or shoes).

Two fairy godmothers, one English and one French, helped put these Sisyphean tasks within reach. A friend from Stanford had given me the phone number of an English woman working for the Ford Foundation in Paris by the name of Marion Bieber. She was the very first person I called, a few days after arriving in Paris. A German-Jewish refugee to London who had lived in Europe, Africa, and the United States, Marion spoke many languages and wasted no time in making friends. Over two decades, before she moved back to London for retirement, she showed me how to set a course by solving problems one by one. At our very first meeting over drinks on her terrace overlooking the rue Saint-André-des-Arts, she introduced me to a graduate student from Cornell who was also looking for an apartment. The two of us rented a bright orange place from a Tunisian who had invested his life savings in a sixth-floor walkup near the Cadet Métro station; the neighbors would not have tolerated his living there, but American students posed no such problem. In subsequent years, Marion found me a language tutor, gave me names of friends who rented flats, lent me her lovely house in the Dordogne for extensive periods, and put me up on whatever spare couch she had available. Even more significant, she made navigating France seem doable and fun in the doing.

Chris White, my newly acquired roommate, introduced me to my second Parisian godmother, a retired schoolteacher and family friend, Madame Faisy. Long after Chris had finished her study of Vietnamese land reform and gone back home, I continued to visit with Madame Faisy. Sometimes I would take her to the Comédie-Française, but only after we had read the play and discussed it at length in the sitting room of her tiny apartment on the rue de Beauce in the third *arrondissement*. Over several meetings we read through *Le Rouge et le Noir* with elaborate discussions before, during, and after a dinner she would prepare for me. Everyone should have such a teacher: patient, careful, enthusiastic about literature and about the beauties of the language. Her favorite meal was *pot-au-feu;* she served the broth first, then the meat, and then the vegetables, as it was "not French" to serve dishes mixed together. She and Marion both had telephones. Our landlord was on a waiting list that reached seven years, he said.

In those first fifteen months in Paris, I did not succeed in learning to speak French perfectly or making a mark among French historians. Far from it. But Paris grabbed hold of me and never let go. When I visited Amsterdam and London for the first time that year, I found them provincial, quaint, and insipid. I did not suffer so much from Francophilia as Parisophilia, for although I enjoyed visiting out-of-the-way places in the provinces, I never developed much fondness for provincial cities, despite being much better treated by archivists and librarians in Troyes or Toulouse, for example, than in Paris. Coming home in the evening after a long day in the archives of Reims or Troyes—I had picked them in part because I could commute from Paris—my heart would always beat faster as the train approached the Gare de l'Est and the familiar landmarks came into view.

It is difficult to pin down the exact source of this feeling. Was it neurotic ambivalence about a place that pulled me in only to push me away? The usual tourist's fascination with the city of lights and the western cultural nostalgia it so brilliantly evoked? Or the midwesterner's hope, shared with Fitzgerald, of breaking free from the confines of low prairie skies and the social claustrophobia of middle American life? The origins of the feeling ultimately mattered little; what counted over the long run, besides the essential personal connections, were the attractions offered by Parisian intellectual life, especially the heady mixture of theoretical and political critique. French intellectuals were never just intellectuals and certainly not just professors. They spoke at antiwar rallies, wrote in the major dailies, sometimes published novels, and, at the same time, offered a powerful critique of the West's most cherished philosophical assumptions.

Although French history—as practiced in France—enjoyed international acclaim in the 1970s, the real intellectual excitement in Paris came from elsewhere. In the immediate post-1968 years of protest and cultural upheaval, Jean-Paul Sartre and Simone de Beauvoir still ruled the roost, but they faced ever stronger challenges from the likes of Lévi-Strauss, Jacques Lacan, Louis Althusser, Jacques Derrida, and Michel Foucault. From my very first year in

France, I tried to ride the intellectual waves that were breaking on shores all over the western world. Existentialist Marxism, structuralism, revived Freudianism, and later poststructuralism: they all flowed forth from Paris. It was hard to keep your head above water but well worth the effort. I went with reasonable regularity to the libraries and archives on my agenda, though sometimes only after playing *flipper* (pinball) in the local café, but I also rushed off to attend antiwar rallies at la Mutualité, religiously read *Le Monde,* and in December 1970 managed to get into Foucault's inaugural lecture at the Collège de France. I did not understand much at first, perhaps, but I sensed that there had to be some link between my thesis research and this extraordinary gush of new ideas about politics, social life, and thought itself.

Unlike some of my history colleagues, I did not view "French theory" with hostility. The tingle of new ways of thinking only intensified my rampant Parisophilia. Over the years, the variants of French theory prodded me to look for the wider significance of my own research. The aim was not to read the meaning of 1789 off some stable theoretical grid. I did not develop a Foucaultian, Lacanian, or Althusserian interpretation of the French Revolution; instead, I found that the French Revolution could talk back to theory. It showed, for example, the Foucaultian power of discourse, but it also demonstrated the limits to that power. Foucault himself repeatedly referred to the end of the eighteenth century as a major turning point, but he never explained how or why that was true. For me, the French Revolution turned out to be the perfect place for investigating the operation of language, social life, and politics because it was a primal moment of rupture with the routine. It laid bare all the conventionalities of social existence and made them a subject of dispute and even study. In many ways, 1789 gave birth to theory in the modern sense. Theory therefore could not help but be relevant.

This interest in the philosophical stakes of the French Revolution inevitably brought me back to François Furet, especially after he published his influential collection of essays, *Penser la Révolution française* (1978). Even though I claimed to a French colleague that I found the analysis "superficial"—a remark that embarrasses me to this day—I wrestled with it mightily for some time, finally exorcising my agitation in a long review in 1981. Despite my dissension from parts of Furet's argument, I marveled at his ability to set forth the theoretical stakes of the event. I would have to write my second book, *Politics, Culture, and Class in the French Revolution* (1984), in direct confrontation with his point of view. When I gave him a copy after publication, he arranged a special seminar on it at the École des Hautes Études, where I had come on his invitation as a visiting professor at the end of 1984. *Et voilà:* the moment so much anticipated and just as much dreaded had arrived.

Officially, my visit consisted of two lectures, comparing the English and French regicides, that I gave in Furet's joint seminar with Mona Ozouf. I can hardly remember those talks, and I am quite sure no one who attended does either. In contrast, the seminar devoted to my book turned into a kind of historiographical summit because François invited not only the relevant historians at the École but also his longtime Marxist antagonist, Claude Mazauric, who had been very friendly to me and other American historians. Mazauric and Furet had not been in the same room for years; their only encounters had been mutual savagings in print. The atmosphere was consequently charged with expectation, not so much about what I would say but about how the discussion period would unfold.

After I gave my presentation—in French, written out word for word—the questions began. Unexpectedly, political differences did not dominate the discussion despite Mazauric's presence. Indeed, Furet and Mazauric maintained cautiously polite stances toward each other. At some point, however, Roger Chartier asked me a long and rather complex, though entirely amicable, question. After I had answered as best I could in my now serviceable but far from eloquent French, Furet turned to him and, his voice laced with irony, queried, "Is the professor satisfied?" François could on occasion take a tone that was knowing and disdainful, which did not always win him friends. The tension was palpable, but I was home free. I had been the triangulation point of intra-French jousting rather than the direct object of attack, but this in no way disappointed me. I was no longer on the outside looking in.

A small group of my American friends in French history went out for drinks afterward to dissect the event. More than one Kir Royal was required to bring me back to earth. I had many acquaintances among French historians of France, and several became friends in the next decades. But what sustained me as a historian of France, at least until the mid-1980s, when my reputation as a French historian became more established, were my American colleagues and students. The community of American historians of France has always struck me as remarkably cooperative, collaborative, and congenial. Envious colleagues in British or German history tend to attribute it to our collective captivation with French food and wine. And we do share a certain feeling of vicarious superiority because of our connection with France. That it is so much more tiresome to procure a reader's card at the Bibliothèque nationale than at the British Library or the Library of Congress only adds to our sense of hard-won fellowship.

Many of my most lasting and significant professional friendships have been not only established but also sustained in Paris, rather than in the United States, where we French historians are often separated by great distances. No matter the time of year, I know I can go to the Bibliothèque nationale the day after arriving and run into someone I know. When I arrived one night after dinner at the door of the apartment that the École had arranged for me to rent and found a *clochard* sleeping across the threshold, I briefly panicked, but I also knew that it would make for a hilarious story when I told it to Tip Ragan, a former student with whom I had just had dinner. My friendship with him, as with not a few others, was solidified by countless adventures that could only be shared in France: in his case, a desolate walk to the Mammouth cafeteria, the closest lunch place to the departmental archives of the Pas-de-Calais; a glorious one-star lunch in the restaurant of the Arras train station; food poisoning after lunch in Amiens; the gigantic, intimidating *plateau de fruits de mer* in Brittany—yes, it is true, we French historians tend to remember meals and their consequences. My life's terrain would be so much less loamy without these unplanned enrichments, the cognacs sipped late night in cafés, couches offered, stories told, complaints heard, hopes declared. In my mind, the profession is made up of chains of such shared experiences. Each of us has been drawn to French history for a different reason, but surely Paris and France enter into everyone's equation. French history has never been just another possible field of study.

My seminar that day at the École was only one of many during that period that marked a gradual sea change in Franco-American historical relations. Furet, then president of the École des Hautes Études, had been one of the first leaders of the French historical community to master English, incorporate Anglo-American research into his own writing, and teach regularly in American universities. The up-and-coming generation of my counterparts in France—Roger Chartier and Jacques Revel, for example—developed skills in several languages, connections with many American (and other foreign) universities, and relations with students and professors from all over the world. Historians from elsewhere had always been welcome in France, albeit with a certain condescension on the part of their French hosts, but from the 1980s onward, their research and writing began to have an impact among French historians. The arrow of influence stopped pointing in only one direction; we did not just follow the French lead. My odyssey was not such an individual journey after all. It was part of the steady internationalization of historical study.

In the very first issue of the journal *French Historical Studies,* published in 1958, David Pinkney famously argued that American historians of France should concentrate on writing syntheses and leave deep archival research to the French. American historians largely ignored him, and by the beginning of the 1990s even he had given up on this view. By then, he had to admit, the French had begun to favorably review Anglophone publications and incorporate the findings into their own research. But I wonder if something has not been lost in this much-celebrated process of integration and more generally of globalization. The *"maîtres penseurs"* of the 1970s and 1980s are now all dead, with no successors in sight. French historians no longer hold the leading strings of the international profession. It is not necessary to go to France for croissants, decent coffee, or hundreds of varieties of cheese. Indeed, Paris becomes every day more like Venice, a city as museum, and graduate students find it increasingly difficult to live there and have money left over to eat. A cognac in a café is an unattainable luxury for most of them. Will French history become just another field of study, in which students go for blitz research trips, learn just enough French to read their documents, and feel no *frisson* about the choices they have made? Even Fitzgerald preferred to spend his declining years in Los Angeles. I make no such prediction. Youth and Paris, like hope itself, spring eternal, and there is no tamping them down.

CHAPTER 5

Défense d'afficher . . .

Steven Laurence Kaplan

France had no place in my Brooklyn childhood, which was drenched in schmaltz rather than *sauce béarnaise* and framed by deeply ambivalent memories of another Europe from which my grandparents and parents had fled in the wake of World War I. France was one of numerous exotic encounters I had in my first year at Princeton in 1959. I took a "Renaissance-to-Revolution" European survey, small class format, taught by a reasoned and refined yet passionate Francophile, Charles Gillispie, whose rigor and generosity would deeply mark my life in personal as well as intellectual terms. He awed me because he was everything that I was not: ultra-Waspy, ultra-tweedy, ultra-cultivated. He wore a beret and drove a strange bathtub-looking vehicle called a Citroën DS. In those pre-inflationary days, Princeton graded from a lofty 1 to an ignominious 7. Gillispie cruelly accorded me a 6 on my first paper, a prematurely postmodern reading of Montaigne that he found hollow and ahistorical. That set the tone for the rest of my career: an urgently upward climb, tonically Sisyphean.

Two years later, I traversed the Atlantic for the first time, thanks to a Princeton summer-work program. On my first morning in Paris, famished, I wandered into a prosaic bakery on the rue du Cherche-Midi. Only later did I learn that it belonged to Pierre Poilâne, not yet the celebrated founder of the dynasty of the *miche* (round sourdough loaves) who would one day open his oven room to me. Oracular moment? On a whim, I bought a squat, golden loaf with a somewhat pugnacious bearing called a *"bâtard."* I have a vivid memory of my inaugural mouthful, a Proustian inscription: a voluptuous, buttery crumb fused with a crackling, caramelized crust, a toasted nutty impression between sweet and savory on the palette with an intense persistence of flavor after swallowing. This turned out to be the inconspicuous beginning of a long apprenticeship in taste and an unremitting liaison with bread, sensual and cerebral. Several days later I began a job that would last three months and socialize me, sometimes brutally, into some basics of French life as it was actually lived. I worked in a large wine factory located in the Communist-run city of Ivry-sur-Seine. Called Vins du Postillon, the potion we produced, a coarse California-style mix of Algerian and Languedocian *cépages,* was the preferred beverage, according to our publicity, of "nine Parisians out of ten," proof that France had not yet reached the hedonistic pinnacle of the *Trente Glorieuses.* Wine and bread, my Eucharistic summer!

I had listened to my leftist father inveigh against capitalism, I had read some Marx and a bit of Max Weber, but it was here that I discovered social class. I witnessed bitter confrontation between management and labor, subversion of the assembly line, terrible work accidents. I met a worker priest on the job even as I was reading Gilbert Cesbron's gripping novel on these priests, *Les Saints vont en enfer.* Initially I was stunned by the incandescence of the (what I would come to see later as a kind of formalized or ritualized) hostility to the United States. I was beaten up by a handful of young Communist (CGT) union members who did not like my *"sale tronche d'amerloque."** My very assailants subsequently invited me to many party and union political and social events. The tension in behavior between tolerant fraternity and violent sectarianism was mirrored by a tension in attitude between Plutonian pessimism (alienated resignation) and utopian fervor (faith in "struggle"). For some the rapturous perspective of *le grand soir*—the climactic moment of revolutionary apotheosis—was therapeutic consolation, while for others it was a veritable political program. Now that the Front National is France's leading working-class party, it is easy to forget how much influence the Communist Party exercised, politically and culturally, in the fifties and sixties, and how deeply *la France ouvrière* marked the modern landscape.

I do not know why I did not pursue this newly kindled interest in contemporary France when I returned to Princeton for my last year. Partly because I did not have the tools to take critical stock of the mélange of enthusiasm and turmoil I felt. Partly because I did not find a faculty member who evinced a passion for twentieth-century France. Surely also because I was in some sense already rooted in the Old Regime/Revolution, which seemed to be the "be-

---

* Ugly American mug.

ginning" of a story that I should not casually pick up toward the "end" merely because it was palpable and close to me. Charles Gillispie hinted that all the really important questions found expression in the eighteenth century. Despite his despairingly dull lectures and a certain impassibility toward undergrads, R. R. Palmer reinforced this idea in his course on the Revolution. Palmer's preceptor, David Bien, an assistant professor at the time, helped us to problematize the notions that Palmer presented *ex cathedra;* he was a wonderful teacher, became a dear friend, and bears some of the responsibility for the unfolding of my French destiny.

That destiny, however, was not (yet) indelibly inscribed in my itinerary. For before I could acquire a second cultural identity, I had to deal with the putative first, my Americanness. I had never doubted it, but I had never pondered it, until I entered Princeton. I had attended public school, saluted the flag every day, resisted the pressure to sing Christmas carols by merely mouthing the words, worshipped Abe Lincoln. In Hebrew school, we read an acculturating anthology that recounted the invaluable contributions that Jews made to the "triumph of America" (Haym Saloman, financier of the American Revolution; Uriah P. Levy, nineteenth-century naval hero and would-be Dreyfus; Lipman "Lip" Pike, America's first professional baseball player, and so on). My first weeks at Princeton were deeply jolting. All the other guys came from different tribes: ethnic, religious, social. The institution itself seemed to embody a history and culture to which I was entirely foreign. Viewed in this light, who could cavil with the unspoken quota on Jews? After all, they sent us a rabbi on Friday nights so that we could fulfill the mandatory chapel obligation in confessional comfort.

So on one level, without abjuring anything of my Brooklyn heritage, in the myriad senses of the term (including three-manhole stickball virtuosity), I wanted in some sense to become American, or perhaps merely more American. The solution seemed to me obvious: join an eating club, cachet of accommodation/acceptance, and major in American history. The Quadrangle Club, heavily marked by southern presence and practice (grits served every morning by black waitpersons, some of whom descended from slaves manumitted by benevolent graduating seniors), made me a bid in a spasm of proto–affirmative action. I wrote a junior essay on L. Q. C. Lamar, a democratic senator from Mississippi during Reconstruction, under the direction of David Donald, the most compelling and forthright lecturer I have ever heard ("I am a Christian and a conservative"). I did my senior thesis on the "meaning" (a word actually in common use as early as 1963!) of the Philadelphia Centennial Exposition of 1876 under the aegis of John William Ward, a witty and charismatic teacher and cultural historian. Approaching graduation, I entertained two strategies: law school at Harvard or Yale (a sort of social revenge for my father, whose politics had denied him a "successful" career in the bar) or graduate school in southern history—the ultimate assimilation—with Donald, now at Johns Hopkins, or C. Vann Woodward, at Yale. Unable to make up my mind, I turned to the natural (subversive) procrastinating alternative: a Fulbright to France.

It was precisely *because* I wanted to study the French Revolution at Bordeaux that I was assigned to Poitiers, a sumptuous center for Romanesque architecture: at least that was how I interpreted the decision. After my Paris initiation, Poitiers was hard time. It was a small university town, dominated by a tightly knit claustral bourgeoisie-notability, boasting few charms beyond the magnificent churches. De Gaulle had not yet fully cleaned house: a small American military base loomed on a hillside above the town, behind a statue of the Virgin (the only one in town, joked the soldiers, though the black ones I met complained bitterly of townie racism—a plausible claim, it seemed to me, after witnessing numerous anti-African student demonstrations outside the law school). I lodged with an aged *rentier* in an attic room of seven square meters with a cold water sink. The house had several toilets, but I was consigned to use the outhouse in the garden. Shortly after I was settled, the women's auxiliary of the Protestant Temple called on me. They kindly invited me to a recital at their church. Fulbrighters had attended the church for years, I learned: it was assumed that Americans were usually Protestants. Anxious to please—part of the Fulbright pact—I accepted: two hours of "Negro spirituals" botched by well-intentioned French musicians made up in blackface.

Poitiers introduced me to the sempiternal center-periphery, Jacobin-Girondin problematic, figuring a profound abyss in the days before decentralization and giving me a precious lesson on how the State (always capital E in French, in deference to its quasi-sacrality) functioned—and dysfunctioned. Beyond its insularity and self-absorption, however, Poitiers offered me numerous points of entry and interest. I took Jean Egret's course on the pre-Revolution period: a mandarin's *cours magistral,* to be sure, but masterfully produced. Jacques Roger, who would later become a close friend, gave brilliant lectures, treating first Molière and then Buffon. And I went to the archives for the first time, a magical moment, an exhilarating trip into the past, a piquant experience that solicited almost as many of my senses as a bread tasting: the visual signs of oldness and authenticity, the musty odor of age, the specific patter—crackling, clicking, rustling, humming—of old paper or, more rarely, vegetable parchment, the touch that invites me to imagine that I am in contact with the actors themselves, and something resembling a taste of the past, irrigated by the salivation of excitation. I spent many weeks in the reading room, opposite a retired *directeur de l'enregistrement* who smoked mephitic *papier maïs* while examining papal bulls and other precious documents and never tired of reminding me, with a civil servant's organic pride, *"l'Administration a traversé toute la Révolution."** Using police sources, I crudely tried to locate traces of a "history from below" in the style of Georges Lefebvre, a line of inquiry I would never abandon.

I ended up a grad student at Yale, under Woodward's wonderfully gentle yet incisive tutelage. After two years of southern history, and a pre-dissertation paper on politics and frontier capitalism (the Memphis El Paso and Pacific Railroad, part of whose archives were in Paris . . . Texas), I knew that I wanted to turn back (or forward) to France. Push and pull factors favored my emigration. Push: a gnawing, residual sense, despite Woodward's constant nurture, that I was not sufficiently all-American to fathom the American past in the eyes of much of the establishment. In epitome, that was the counsel of his Americanist colleague, George Wilson Pierson, ultra-Brahmin Yalie, who discouraged me from taking his seminar. It was also the message of Carl Bridenbaugh in his address as president of the American Historical Association (1963). He worried that the "environmental deficiency" of the new cohort of historians of "lower middle-class or foreign origins" would make it "impossible" for them to reconstruct "our past" for future generations. (Thirty years later I felt that I had come full circle in the genre of ethnocentric anathema when French historian Madeleine Rebérioux disqualified my remarks in a debate on interpretations of French history on the grounds *"qu'un américain ne saurait jamais comprendre ce qu'est la République [française]."*)† In a climate of burgeoning disarray and rejection of consensus—political assassination, an accelerating civil rights movement followed by ghetto riots, embryonic feminist mobilization, the flowering of countercultures, expressions of a broader contestation of the Vietnam War—I did not resonate with a nostalgia for the homogenized, *Gemeinschaft* culture of the world we had lost—and that I had never known.

Pull: The idea of negotiating alterity seemed to me to be much more frank and congenial and less fraught with barbed ambiguity in a *really* foreign place. Culturally and viscerally, there was an emptiness in me that only France seemed able to fill. I missed the streets of Paris, Les Halles late at night, the early morning noises (*"Paris s'éveille,"* sang Jacques Dutronc), the theater, the food (thinking it as well as eating it), the language, and the constant challenge of ordinary communication and more subtle and/or ludic exchange (for ex-

---

* The administration survived the Revolution from beginning to end.
† An American could never understand what the French Republic really is about.

ample, deciphering the *contrepèterie*, the canonical form of French wordplay). More telling in terms of direction: I had succumbed to the siren song of social history in the manner of the pioneering interdisciplinary journal, the *Annales*. I read every issue from the beginning, enthralled with its intransigent, irredentist ambition. Marc Bloch in particular dazzled me, not only with his learning, but with his range, his versatility, and his capacity to surprise with unexpected concepts and connections. He reminded me of Bill Bradley moving without the ball. Though Yale had no social historians of France, a branch of the Mediterranean flowed through New Haven, thanks to R. S. Lopez (with whom I talked climate, trade, transportation, technology) and J. H. Hexter (who taught me that skepticism rendered enthusiasm intelligent). Fernand Braudel's vast study of the Mediterranean world demoralized even as it exalted me. Of its trinity of Time, Space, and Man, only the latter seemed to be in my reach, and even Man was not easy to seize. Still, I succumbed to the blandishments of *l'histoire totale*. Warmly supportive of my Gallican turn, the courtly and avuncular C. Vann Woodward nevertheless looked at me as if I were mad when I announced that I wanted to do "total" history. This was about the time when Oxford's Richard Cobb unleashed in the *Times Literary Supplement* a savage, anonymous onslaught against the supercilious and narcissistic "*Nous des Annales,*" "*frères-ès-conjoncture,*" and so on.*

Diffusely conceived in my mind, "total" meant on the one hand that it was legitimate to explore every aspect of human existence, from menarche to monarchy (as Peter Stearns once remarked), from weather and disease to sex and food, from emotions to techniques, from crime to punishment, from the bottom to the top, a sort of Voltairean agenda to move beyond official or conventional history in search of "the meatiness of life." On the other hand, "total" signified a relentless attack on a single central problem—a sort of "total social phenomenon" that spoke to the fundamental concerns of an entire society in order to map out the ways in which it played out in all spheres: economic and social, to be sure, but also cultural, religious, psychological, and political.

The incongruity between Braudel's planetary gaze and my resources compelled me from the beginning to engage in a constant readjustment of scale in an attempt to find an object that was intellectually and psychologically plausible. This anxiety about scale, feasibility, and tools probably led me to shift imperceptibly in my pragmatic orientation from Braudel to Ernest Labrousse, though I never relinquished my preference for *La Méditerranée* and *Civilisation matérielle* over *L'Esquisse* and *La Crise*. As if to reassure mere mortals,

---

*Cobb's disdainful evocation of the putatively sectarian brotherhood of *Annalist* historians, given to quantitative orgy.

Braudel later explained that *"globalité,"* as he preferred to say, was not wild hubris but *"simplement le désir, quand on a abordé un problème, de le dépasser systématiquement."**

Total history intoxicated me, but intellectually I feasted on LSD, the sixties' *plat de non-résistance.* This was the shorthand I used to define my framework to my jerry-built thesis committee in early 1967: *Longue durée,* Structures, Daily life. Braudel's articulation of time marked me indelibly. Although I never became a veritable long-runner, the concept shaped all of my research. The idea that time was multiple, multi-layered, overlapping, textured, simultaneously continuous and discontinuous, remote and nearby, aloof and intimate, misanthropic and hospitable, hot and cold, orderly and chaotic, determined and contingent, dense and diffuse, prolix and pithy—this was all revelation to me.

If I did not explicitly practice the long run in my research, I was certainly a *frère-ès-structure.* Yale was then awash in structuralism—literary, linguistic, anthropological. I remained convinced that the diachronic was our *fonds de commerce,* but I did not view the synchronic necessarily as an assault upon historicity. Structures were both quasi-everlasting and manifestly impermanent, very constrictive and less so, prisons to be sure, but not always high-security prisons from which escape was virtually impossible. Braudel offered a definition of structure that promised considerable analytical latitude: assemblage, architecture, highly resistant realities that perdure.

Far from a precocious apologist for the "agency" of historical actors (not yet a fighting word in the sixties), I was nevertheless troubled, philosophically and pragmatically, by Braudel's gloomy rendering of man "enclosed in a destiny that he barely has a hand in making." Braudel's uncompromising contempt for the event and his cavalier attitude toward politics that, under the nascent influence of Michel Foucault, we were beginning to think of in terms of power, aggravated my malaise. Structure seriously delimited man's freedom, of that I was sure. But did that authorize or require historians to bypass the struggle in which they engaged against those constraints? Braudel inveighed against social-science abstraction, but if he refused to view daily life day by day, if he did not accept the *social vécu*—lived life—as a valid terrain of observation, then didn't these endless repetitions, reduced by moving averages to tiresome sameness, merely congeal into a more or less mechanical abstraction?

Using an image that speaks to my sensibility, years later, the fervent Labroussean Michel Vovelle affirmed what had become the *nouvelle histoire* doxa: that the short-run time of the event, which is also the quintessential time

---

* Simply the desire, when one addresses a problem, to systematically go beyond it.

of politics, "deals only with a tiny, superficial crust [*croûte*] of human history." In retrospect, it is clear to me that as others were Trotskyist or Lambertist or Frankist in the sixties, I was a *croûtiste*. I was much less certain than Vovelle, and a fortiori Braudel, that "*la vraie histoire, comme la vraie vie, est ailleurs.*"* Passionate student of bread, equally enamored of crumb and crust—infrastructure and superstructure, I infer from Vovelle's choice of the image, not from his ideological itinerary—I know from having *mis la main à la pâte* that the crust, far from an accident or a décor or an illusion, is ultimately the expression of the same forces that construct the crumb and provides crucial clues concerning the state of the whole loaf—or should I say the *miche totale*?

In any event, as I wrote my dissertation prospectus (a thirty-year plan!) in early 1967 on the multiple ways in which bread (and its antecedents) framed and governed life in the Old Regime, I knew that, along with attentive scrutiny to numerous long-run *structures structurantes* and to "conjunctural" variables, I would have to look closely at politics, from above as well as from below; at subtle and more brutal ways in which power was exercised, exchanged, resisted, and reappropriated; at the structures as well as the protean features of everyday life; at the everyday order and how it was sustained and subverted; and at the way crises took root at the confluence of extremely long, middle-range, and very short time. While I worried that I was betraying my masters, I continued to flatter myself that my inspiration and my thinking remained fundamentally *Annaliste,* deeply if deviantly Braudelian, and elliptically Labroussean.

My *gagne-pain* seemed to be too good to be true. Could it really be that this crucial problem had not been tellingly attacked before? After weeks of ulceration in the library, I found that the terrain was miraculously clear. I set off to France in 1967 for a stint of two years. I obtained from Henri Peyre, a celebrated *littéraire* at Yale, a letter of introduction to his classmate at the École Normale Supérieure, Jean Meuvret, the great historian of the subsistence question and what I would later come to call the "*filière blé-farine-pain*" (the grain-flour-bread sector). François Furet helped me clarify my *problématique* and put me in touch with numerous other historians at the Sixième Section (E.P.H.E.), including Denis Richet and Emmanuel Le Roy Ladurie, replete with ideas and energy, and willing to discuss. In those days Furet readily intoned the *Annales* mantra that "*il n'y a d'histoire que sociale*" and even upped the doctrinal ante: "*il n'y a d'histoire sociale que quantitative.*"† Le Roy imagined the historian of the future as part computer programmer. Nourished by

* Real history, like real life, is elsewhere.
† The only history is social history; the only social history is quantitative history.

the quantitative environment, which Chuck Tilly would soon expose as a well-intentioned Potemkin village, I would later spend countless hours in Ithaca—Cornell University hired me in 1970—typing the data of marriage contracts and after-death inventories onto IBM cards and "running" myriad canned social science programs on the forbidding mainframe, available to "humanists" only at low-priority times in the middle of the night.

Different in his social origins, politics, and intellectual style from my other French mentors, historian Pierre Goubert welcomed me into his home (*"Ah! Le boeuf en daube!"*) and into his lively seminar, where he practiced an eclectic brand of (basically but not exclusively) history from below, informed by moral and visceral need, as he put it, *"de m'intéresser à tous les hommes, et non seulement à ceux qui brillèrent par leur naissance, par leur état, par leur fonction, par leur richesse ou par leur intelligence."** François Billacois, another contact in the Normalien nexus who was also in Goubert's orbit at the University of Nanterre, recommended that I see some police papers at the Bibliothèque Historique de la Ville de Paris. I was refused access on the grounds that these papers were "reserved" for a reader, protégé of the head librarian. I complained to the reference librarian, a strapping man about my age named Jean Dérens. At considerable professional risk, he gave me access to the documents ("a matter of principle") and then over a beer expressed keen interest in joining me in the gymnasium basement of the American Church of Paris for a weekly night of basketball, followed by some fraternal drinking. I dredged up a handful of Americans, and Dérens recruited a half dozen fellow graduates of the École des Chartes, including a future director of the Archives nationales, a future chief curator of the manuscript room at the Bibliothèque nationale, and the future founder of the Pompidou Center's public library. Save for Dérens, a merciless rebounder, they were awful players (no hands, slow reflexes, locked onto archaic zone positions) but delightful company. They were the nucleus of a ramifying network of *chartistes* throughout the Hexagon—graduates of the elite school that trains archivists and librarians—who facilitated my work immensely wherever I conducted research, especially in the almost fifty departmental archives I visited for my thesis.

May '68 threatened fugitively to annihilate all the "mandarins," some of whom were my mentors. I lived it with a mingling of apprehension and exhilaration. Young historian with a keen interest in revolt and revolution, I knew that I was traversing a historic, perhaps a revolutionary moment. I bought the last bicycle remaining in La Samaritaine minutes before the de-

---

* To inquire about all men and women, not just those who shone by their birth, their status, their profession, their wealth or their intelligence.

partment store was shut down by the proliferating strike movement, thus obtaining a precious instrument of mobility that enabled me to roam widely on the various battle fronts, whether verbal or physical. At the Sorbonne, I witnessed the abortive efforts of a number of professors, including distinguished and powerful historians, to resist or canalize the tide of contestation. At the Odéon theater, the mood was festive, Woodstock in part, but with a febrile shared sense that the young people could and would change the world. The widespread *prise de parole* was in some ways more important than what was actually said. Stakhanovite, I even managed to get some work done in the only archive that remained open, thanks to its self-proclaimed Gaullist *magasiniers* who deplored the events as a bacchanalian orgy choreographed by the demonic *Katangais,* as certain so-called "outside agitators" were called.

Many of the leaders were my age; I felt a deep empathy with their outcry. The *manifs* gave me a vivid sense of what it felt like to be in a crowd in action. I witnessed brutal violence on the barricades, saw eyes pop out and heads split, and marveled in the end at the relatively low human cost of the clashes. I peddled to Ivry to try to understand why my Communist Party friends remained so stubbornly refractory. I was running one morning in the Bois de Vincennes when the paratroopers took possession of the space. When de Gaulle disappeared, like many others, I feared civil war.

Did this experience make me in some sense a historian of the '68 generation? May '68 deepened my faith in the capacity of France to place itself into question, and it focused my attention on the long-term trajectory of social movements of all sorts. It stimulated me to rethink notions of authority and legitimacy, of order and disorder, of morality and immorality, of carnival and social control, of (social) production and reproduction, of power and powerlessness. It impelled me to challenge common assumptions about the relations between "economy, society and civilization," the *Annales* trinitarian hierarchy.

It may be that May '68 was midwife to my own cultural/professional revolt, an insurgency doubtless shared by other American historians. May '68 did not deliver me from the deep respect I felt for the grand figures of French historiography in France, though what was a sense of (starkly vertical) deference gently metamorphosed into (a more horizontal) esteem. I rejected the role into which we Americans had been implicitly cast, by (many of) our own teachers and by (many of) our French hosts, as derivative or supporting actors, in a category apart, journeymen destined never to attain mastership in the Franco-French corporate universe. On the one hand, I could no longer abide R. R. Palmer's view that it was fruitless to attempt to practice French history as French historians did it, for the playing field could never be even given our distance from the archives and libraries and from the culture. Instead he urged

that we locate our comparative advantage in more synthetic works, converting our estrangement into a virtue and taking advantage of the myriad un-
tapped veins of signification that lay fallow in the gargantuan French theses.
On the other hand, I bristled every time I read a review of an American monograph in a French publication that grudgingly allowed that the work was not
so bad *"pour un anglo-saxon."* (This had nothing to do with my egregious lack
of Anglo-Saxon credentials.) After May '68 it was clear in my mind that I
wanted to *"jouer dans la cour des grands."** If I were good enough, I wanted to
be judged *sur pièces* and not prejudged, and I wanted to be evaluated by universal criteria, not by local barons. I now saw this as a sort of political as well
as intellectual battle.

This issue had very little, if anything, to do with anti-Americanism, a very
old story in France, embedded on the left as well as the right, a chronic condition that erupts periodically, with more or less ferocity. It varies not only in
intensity but in nature: all anti-Americanisms are not equal. Indeed, certain
expressions strike me as reasonable and perhaps even necessary. By and large,
in our circles, I think we historians encounter much more philo- than anti-
Americanism; the former can sometimes be as burdensome as the latter. Certain French historians, surely a small minority, resent Americans as poachers,
imperialists surfing the tide of American hegemony—individual analogues to
voracious American pension funds—to gobble up rich chunks of the national
patrimony. Others have a more narrowly defined proprietary attitude about
encroachment on terrain they have staked out as *theirs;* this attitude, both understandable and a bit paranoid, is hurtful particularly to our grad students,
though it can often be inflected by negotiation. Then there are the curmud-
geonly French positivists who revile the United States for exporting to France
toxic theory, to wit, Derrida, Foucault, Jacques Lacan, or Michel de Certeau..

A more interesting and elusive question concerns the (eventual) impact,
conscious or subliminal, of anti-Americanism(s) on the way American historians of France do their work. This is, again, a highly variable phenomenon
because we are a highly variable group: what strikes one of us as vilification or
caricature may impress another as ethnographic description. Today, perhaps
more than ever before in my experience, being American carries a lot of
baggage, especially in France, which has multiple domestic as well as global
reasons for heightened susceptibility. We are in a moment of enormous Mani-
chean temptation: France has principles, America has interests; France is from
Venus, America is from Mars; Americans go bowling alone, the French are
solidarist; America is generous, France ungrateful. This climate may weigh

---

* To play in the major leagues.

more heavily on American historians who study *"questions sensibles"* (Vichy, colonialism, the cold war, anti-Semitism) than those of us more insulated from hot controversy. Yet it is precisely when we are shocked or angered, by information we have uncovered in our research or by events in our environment, that we tend, by a kind of scholarly hygiene, to take some distance and to respond as soberly and rigorously as possible. Still, it is not always easy to remain serene, and it is parlous to imagine that the historian can stand immune from emotions that roil the citizen. If I did not quite vibrate with Foreign Minister Dominique de Villepin's lyricism, I ardently opposed the Iraq War. Once it began, however, I detested the moral narcissism of numerous French commentators and the schadenfreude of many reporters in the early days whenever things seemed to be going badly for the Americans.

Contemporary preoccupations have always informed my historical regard, be they American or French. One of my abiding interests, for example, concerns the Tocquevillean tension between liberty and equality. It frames the history of the subsistence question (Old Regime), crucible of French liberalism, in which a Gallican version of the moral economy confronts the egocentric market principle. It is at the core of Turgot's assault on Colberto-corporatism. It pervades the Revolution, from the abolition of the guilds to the affirmation of Jacobin centralization and the imposition of the General Maximum Law and the "bread of equality." It is the leitmotif of the tripartite struggle between the State, the millers, and the bakers (1946–1958), part of my current research project. This same tension structures the contentious debate on the character of contemporary France: Prime Minister Lionel Jospin's momentous 1999 statement that *"l'État ne peut pas tout"* (the State cannot do everything) in front of the Michelin tire factory contrasted with Jacques Chirac's rampant rhetorical Jacobinism, the frantic allergy to the scapegoated "Polish plumber" during the debate on the European constitution, the horror of "neoliberalism," the apotheosis of the French social model, the curse cast on affirmative action and the reluctance to question the efficacy of the Republican model of integration, the tocsin of "economic patriotism" and its aporias (Danone yogurt on all future menus of the Society for French Historical Studies!), the notion of *"devoir citoyen"* and civil disobedience, the chronic problem of social representation that has galvanized my attention since 1962, the proclamation of the French cultural exception, and so on. The controversy over all these issues feeds back into my work, sometimes directly—see *France, malade du corporatisme* (2004), which I coedited with Philippe Minard—usually more diffusely. My view of France in past time is also shaped by the way France looks at herself. How can one remain indifferent to the swagger of the Gaullist moment of *"défense tous azimuts"* or to the declinist-anomic-loser's gloom of the Chiraquian *fin-de-règne?*

With world-class scholars in many fields, by 1980 American historians had freed themselves from psychological and intellectual heteronomy vis-à-vis the French. It is my impression that scholars on both sides of the ocean simultaneously moved closer (the French began to visit us for long sojourns, to read us more attentively, to speak English) and further apart (American researchers no longer made scholarly choices in strict reference to the French *champs*). We had many conversations together on both sides, but in some important ways, for the majority of the players in France and the United States, preoccupations diverged. Americans, who had always paid vigilant attention to French historiography, began to sense that the French had lapsed into a certain stagnation and, following the not wholly consummated "critical turn" of the *Annales,* a certain disarray. The French, by and large, continued to do what they had always done, and continued to do it very well, without paying much heed to the rest of the world. They did not worry much about the concept of agency, did not take the full measure of gender, blanked on queer theory, vaguely took note of poststructural currents and critical theory in historiography, regarded postmodernism as largely fatuous and in any event irrelevant. The linguistic turn was not the object of impassioned debate it was in the United States. Pushed by their students, many French historians were swept up in the culturalist tsunami but not always as a result of serious reflection, epistemological or methodological. They shrugged off the violent attack on social history, which in the United States had left some dead (often suicides) and many wounded.

I tried to play the game—actually several games—on both sides. Upon arriving at Cornell in 1970, I immediately invited Foucault for a month, followed by scores of other French historians over the years, mostly social and cultural, for stays of varying length. I read Derrida alongside my friend Dominick La Capra, with whom I pondered the ways of intellectual history. I tried to get to the archives every year and spend every fourth year entirely in France. I wrote about subsistence and work, the "two mammaries of France," in Pierre-Joseph Proudhon's formula. With indispensable help from Maurice Aymard, Jean-Louis Flandrin and I founded in the eighties the first scholarly journal on the history and culture of food, addressing at once our sybaritic and scholarly selves. The trenchant editorial committee debates in Paris among sociologists, anthropologists, psychologists, and historians were among the most stimulating exchanges I have ever had; they reinforced my conviction that future social historians needed to study what Braudel called the "auxiliary sciences," even if history was no longer destined to serve as the queenly "feder-ating" discipline of the "human sciences." Without abandoning *all* of its golden-age pretensions and without abjuring its post-positivist concern for proof and demonstration, I believed that social history had to rethink means and ends, elaborate or appropriate better theoretical tools, pay as much atten-tion to the symbolic as to the material, articulate short-term and long run time frames and micro and macro scales of action, and practice close reading as well as social analysis, among other tasks. I defended social history vigorously in my book *Adieu 89* (1993).

When the Bicentennial of the French Revolution beckoned, I could not re-sist: a legitimate opportunity to confront the eighteenth century and the twen-tieth—the two Frances in which I lived—and to reflect on the Revolution and on contemporary French politics and culture for the first time. Fruit of several years of intense research throughout the country, in the archives and in the field, the project, as I construed it, was a historical investigation and an ethnog-raphy, not a "work of circumstance." *Adieu 89* traces a portrait of France in 1989, its dreams and contradictions as it once again confronted its collective memory. How to deal with a founding event that was also a lacerating rup-ture? Celebrate? Commemorate? Execrate? Take the Revolution "as a bloc," heeding Clemen-ceau's warning that one could not *"distraire"* any part with-out doing violence to historical truth? Or pick and choose, as a function of what now seems worthy or memorable. Was the Revolution finally *"terminée,"* as the school of the new vulgate energetically claimed? Or was the Revolution still incomplete, a constant challenge to achieve a more just world? From the mid-eighties, politicians, prelates, journalists, historians, and citizens strug-gled over how to handle this event; for most of the leaders, it was a thorny predicament and an uncomfortable, even unwelcome obligation. The resur-gence of a muscled, virulent anti-Revolutionary current further complicated the landscape. The debate generated by the Bicentennial was often acrimo-nious. Beyond the Revolution, there loomed in my view two critical questions: What is a democracy? How does one write history? In a long section dealing with the "French *Historikerstreit"*—a separate volume in the American edi-tion—I subjected to critical scrutiny the new vulgate that cast the Revolution as a discursively determined enterprise, ideologically tainted and driven from the outset, largely independent of the play of contingencies, and dangerously toxic to the democratic project.*

Warmly praised by many, in some circles my book was considered to be as

---

* *Historikerstreit:* the sometimes vitriolic 'historian's' quarrel' concerning Hitler, Nazism, the Holocaust, etc. that buffeted Germany in the seventies and eighties.

radioactive as the Revolutionary ideology. The center-left weekly *Nouvel Observateur* had crowned France's leading "revisionist historian as "the king of the Bicentennial." I was guilty of lèse-majesté for contesting the newly sacralized reading of the Revolution and the "networks of power" on which it was built. I did not remotely foresee such a violent reaction. For the first time, a book I had written was denied a subvention by the Centre national des lettres. My publisher came under stiff pressure not to bring it out. Two major weeklies and a daily refused papers on the book from regular collaborators. On the radio, several debates took place—but with surrogates rather than the protagonists. The latter refused to participate in conferences in which I was involved. Invited to fly to Paris for the grandiose Bicentennial colloquium organized by the Institute d'histoire du temps présent, I was refused the right to reply after the tightly controlled round table organized around their interventions. A "scientific colloquium" with no debate. This was hardball: the notion of academic freedom did not seem to have much purchase among those who identified themselves as liberals. An intellectual and moral shock, the *Adieu* affair was at the same time a salutary wakeup call. In my preface to that book, I noted innocently that I had a tendency to forget that I was American, so immersed was I in things French. Here was a shrill reminder that I was after all *gaijin*. Now I am inclined to brandish this status as part of a double identity: part insider—always outsider: *francophile critique*.

It may have been naïve to expect a climate of tolerance in a place where ideas matter so much and carry stakes that we rarely observe elsewhere. As Clemenceau remarked: "*La tolérance! La tolérance! Il y a des maisons pour cela.*"* Fortunately, there are many mansions in the House of France. When I published *Le Meilleur pain du monde* in 1996, *Le Nouvel Observateur* warmly celebrated my "return to the fold" after a transient Jacobin aberration. Bread invites communion. Why France? Beyond the archives and the bakeries, beyond France for the historian is France for the man. I have opted since the nineties to live most of my life in France in part because I experience there a grand respiration that I cannot achieve in other places, a particular taste of freedom, a space for irony, and a shared intelligence of everyday things. When Janet Jackson bared a breast in the Super Bowl extravaganza of 2004, the entire Moral Order convulsed with rage and imposed sanctions and safeguards. When actress Sophie Marceau exposed a breast while climbing the steps at Cannes in 2005, all of France and Navarre vibrated with joy.

---

* *Maisons de tolérance* are brothels that once enjoyed legitimate business status in France.

CHAPTER 6

❧ France for Belgium

Gabrielle M. Spiegel

It is my profound conviction that what we do as historians is to write, in highly displaced, usually unconscious, but nonetheless determined ways, our inner, personal obsessions. At least this holds true for the historical work that we feel we *have* to do, as opposed to the manifold professional obligations undertaken as part of the normal course of a career. In my case, the governing inner agenda remained unknown to me until I reached my mid-forties. But looking back, I can see how it shaped both my need to be a historian in the first place and the circuitous paths I pursued in the shaping of what, on reflection, seems to have been a reasonably coherent intellectual trajectory. This account of my personal investment in and intellectual itinerary through historiography may seem unduly self-absorbed. But I believe that the trajectory of my work—from an early concern with the "truth" and "fictionality" of French medieval representations of history and with the ideological investments that conditioned and constrained the medieval approach to the past to an increasing awareness of the constitutive force of representation as such—is characteristic of a significant segment of the academic generation to which I belong. This is especially true in the United States among those of us who engaged deeply with "French theory." Of course, to say this begs the question of the autobiographical genesis of those "obsessions" that led me to French history and the motivations that prompted me to study medieval and, ultimately, contemporary historiography from a theoretical perspective. In order to explain I must make a detour through various slices of my past.

I was born in the United States to a family that had only just emigrated from Antwerp, Belgium, arriving in New York in late 1938, in flight from Hitler's Europe. My father was Belgian, my mother Viennese; although prescient to some degree in their hasty departure, they certainly had no thought of staying in the United States should the situation in Europe improve. Thus, I grew up among the Belgian and Viennese refugee communities in New York City, a group sufficiently large that my parents felt little need to mingle with the Americans among whom they had, by force of history, landed. Nor did they initially think it necessary that their children learn to speak English, since clearly the war would be over before too long and we would return to Antwerp, at that time still a predominantly French-speaking city. It was not the case that they could not speak English—indeed, my mother had been pursuing a doctoral degree in English philology at the University of Vienna before marrying—but rather that everyone they knew spoke French and German. We four children, therefore, were initially sent to school speaking only French, though once we switched to English, my parents switched to German, a more comfortable language for my mother and a matter of indifference to my father, who spoke eleven languages, including Malay, with ease and fluency. Thus French became the lost common language of our family, although my older sister, born in Antwerp, kept up her command of the language in a more decisive way than the rest of us and eventually married a Frenchman. The German spoken at home, on the other hand, became the mark of our difference from our schoolmates and thus to be avoided at all costs, a feeling strongly reinforced by the course of German history during the war. Needless to say, by war's end, everyone who had not left was dead, and there was no thought of returning to Antwerp. And so, for better or worse, we became "Americans."

I offer this family linguistic history because I believe that it left us children with a profound sense of marginality in relation to the worlds we inhabited, whether at home or at school, and also—at least for my older sister and me, though not for my older brother or, interestingly, my twin sister—with a deep sense of nostalgia for the French language and things French, which we doubtless did not distinguish very clearly from things Belgian, since our only relationship to Belgium was linguistic, via French. I am now convinced that it was this perduring sense of not belonging, of intense marginality and linguistic discomfort, of having lost a past and personal history for which I felt that I had been intended but which had been taken away from me by history itself, that generated my need to be a historian, albeit a historian of a type quite different from that typical in the United States. But that is part of a later story.

I decided to become a medieval historian at the age of thirteen, or at least I then first identified medieval history as the subject to which I was drawn, since I had no idea what it meant to be a professional historian and would doubtless have resisted the thought if I had known. I was introduced to medieval history when, bored with the rather minimal history curriculum offered in my eighth-grade class, I asked my teacher—a marvelous and inventive man to whom I still owe much of the ways that I think about history—for extra reading. For reasons that can never be recovered, he assigned me Henri Pirenne's *Mohammed and Charlemagne*. This encounter with Pirenne set me on the path of medieval history, from which I never wavered. I was utterly captivated by . the argumentative structure of *Mohammed and Charlemagne* and saw in it a way of approaching history, of understanding the underlying forces and conditions that promoted long-term historical change, which resonated somehow with my own ways of thinking.

Looking back, of course, it seems clear that the decisive factor was that Pirenne was both a medievalist and a Belgian, the former because I intuitively fastened upon the idea that medieval Europe represented in emblematic form the Christian world whose prejudices had led to the death of so many members of my family and deprived me of my history, both past and future. In becoming a French medievalist, as I was to do many years later, I thus sought to understand the Christian world at whose bidding so much of my personal history seemed to be governed and ultimately—in making the deconstructive turn that my own practice of history eventually (and I now think inevitably) took—to deprive it of its power to rob me and others like me of our legitimate places in history. In short, if I could not have the history for which I was intended, neither could Christian Europe, since the deconstructive readings I eventually applied to medieval history suggested the linguistic nature of all historical accounts, hence robbing the past of its status as objectively "true." But before that could happen, I needed to "master" the past, hence my obsession with history and desire to become a medieval historian.

That such fantasies unconsciously governed my life choices may seem irrelevant to the ways in which, eventually, my own work fit into larger professional contexts. Yet I persist in believing that my losses—of history, language, homeland, identity—were shared by an entire generation in both Europe and (to a lesser extent) the United States and made themselves felt in the need to confront, in a philosophically displaced form and forum, an epistemological loss of certainty in the truth and utility of history, a loss we no longer could, or cared, to mask beneath the modernist guise of continuity and progress. For ours is a generation that has labored under the sign of loss, itself symptomatic of the postmodern conundrum generated by the simultaneity of our desire for history and our recognition of its loss, a recognition that paradoxically nourishes the very desire it can never satisfy. In that sense, we hover between a desire for the past and the sense of its irretrievable absence. Our desire for history has an elegiac component, by which it becomes a kind of mourning for the unpossessed dead that is the past. In postmodern history in general, I would argue, the tension between our sense of the past's erasure and our desire for history harbors a longing for presence, a presence we simultaneously acknowledge as always already absent and thus, like the past itself, an unattainable object of desire. The double gesture driving my own relation to the past is the double gesture that lies at the core of what has since come to be called postmodernism, although in the fifties and sixties, as I embarked upon my career as a French medievalist, no one in the United States, I suspect, could have articulated this core feature of contemporary historical consciousness.

I studied medieval history during my college years at Bryn Mawr, where I had the privilege of working with David Herlihy, who urged me to enroll in graduate school and pursue history, a choice I resisted for several years, perhaps fighting on some level the pull to history that constituted the inner narrative of my unconscious life. Since I was living in Baltimore at the time (this was the mid-sixties), eventually I succumbed, applied to Johns Hopkins, and began a lifelong involvement with both French history and Hopkins.

The history department at Johns Hopkins was probably the premier institution in the United States for the study of premodern French history, boasting a faculty that included the medievalist John Baldwin, who became my doctoral mentor, and the early modern French historians Robert Forster and Orest Ranum, with whom I studied. Indeed, the sixties marked a moment when Americans turned from the study of British history, which certainly had been dominant at my undergraduate institution, to the study of France, in part because of the postwar éclat of the *Annales* school (which Forster and Ranum did much to promote in the United States) and in part due to the availability of fellowships such as Fulbrights that made extended study abroad possible for large numbers of American graduate students. And my own linguistic relation to French made the choice of being a French medievalist both logical and overdetermined.

The choice of medieval historiography as the subject of my dissertation was less obvious. In the mid-sixties, scholarship in medieval historical writing was largely devoted to the identification of what could be accepted as historically "true" in chronicle accounts of the past and the radical expurgation—most often in the form of scornful neglect—of everything that could not. To the extent that medieval historiography was studied at all (and it was barely a subject of investigation at the time), the prevailing approach lay well within the frame-

work of empirical work, serving the needs and interests of institutional and social history. Like many Capetian historians of my generation, I was trained to
study bureaucratic and institutional history, with a strong focus on royal king-
ship in France. I chose historiography as my field of Capetian history because I
was married with two small children and could not spend a year away in the
archives (ruling out social, institutional, or any archive-based history as an option) and because of the emergence of historiography as a serious center of investigation for medieval French history among scholars such as Robert-Henri
Bautier and, especially, the group centered around Bernard Guenée in France.

I remember distinctly the strong feeling of homecoming that came over me
when I first arrived in Paris to work on manuscripts at the Bibliothèque nationale, a rather paradoxical sentiment since I had only been to Paris once, for
a one-week visit at the age of sixteen, dragged there—with my twin sister—
by my mother for a relentless round of visits to museums. Although my French
was more than passable, thus relieving me of some of the difficulties experienced by many novice American researchers in French archives and libraries,
this was hardly a guarantee that I understood the ways in which both French
institutions and French society operated. And so, like everyone else, I went
through the arduous task of becoming socialized to the ways of Parisian life,
learning to pay for purchases at the *caisse* in the cheese store before asking for
the package and to fill out the series of *fiches* required to get a manuscript delivered for perusal in the Salle des manuscrits of the Bibliothèque nationale. I
also suffered the lesson that one could not go to a real French restaurant at
lunchtime and order *salade niçoise* and nothing else (at least not in those days:
that sort of meal was relegated to cafés).

In truth, once absorbed, the particularities of French social and culinary
mores make for the most pleasant sort of living; I cannot think of an American scholar who does not rejoice in the wisdom of having chosen Paris as the
locus of his or her research. Since my visits generally were limited to four to
six weeks over the summer, I never attempted to master the intricacies of
French wine and food and to this day remain relatively indifferent to French
cuisine. My accent, derived from having learned French among Belgians in
New York City, made me almost unplaceable: certainly not French yet not rec-
ognizably American—or even Canadian (the perennial question of where I
belonged thus foisted upon me once again)—but I suspect it spared me of some
of the difficulties experienced by my colleagues doing research in Paris during
the late sixties, a period when American scholarship was scarcely acknowledged, much less valued, and most French academics viewed with trepidation
the annual summer flooding of seats in the Salle des manuscrits by Americans.

My first book on royal historiography, *The Chronicle Tradition of Saint-Denis,* involved me in the question of how French society understood and deployed its past, beginning as early as the Middle Ages, a topic that would run like a leitmotif through much of my subsequent work, although displaced in a wide variety of ways. This work was relatively straightforward since much of it concerned the evolution of the chronicle tradition itself. I studied it in order to trace the ways that the past, as constructed by the chroniclers, constituted an ideological structure of argument, one that sought legitimacy from the borrowed authority of history understood as a putatively real, though highly permeable and fragile, tradition, hence an artifact of historiography. What made the writing of history important in the Middle Ages was its ability to address contemporary political life via a displacement to the past, to embed both prescription and polemic in an apparently "factual," because realistic, account of the historical legacy the past had bequeathed. My approach shared the basic orientation of the work being done by Bernard Guenée, Robert-Henri Bautier, and their students, many of whom I met while working at the Bibliothèque nationale, having been graciously introduced by Guenée and Bautier, both of whom had strong ties to my mentor, John Baldwin.

This early work probably represents the moment when my own ways of doing history were closest to those then practiced in France. It was grounded in manuscript work, strove for deep and technical knowledge of its subject, and addressed concerns at the time widely shared by the group of French scholars who worked on historiography. The most important of these concerns was the ways in which the "truth" of the past underwrote the utility of historiography for medieval rulers and political actors, whose interests were not to produce an account of "what actually happened" but to legitimate their propagandistic and political goals. It thus addressed primary questions of French social and political life, matters always close to the heart of French historical writing, and it made for a happy period of communication and even collaboration with French scholars.

However, even during this early, apprentice-like period of writing history, I felt dissatisfied with my readings of texts. In part, there were good intellectual (as well as underlying psychological) reasons for this discontent. They stemmed from the fact that medieval historiography, like all historical writing, foregrounds the problem of how to represent reality—of the relationship between text and referent—by its deployment of a "realistic" style. But medieval historical writing does this is an especially disturbing way, since in sharp contrast to modern historiography, where "content" (facts, data) is presumptively real and style is to some extent optional, medieval chronicles tend to employ a realistic style, while including as morally serious "content" a vast range of materials that are excluded from the precincts of modern historical realism: miracles, resurrections, saints, myths, and visions, inter alia. To ask what were the minimum requirements for realism in medieval historiography was tantamount to asking: what was the generative grammar that defined historical writing in the Middle Ages, the linguistic protocols that transformed the past into historical narrative?

To answer this question, I investigated the literary character of medieval historical writing, drawing on the work of Hayden White in *Metahistory* and, eventually, the whole apparatus of structuralist and poststructuralist thought—anthropological as well as literary—then being imported from France and spreading rapidly through the American academy, first in literary studies and later in cultural history. In examining the literary modes and narrative economies of medieval chronicles, I was, of course, employing a technique of interpretation that in its largest sense has been termed the "linguistic turn," the hallmark of which has been a growing awareness that perception, cognition, and imagination are mediated by linguistic structures cast into discourses of one sort or another. Although inspired by French thought, this work would increasingly draw me toward critical theory and historiography *tout court* and thus away from French history in its traditional sense.

That French historians remained relatively impervious to the influences of "French theory," a complex of ideas and critical theories that some writers have argued found its true destiny in the United States, is one of the more perplexing aspects of Franco-American intellectual relations during the late seventies, eighties, and nineties. The easier part of the equation to explain, I think, is the French rejection—or rather neglect—of theory as a method of historical investigation. To the extent that "linguistic turn" historiography questions the historian's ability to garner certain knowledge about the past, it disrupts any confident approach to social history, which, indeed, in the United States experienced a sharp decline in favor of cultural history based on the analysis of discourses. But since French history in the modern period, and especially in the heyday of *Annaliste* historiography after World War II, tended to privilege a profoundly structuralist social history, it proved inhospitable to the genealogical and deconstructive turns in the work of authors such as Michel Foucault and Jacques Derrida. And since it is my belief that French history is principally, if not exclusively, "about" French society past and present, to take up the "linguistic turn" risked decentering the place of French history in French social life. This was a path that most French historians did not care to pursue, especially during the halcyon years of *Annaliste* dominance over the French historical scene.

That Americans, for their part, would be so powerfully receptive to French theory is somewhat more difficult to understand. One reason, no doubt, was that, like other sectors of American society and economy, historical studies in the United States during the sixties and seventies experienced upheaval and change, in this case involving recruitment into the profession and the importation of the new attitudes toward the past that inevitably followed. In addition to the entrance of women and African Americans into the American academy, there was a new wave of participation among classes and what, for lack of a better word, can be called ethnic groups, among them Jews, who entered universities in large numbers in the early sixties, constituting both a clientele whose interests needed to be addressed and a pool for future professionals.

The experience of these new groups during the "sixties," when the civil rights movement, the Vietnam antiwar movement, the rise of feminism, and the utopian critique of American culture represented by the growth of the "counter-culture" were in full swing, is obviously relevant. Members of this generation, which came to consciousness of their place in history in an atmosphere of deep ambivalence toward authority and power—both political and cultural—developed their own, distinctive vision of the past, which they approached with the same suspicion of order, hierarchy, authority, and patriarchy that had characterized their involvement in the contemporary world. Nor were Americans alone in this tendency, although the openness of the American academy to new groups and new ideas certainly facilitated the pace with which they were accepted in comparison to Europe, France in particular. Eventually, however, a group of historians, led by figures like Roger Chartier, made inroads into the predominantly social orientation of French historiography.

One should not shy away, I think, from the specificity of this American pattern of social recruitment, particularly with respect to the entrance of Jews. For ours is the first generation of those immigrants, drawn from both the dispossessed of the "old European order" and the refugees from Hitler's Europe, to enter the American academy in large numbers, trailing all the ambivalence toward and desire for mastery over worlds that we had all, in some deep way, lost. In my case, the pull to deconstruction and Derrida now seems a foregone conclusion. And yet, though irresistibly drawn to it, I never wholly or uncritically espoused it, being unable to accept what we all then believed to be Derrida's radical notion of textuality. Nonetheless, like other scholars engaged with postmodernism, I became convinced (not least through my reading of Derrida) that the positivist notions of referentiality and empirical truth that had shaped "scientific" or objective historiography since the nineteenth century was untenable, at least in the epistemologically uncompromising terms in which it had been framed. Because I could accept neither the erasure of the past implicit in some poststructuralist accounts of textuality nor the plenitude of presence implied by positivism, I found myself caught in a commitment to the middle ground. It was this double, and to some extent self-canceling, epistemological ethic, veering haplessly between an awareness of the past's absence and the need for its recuperation, that spawned my concept of the "social logic of the text."

This concept seeks to combine in a single but complex framework an analysis of a text's social site—both as a product of a particular social world and as an agent at work in that world—and its discursive character as "logos," that is, as a literary artifact composed of language and thus demanding literary (formal) analysis. The play on "logic" as signifying at once a mode of linguistic performance and an objective description of a social reality (albeit one mediated in language) was intentional. In framing this position, I was aware of its inherent epistemological contradiction: asserting the reality of a past that cannot be reached except through language and yet, at the same time, asserting the past's objective, if absent, existence. Implicit in the concept of the "social logic of the text," therefore, is the belief that we may recover some sense of the material world of the past but also the recognition that language intervenes and mediates the ways in which we know and constitute it. Translated into autobiographical terms, it expresses the dual gesture that stands at the core of my work: the desire for history and commitment to its recovery and the equally powerful belief in the past's erasure and loss.

It should come as no surprise that this work led me further and further away from a direct relationship to French history, although I later wrote another book on the rise of vernacular prose historiography in France in the thirteenth century. Once again, I sought to enjoin poststructuralist theories of language and textuality while holding on to a notion of the social roots of discursive behaviors, that is, to a double (and somewhat contradictory) vision of history as governed at once by material, social contexts of life in the past and by their linguistic constitution and expression. Along the way, I became obsessed with the relationship between memory and history, a question that for me was directly involved with the Holocaust and my own oblique relationship to it. In this, I was following a path that would also, if in a very different way, come to preoccupy French historiography (although the study of French medieval history remained relatively untouched by it), as French scholars finally confronted the question of France's role in the genocide of French Jews and their decades-long silence about it. About the same time, Pierre Nora and other French historians associated with his massive volumes on *Realms of Memory* sought once again to connect questions of French memory to those of

French society, thus remaining faithful, in their own way, to the profound commitment of French historiography to the investigation of social and socio-cultural currents in French society and life.

The intellectual journey described here traces, therefore, the progressive awareness of a need to confront a generation's profound loss of certainty in older ways of knowing, conceptualizing and experiencing the past. Postmodernism has challenged us to elaborate new forms and new philosophies of writing history. If, as Jean-François Lyotard argues, there are no longer master narratives, still less are there certainties about the nature and status of history itself, whether as an object of study or subject of practice. Our confidence in the totality and ultimate unity of the greater historical enterprise is gone. Like so much else, history has been subject to the fracturing and fragmentation that has beset all aspects of postmodern thought.

But it would be wrong to leave the impression that loss is the only sign under which we have labored. The abandonment of traditional models of historical writing has been at the same time exhilarating, liberating, and enormously productive. It has expanded, enriched, and deepened our historiographical practice while freeing it from its positivist illusions. If we have now left behind the positivist certainties and foundationalism of the "old" historicism in favor of new and as yet unsettled historical practices, perhaps this is not cause for regret. A historiographical practice grounded in an awareness of its own philosophical (and psychological?) commitments will not diminish but rather strengthen our appreciation both of the past as the object of our study and of the present as the site of our inquiries into the past. In the final analysis, what is the past but a once material existence, now lost, extant only as sign and as sign drawing to itself chains of conflicting interpretations that hover over its absent presence and compete for possession of the relics, seeking to invest traces of significance upon the bodies of the dead by putting words where silence reigns?

CHAPTER 7

✤ Why Paris?

Barbara B. Diefendorf

My Dutch grandmother explained my fascination with French history as the product of the small drop of French blood flowing in my veins from the seduction of one of my Dutch foremothers by a French soldier during the wars of the Revolution. She waited until I was in my mid-twenties to tell me this, presumably so as not to shock me, because at the same time she warned me not to be judgmental: "Times were different then." The story came to mind as I pondered the paths this autobiographical sketch might take. I am acutely aware of how the narrative strategy I adopt at the outset of this account will shape the story I have to tell. One set of choices will make my career look like an accident, the result of a long series of fortuitous events; another will make it appear overdetermined, the product of an inevitable march of events. And yet, however much Dutch Calvinist blood still runs in my veins, I do not believe in predestination of either a spiritual or a worldly kind. It is tempting to recount my personal history as if each step led neatly to the next, but it simply would not be true. I can date my fascination with France—and especially with Paris—to a youthful infatuation; it is harder to explain why that interest took an academic turn. Never once as an undergraduate did I look up in class and imagine myself on the other side of the podium, as teacher instead of student, much less as a teacher and scholar focusing on the history of sixteenth- and seventeenth-century France, a period I did not even encounter until my second year of graduate school. I would like to take credit for careful planning and ambition, but in truth my career trajectory owes far more to happenstance and to choices made by following my heart with little thought as to where they might lead.

In this I am a product of my generation as well as of my temperament. I graduated from college in 1968, a pivotal year but not a good one for career ambitions. Having never had a woman professor, I had no role models among my teachers, and, although I had read *The Second Sex* with interest one summer while still in high school, I did not see a connection to my own situation when, having graduated Phi Beta Kappa from the University of California at Berkeley, I found that the only job for which I was qualified was as a glorified file clerk for an executive recruiting firm in San Francisco. Within a few months, I was pondering two choices: scrimp and save enough money for a plane ticket to Paris without worrying about what I would do when my money ran out or return to school in the hope of finding something more satisfying to do with my life. School won when my boss agreed to let me continue part-time while attending classes. I was nevertheless still uncertain enough about what I was doing that I would only have applied for the M.A. program had one of the professors I asked for a recommendation not advised me that I would not be taken seriously unless I applied for the Ph.D. I took his advice and applied to study nineteenth-century French history.

Why France? Because it was the foreign language in which I was most proficient; because it was the field of history for which I could write the strongest application; because I had spent my junior year there and wanted to go back; because I was still in the grips of a childhood fascination and did not even consider other possibilities. On some deeper level, this was a way of seeking out my European roots without the more painful confrontations with the past that would have come from going to the Netherlands, which my father had left on the eve of World War II and to which he had never returned. But I only realized this much later, at the same time that I recognized my preference for studying problems like religious violence and gender inequities at one remove, by locating my studies in the distant and not the recent past.

I grew up in the San Francisco Bay Area, in a town just north of Berkeley, where my mother was living when she met and married my father during the war. She was a high school teacher, the first member of her family to get a college degree. He was an engineer on a Dutch merchant marine ship carrying American troops to the South Pacific. A recent graduate of the maritime academy, he had been at sea when Germany invaded the Netherlands. Like others lucky enough not to have been in Dutch ports at the time, his ship had sailed for London, joined the Allied war effort, and carried supplies across the North Atlantic until, after Pearl Harbor, it was sent to the West Coast to serve in the Pacific theater instead. My father always claimed that he would not have returned to live in the Netherlands even if he had not had an American wife and the beginnings of a family to keep him here. He was never very specific, but I knew that he had ambivalent feelings about the country where he was born and the family that remained there; the blue air letters that arrived periodically from my grandparents were seldom occasions for joy. I attributed this to the experience of being raised in the port city of Rotterdam during the Depression, the son of narrowly pious parents who expected him to spend most of each Sunday in church.

Only later did I learn the deeper source of strain. My father's only brother, who had also been in the Dutch merchant marine when the war began, had apparently gone over to the German side at some point. Inconsistent and conflicting stories about how and why this took place added to the tension and made my father wonder just where his parents' sympathies had lain as they endured the war in occupied Rotterdam with a son in each camp. With no real understanding of the true reasons for his disaffection, I nevertheless identified with my father's negative feelings and had little desire to explore my Dutch roots. Instead, I fixed my affections on a country I could view with more detachment, drawn to its self-presentation as a beacon of civilization and naïvely unaware that it too harbored complicated histories of collaboration that made it difficult to face up to its recent past.

Like many young Francophiles, my fascination with the country went through a number of stages, from a first passionate encounter with Impressionist art at about the age of twelve to perplexed attempts a few years later to grasp existentialist philosophy and New Wave cinema, which I did not understand but thought incredibly chic. From the time I was put into my first French class in the seventh grade, I learned the language with the hope and expectation of someday using it in its native setting. I started college with just one idea in my head: I wanted to spend my junior year in France. The University of California's Study Abroad Program gave me that opportunity.

I arrived in France in August 1966. No one knew at the time that this was the calm before the storm. France was undergoing big changes, but most were not yet as visible as the few pristine monuments that had begun to emerge from the recently ordained project of cleaning Paris's soot-darkened buildings. Bordeaux, where I studied, still had its grayness intact and remained a sleepy, somewhat gloomy city, even if changes were clearly in store. University classes still met in the old Faculty of Letters, in the heart of the old city, though the move to the new, American-style campus at Talence was planned for the following year. Classes remained formal, with students rising from the worn amphitheater benches to salute the professor's entrance. Formality also dominated in the very traditional Catholic family from whom I rented a room. I took my meals at the student restaurant and showered at the public baths; the only full bath in the house where I lived lay within the inner sanctum that I penetrated only rarely and by special invitation. Normally I climbed to my third-floor room past closed doors of dark, solemn wood. I seldom heard the sounds of the life lived behind those doors, though the odors of good cooking perfumed the halls every night and after the family returned from mass on Sunday. The meals I was invited to share were ritually presented and carefully explained—why one ate *crèpes* for Chandeleur, why *boudin* sausage with Arcachon oysters was a typically Bordelais specialty. My hosts impressed upon me the importance of the table as a definer of French identity but also, more subtly, a sense of cultural superiority that, although occasionally an irritant, most often simply set me to thinking about just what this cultural heritage was that they took for granted and I, it seemed, had come to find.

Once a week, I visited a Protestant family for tea. It did not matter to them that I practiced no religion, but it mattered a lot that I came from good Calvinist stock. They had specifically requested that their weekly visitor not be a Catholic. In my ignorance, I found the request very strange, just as I found puzzling the family's cloistered separation from French society at large. Although they tried to educate me about the troubled history of Protestants in France, I found their clear sense of outsider status perplexing, especially by contrast to the cultural assumptions of the family with whom I was lodging. I also had a hard time comprehending how much of their sense of aggrieved separateness came from their Protestant identity rather than their return to the Hexagon in the recent French exit from Algeria, where they had long resided when the battle for independence began. I really only understood what they told me years later, when I had made the Wars of Religion my area of expertise. It is clear in retrospect, however, that my experience with both families helped orient my interests toward the social, cultural, and even religious dimensions of French history. It is equally clear that living and studying in France prior to the upheavals of 1968 has intensified my awareness of both long-term continuities and more immediate processes of historical change.

However interesting I found Bordeaux, it was Paris that excited my imagination, and I spent as much time there as possible. On my first arrival, Paris fascinated by appearing both startlingly familiar and totally new. The landmarks we passed as we were bused to our hotel in the Latin Quarter amazed me with their familiarity, having been captured so often in photos and films that every first glimpse felt like a homecoming, and yet my many miles of almost random exploration kept revealing unexpected scenes. As I wandered, my sense of the historical city deepened. Like most visitors, I was charmed first by Haussmann's nineteenth-century boulevards, with their wide streets and harmonious façades. I had had no experience with medieval cities and could not yet regret Paris's losses, though I quickly learned to appreciate the small tangle of streets around the church of Saint-Séverin more for the hints they gave of an earlier Paris than for the cheap ethnic restaurants that abounded there.

When in Bordeaux, I fed my craving for Paris on the novels of Balzac and Zola. Unconsciously, at least at first, I ignored the novels that dealt with provincial life and read only those set in Paris. It is clear now that my interests were already more historical than literary, as even my choice of authors must suggest. I was more intrigued by the portrayals they offered of Parisian society—the tensions between old and new nobility in *Père Goriot,* the ambitions of the parvenus in *La Curée*—than by the formal devices they employed to develop their characters and plots, but I did not yet recognize that the questions I was asking could (at that moment at least) be better answered in classes on history than on literature. My studies of literature in Bordeaux were devoid of theory. We did a broad survey that began with the *Chanson de Roland* and ended with Albert Camus, and we spent more time analyzing the brief excerpts in all six volumes of the Lagarde and Michard textbooks that were then common currency in French high schools than reading and discussing complete works. It was only when I returned home and began my senior year at Berkeley as a French major that I learned not only that my favorite authors were completely out of fashion but also that the questions that interested me about the social context for literary creation were out of fashion as well, at least in the Berkeley French department.

The history department proved a more welcoming place to pursue these interests, so I added a second major in that field. A proseminar on "The Novel in French History" meshed perfectly with my desire to explore how authors both commented on and transformed their societies in their works of fiction. A senior seminar on "Positivism and the Symbolist Reaction" gave me my first taste of the pleasures and pains of original research. However far my historical interests have since moved, I recognize in the paper I wrote for that seminar, on the literary impact of Joris-Karl Huysmans's *A Rebours,* the same blend of social, cultural, and literary sources and methods that continues to characterize my work as a historian.

Literary sources also provided the initial impetus for my first graduate seminar paper, a study of the transformation of Paris's place Maubert under the pressures of Haussmannization, but so did Honoré Daumier's image of a smug landlord looking out on the city and saying, "There goes another building; I can raise my rents again." What did Haussmann's rebuilding projects mean for those who lived through them? How did they transform the urban fabric of Paris but also its social texture and relationships? I began an outside field in urban studies and might happily have developed into a nineteenth-century urban historian had not the professor for whom I wrote the seminar paper intervened to warn me that I had choices to make. Modern French history was at that moment in crisis at Berkeley. I could complete the M.A. and go somewhere else for the doctorate, or I could change fields, moving into the more distant past but working at the same nexus of society, politics, and culture with a historian who would be joining the Berkeley faculty the following year.

I chose the latter option, for reasons more personal than professional. I was still too uncertain about what I was doing to move half a continent or more away, and I had met someone in my first graduate class, a proseminar on the French Revolution, who was a powerful inducement to stay. Jeff has an important part in this story as the man who still shares my life, but from the beginning he also played an important role in my transformation into a professional historian by taking my work as seriously as he did his own. I found that I liked the rhythms of research and writing and that, given his companionship and that of the friends I made through him, I thrived in an atmosphere in which these rhythms were taken for granted. I did not know that we would marry and that many of the friendships made in graduate school would continue to this day, but I did know that I liked my life and did not want to abandon it and begin anew.

I slipped back into the *ancien régime* with an independent study of the area around Richelieu's new palace (now the Palais-Royal) in seventeenth-century Paris. The period was new, but the project had similar aims to my study of place Maubert. I wanted to understand the impact of an ambitious development project on the urban fabric of Paris. As a research paper, the project was only a partial success, but it opened new doors by giving me my first introduction to archival research. I took six months off after completing my M.A. to join Jeff in Germany, where he was doing research for a dissertation on the impact of the French Revolution on Rhenish businessmen. His research would take him to Paris in the summer, giving me a chance to work in the Archives nationales and Bibliothèque nationale as well. My time in Paris was too short to do justice to my subject, but the experience taught me the thrill of archival research. I loved shuttling back and forth between the Bibliothèque nationale and the Archives, but most of all I loved the sense of expectation that came with every new box of documents or register. Would it contain records that fleshed out the picture I had gleaned from secondary readings? Would it offer clues to connections I had not foreseen? I did not yet know where my research would take me, but the pleasure I took in archival work was a strong incentive to carry on. So was the pleasure I took in being again in Paris, exploring old haunts and observing the changes that were underway. I remember in particular one lunch at an outdoor table adjacent to the old market of Les Halles, which was being torn down quite literally as we ate. The huge construction site was framed by the few elegantly arched columns of Baltard's markets that remained standing, while wrecking balls swung and bits of ash from burning debris floated in the air.

When I returned to Berkeley, I scheduled a meeting with the new French historian the department had hired. Having no background in the sixteenth century, I did not know Natalie Zemon Davis through either her growing reputation or her works. It was thus sheer luck that brought me to her first Berkeley seminar and gave my research interests a stable course at last. After consulting with prospective members of the seminar, Natalie announced our subject as the history of the family in sixteenth-century France. When it came time to decide on a research project, I turned naturally back to Paris, where I felt geographically at home, even if the chronology and subject matter were new. The paper that emerged, a study of marriage practices in sixteenth-century Paris, was the seed for the dissertation I later wrote on the families of the civic elite.

Quantitative social history was then the fashion, both in France's *Annales* school and among Anglo-American social historians, and a published inventory of Parisian notarial contracts gave me a sketchy but sufficient database to analyze patterns of endogamy, dowries, and other questions then of interest to social historians. As with my earlier work, however, literary sources helped me formulate the questions that ultimately transformed the study from a simple exercise in quantitative history to a program for future research. Rabelais raised important questions about clandestine marriage and parental consent; Montaigne about the preservation of patrimony and struggles between widows and their grown sons. I realized that I could not study marriage in isolation and had to reconceptualize questions of family alliance within the broader context of strategies that also involved inheritance patterns and career choices. Recognizing that these strategies reflected local customary law but also, more amorphously, unspoken ideas about status and mobility that might be particular to a given group, I sought to identify a logical but finite group for study. I spent some months floundering in the archives, teaching myself to read sixteenth-century documents, before deciding to focus on the families of the Paris city councillors at the moment of their transition from a largely mercantile to a predominantly noble, officeholding elite.

As with so many other choices made in the course of my career, this decision had unforeseen consequences. It led directly to the subjects of my dissertation and first book, *Paris City Councillors,* and, only a little less directly, to the two books that followed. The Parisian elite became a kind of testing ground on which to explore questions of social and cultural values. *Beneath the Cross,* my second book, had its origins in questions about the religious divisions that I increasingly recognized in this supposedly unified Catholic elite. What did it mean that one in three of the city councillors I had studied had at least one close family member who had gone over to the Protestant faith? And how could I reconcile not only these divisions but also the civic humanism I had identified in the councillors with accusations that city officials had played a leading role in the terrible massacre of Parisian Protestants that occurred on Saint Bartholomew's Day? My newest book, *From Penitence to Charity,* also stemmed from questions about the religious beliefs and cultural values of the Parisian elite, only this time it was not Protestant-Catholic splits but rather divisions among Catholics that intrigued me. Why did I find so many members of this upwardly mobile social elite, particularly among the women, adopting world-denying forms of penitential asceticism during the final stages of the Wars of Religion, and how did these spiritual choices affect the Catholic revival that followed? Approaching the Catholic Reformation from the perspective of its Parisian participants brought me to challenge traditional interpretations of the movement on several levels, including its chronology, the role women played in it, and the fundamental unity of aims and values that was often presumed. In an important way, then, acquaintance with an expanding and yet defined group of people living four hundred years in the past continues to animate my work as a historian. The questions have evolved and broadened, as have the sources from which I have sought answers, and yet, on some level at least, isolating specific individuals and cohorts whose behavior and values I then can query remains my chosen tool for attempting to bridge historical distance.

This is not to say that my scholarship takes place in a vacuum, or even in a conversation uniquely with my fragmentary documents and the spirits they evoke. On some level contemporary issues are reflected in the questions that preoccupy me—problems of sectarian violence, for example, or the limits and opportunities for women's initiatives—though I try to ensure that my reactions to contemporary events open me to new historical questions without predetermining their answers. Memories of televised crowds tearing at the shroud of Iran's Ayatollah Khomeini may have been playing in my mind when I wrote about the funeral of one of Paris's radical preachers early in the religious wars, but the comparison was ultimately more instructive for the differences I observed than the similarities, and I tried at least to ensure that I did not make unwarranted generalizations about the nature of religious violence.

My work also inevitably reflects my own past influences and experiences.

Although I was scarcely aware of it at the time, my interest in the religious divisions of the sixteenth century was in some measure sparked by a desire to resolve questions provoked by witnessing the "outsider" mentality of the Protestant family I got to know in Bordeaux. The contrasting (and apparently unquestioned) assumption of the Catholic family with whom I lodged—that they somehow embodied a true (and unified) French identity—also lurked somewhere in the margins of my thinking as I formulated the problematics of *Beneath the Cross*—but that is also true of *From Penitence to Charity,* which explores conflictive elements in Catholic practices of piety. Still more obscurely, I seem to have been wrestling with my own family's past in my questions about divided families in *Beneath the Cross.* The knowledge that my uncle chose the German side in World War II profoundly shamed me, but it also prompted questions about wartime experiences and the choices people made. What did it mean for my grandparents, living in the occupied and bomb-flattened city of Rotterdam, to have one son supporting the Allied war effort and another fighting for the Germans? More abstractly, how do we weigh the respective roles of circumstance, ideology, and pragmatic self-interest in the choices people make under the pressures of war?

At the same time, my work takes place in dialogue with other scholars and has consistently been nurtured and stimulated by teachers and friends. Natalie Davis opened my mind to the sixteenth century but also continued to inspire me with the example of her own work and the insightful questions that pepper any communication with her. Her role as my dissertation director was perfectly complemented by that of Gene Brucker, my second reader, whose studies of Florentine society offered elegant models of the sort of seamless combination of social, political, and cultural history that I aspired to write for Paris. The third senior scholar who most profoundly influenced my work is Denis Richet. Robert Descimon, who introduced himself in the archives when he learned the subject of my dissertation research, coaxed me to attend Richet's seminar at the École des Hautes Études when I was still too timid to introduce myself, despite Natalie's urging and insistence that he was "the man" on Parisian history. Denis's keen insights into both the religious conflicts in Paris and the important role of women in France's Catholic Reformation were starting points for my own thinking on these subjects, and I appreciated his lack of condescension, his encouragement, and his openness to Anglo-American contributions to early modern French history, which still tended to be treated as a closed preserve. Friendships that grew out of this seminar remain precious to me, as do friendships with a number of the American historians working in my field. In the United States, early modern French history has traditionally enjoyed a reputation as an area in which scholars are mutually supportive rather than competitive, eager to build on one another's work rather than to tear it down. Certainly this has been my experience. Scholars on both sides of the Atlantic have been generous in sharing elusive sources and citations, as well as providing the companionship necessary to balance the lonelier aspects of research and writing.

✤

Most of the American historians of France that I know share the same affection for French culture and for Paris that propelled me into the field. This Francophilia may have been tested in different ways over the years, but it almost always survives and is manifest in the ways we relate to both the process and products of our research. It is manifest also in our patterns of sociability and a shared assumption that the best conversations take place at the table, over a multi-course dinner that is French in inspiration and cuisine. It is a rare historian of France who does not love to cook or enjoy fine wine, and almost universally, I expect, we can trace this appreciation not to dinners in fine restaurants (which we could not afford as students and still find expensive now) but rather to leisurely meals with French friends. My own sense of the pleasures of the table as a defining feature of French culture goes back to my year in Bordeaux—to the memory of meals shared but also those only imagined from the delicious smells that wafted up to my room. The intervening years have provided many fond memories of fabulous dinners in Paris apartments, on a terrace above the Côte d'Azur, at a farmhouse in the Périgord . . . the list goes on, but in the end, the memories center less on what was consumed than on the stimulating exchange of ideas that took place at the table.

I recall, for example, dinners with the French co-directors of Boston University's Study Abroad Program in Grenoble, for which I served as the resident American director in 1989–1990, as occasions for pondering the implications of the fall of the Berlin Wall. Jeff spent the year in Cologne on a fellowship, and his visits prompted long discussions with French colleagues about the future of the new Europe and France's place in this future. "*L'affaire des foulards,*" the debate about Muslim girls wearing head coverings in French schools, made headlines the same year and similarly fueled conversations and debates. Initially astonished at the vehemence with which our program's housing supervisor, who was also a high school teacher, insisted that the scarves should be forbidden as a violation of the secular space of the public school, I came to recognize the profound differences between French and American notions of the separation of church and state. I could understand the historical roots of the French insistence on viewing the public school classroom as an extension of the secular state but remained unconvinced that the mere wearing of a headscarf by a student constituted a dangerous form of religious proselytization. The discussions occasionally grew heated, as my reluctance to concede this point inevitably led to the suggestion that I could not, as an American, be expected to appreciate the need for immigrants to conform to the mores of the country they had chosen, because the United States had no common culture to which to conform. I learned with time not to take this personally, or even as an expression of innate anti-Americanism, and to recognize instead the underlying questions about human and civil rights, but also about the very nature of French identity, that were being aired. The intensity of the feelings aroused by the issue was brought home to me a number of years later, when I watched the discussion at an international conference on religious differences dissolve into acrimony and mutual accusations among the French participants. It is perhaps the only time I have witnessed less than civil and urbane debate among French colleagues.

My own feelings about the question remain mixed, as is appropriate to my outsider status. I have taken the issue into the classroom and used it to spark discussion in courses on "Women and Gender" but also on the French Revolution and its legacy of civil and human rights. But I have also used it—along with other issues encountered in my long and affectionate absorption with French values and culture—to question my own inherited cultural values and assumptions. Standing on the margins of French culture has moved me closer to the margins of American culture, but in a useful and productive way, one from which I have benefited as a scholar, as a teacher, and as a person.

My relationship to France and things French, then, has been an ongoing learning experience, but one I view more in terms of continuity than change. I have never quite recovered from my original love affair with Paris, however much noisier and more crowded I find the city today, and I still take enormous pleasure in wandering Parisian streets, which are more familiar to me than those of any American city, including Boston, where I have worked for twenty-five years. Large chunks of the Métro map remain lodged in my brain on account of the many different neighborhoods in which I have lived. I have put up with the din of constant traffic in order to reside a short block from the Palais-Royal but also relished the peaceful north face of Montmartre and watched the removal of the Baudricourt slums and gradual implantation of a vibrant Asian community in the area southeast of the place d'Italie over the course of a number of years. A long time has passed since my studies shifted from the physical city to the political, religious, and domestic passions of its early modern residents, but something of the curious urbanist lives on in the lively pleasure I continue to take in observing the city's evolution and in witnessing the relative success or failure of controversial attempts to mix old and new. Some of my favorite places have been modernized out of existence, and yet the city itself retains an indelible charm and a fascination rooted in its ability to constantly remake itself while remaining in some essential way the same city that bewitched me long ago.

My attachment to Paris is simultaneously visceral, emotional, and intellectual. I walk its streets in the company of the ghosts of the men and women who populate my books, even as I observe recent urban changes while strolling to meet a friend in a neighborhood café. I wonder if the revolutionary soldier who seduced my Dutch ancestress was a Parisian; maybe he walks these streets with me too.

CHAPTER 8

✦ Catholic Connections, Jewish Relations, French Religion

Thomas Kselman

I can imagine many explanations as to why I ended up studying the religious history of modern France. From a professional perspective, the shrine of Lourdes was a topic ripe for the picking in the 1970s, a way to combine concerns for social movements in the nineteenth century with the growing realization of the power of religion as a mobilizing force. I have no doubt that professional considerations played a role in my decision to study France, but it seems to me that personal factors were equally important, and that the place to begin any explanation of why I did so is my Catholic upbringing in the United States during the 1950s and 1960s.

It is hard for a religious skeptic, which is what I am now, to understand religious belief and devotion. And to judge by my experience, it is surprisingly hard even if you yourself were once a believer. I wonder a great deal about why so many people in nineteenth-century France visited shrines, made novenas, received the sacraments, and prayed for the dead. But these questions have a personal dimension as well, for through them I recall and ponder my own Catholic devotionalism as a child and adolescent. My answers to the historical questions are almost certainly influenced by my answers to the personal ones.

I am convinced that despite my current skepticism, my formation as a Catholic in the United States in the twentieth century allowed me to have some sense of what it was to be a nineteenth-century French Catholic. Such a claim can sound like an ahistorical assertion that there is a Catholic essence that endures outside of history, but that is not at all what I intend. Certainly there are important differences between the French Catholicism of the nineteenth century and the American Catholicism that I lived, the most obvious of which is the much more intensely politicized religiosity of the French case. Nonetheless, I have found myself oddly at home when I page through a French missal or devotional tract, read a sermon, or consider a description of a religious ceremony. Perhaps as a testament to the success of ultramontanism, the Church's centralization and standardization of worship and decision-making in the nineteenth century, the Catholicism I grew up with in the 1950s and the French Catholicism I study seem to me different expressions of the same religious culture. Like devout French Catholics, I grew up believing in the absolute truth of fundamental Catholic doctrines. I was convinced of the efficacy of the sacraments, of their ability to open up for me an eternal life in a blissful heaven. I was convinced that the Catholic Church (and its clergy) had unique access to the grace made available by the suffering of Christ to redeem my sins, and that other religious beliefs were to be pitied for their deficiencies.

If my religious education has made me feel at home in the world of French Catholicism, it was not just because of shared beliefs. I still recall the power that the Catholic liturgy could exercise at early morning low masses sparsely attended by a few devotees and at Midnight mass on Christmas Eve, with the church full to overflowing. And I remember as well feelings of consolation after confession, when my anxieties about hellfire were relieved, the satisfaction that came with receiving Communion, and the pride that accompanied processions around the church on major holidays. I do not take a naïve view of such religious sentiments and have learned to see them through the eyes of a social scientist. But however much I read such feelings as rooted in psychological and sociological contexts, I continue to appreciate as well their power to transcend these, to escape from the limits of an intellectual analysis that tends always to look away from religion even as it claims to study it.

Finally, in thinking about how my upbringing has led to my particular path into French history, I should emphasize that my association with Catholicism did not end when I stopped believing. My two brothers were ordained as Catholic priests, and my parents were devout Catholics, profoundly consoled by their faith as they faced death. This was especially the case for my mother, who told me before she died in 2000 that she was absolutely convinced that she would join my father in heaven. I find myself both skeptical and respectful of such beliefs, no longer convinced of them, nostalgic perhaps for the comfort and reassurance they provide, anxious perhaps about my own future. My feelings about Catholicism are thus complex, for I no longer believe, and there is much about my upbringing that I regard critically. But I also feel resentment when Catholicism is disparaged, and I have sometimes found myself on both sides of the argument when I come across exchanges between Catholics and anticlericals. I see my ambivalence about Catholicism as a quality that allows me to move into and out of a sympathetic reading of Catholic culture, aware of its tensions and complexity.

The Catholic education I received did include an introduction to France, for in addition to the obligatory Latin (all of which I've forgotten) I studied French for three years at St. Mary's High School in Perth Amboy, New Jersey. This choice was not based on some incipient attraction to France, which at the time was a total abstraction to me, but because the alternative, German, was taught by a sister with a notoriously bad reputation. High school French in a small Catholic school in central Jersey was not training at the highest level, certainly, but Sister Harold had been to the summer immersion courses at the University of Laval in Canada, and she provided me with the basics that I have relied on ever since. Catholic education continued through my college years, when I attended St. Joseph's College (now University), a Jesuit school in Philadelphia. When I entered St. Joseph's in 1966 I had no particular goal in mind, other than a general sense that becoming a lawyer would make my parents happy. I chose history as a major because of the wonderful teachers in the department at the time, and I was particularly influenced by the late Ray Schmandt, who guided me toward the University of Michigan, where he had done his graduate work in medieval history. But when I entered graduate school in 1970 my major interest, like so many other undergraduates, was in twentieth-century Germany. I was particularly interested in the behavior of Catholics during the Nazi era, and was shocked and convinced when Guenter Lewy and Gordon Zahn demonstrated a level of Catholic complicity in Hitler's regime. But at St. Joseph's I certainly had no idea that I would study the history of religion in graduate school, and that I would become a French historian.

Catholic students in the 1950s and 1960s were always told that there was great danger in leaving the world of Catholic education, that it was hard, if not impossible, to retain one's faith in secular institutions. I don't know if this proposition has ever been tested, but it certainly describes what happened to me at the University of Michigan in the 1970s. I can imagine the nuns who taught me in elementary school blaming what they would call my "loss of faith" on the secular atmosphere that pervaded Ann Arbor and the University of Michigan, where I spent the 1970s. They would have a point, I suppose, but from my perspective Michigan was a liberating experience, a time of gain and not of loss. But even as I left the Catholic milieu in which I had been raised, I remained fascinated with it. At the University of Michigan I found in modern France a kind of laboratory where I could observe and ponder religious beliefs and practices that remained oddly familiar, because I could recall through them my own participation in Catholic culture.

Ann Arbor was an exhilarating place to live, and it's hard now not to romanticize the experiences, personal and intellectual, that I recall about those years. French history was especially in fashion at Michigan, where Chuck and Louise Tilly served as charismatic mentors for an impressive cohort of students, many of whom have gone on to distinguished careers. While I became friends with many of the French history students, I was always on the fringe of the Tilly group. I was initially interested more in the history of ideas, and I found myself in seminars with Stephen Tonsor and Charles Trinkaus. Michigan at the time allowed students to do a field outside of the department, and in a course on the philosophy of religion taught by Robert Adams I read Emile Durkheim's *Elementary Forms of Religious Life,* a book that I found liberating, for it provided an analysis that linked religion intimately to social institutions and fundamental categories of thought. As I read Durkheim, the veils parted, for I now had a way of thinking about religion that combined rational explanation with a deep sense of respect. I know that Durkheim is not the most fashionable of religious theorists, and that many scholars view him as a reductionist thinker, who saw in religion only the projections of collective ideals. But for me, Durkheim does not so much equate the sacred and the social as much as he moves back and forth between them, sensitive always to their complex interrelations. With Stephen Tonsor I read Durkheim's teacher Fustel de Coulanges, who shared his views that religious ideas and rituals form the basis of social categories and institutions.

My reading of Durkheim and Fustel was more philosophical than historical and did not bring me very far into the world of France and of French history. Nonetheless, I could have become a historian of ideas, focusing perhaps on French religious thought. But at Michigan the appeal of social history was powerful, and when it came to choosing a dissertation I looked for a way to combine my interest in religion with questions derived from social history. A number of concepts were floating around that suggested ways to link the two. The study of millennial movements in the Middle Ages illuminated the power of religion to generate massive social protest, and E. P. Thompson's approach to English Methodism and Eric Hobsbawm's *Primitive Rebels* provided glimpses of similar developments in the modern era, read from a Marxist perspective. The concept of "popular religion" opened up the possibility of exploring religion from the bottom up, looking at the laity rather than the clergy, and of examining the practices that priests might regard as superstitious. I soon found the relationship between priests and people to be a complicated negotiation in which both sides made important concessions. But "popular religion" was nonetheless a valuable category, for it encouraged me and others to think about the ways that Catholic devotions and shrines that exist outside the formal sacramental system helped provide ordinary believers with access to the supernatural, constituting a source of social remedies and cultural significance. In addition to Durkheim, other writers who pushed me in this direction included Keith Thomas (*Religion and the Decline of Magic*) and the cultural anthropologists Clifford Geertz, Victor Turner, and Bill Christian Jr. At the time (and now as well), I made little effort to combine all of these guides into a systematic theory of religion; it seemed to me more useful to draw on them as needed in contemplating specific evidence, which perhaps betrays my empiricist bias.

I cannot recall exactly when I made a decision to study miracles in nineteenth-century France, but it must have been 1973, after my doctoral exams, and I do remember that the multi-volume collection of documents on Lourdes edited by René Laurentin provided the starting point for a dissertation proposal. In making this decision I had the very good fortune to work with Raymond Grew, who directed the thesis that eventually turned into *Miracles and Prophecies in Nineteenth-Century France.* As a mentor, Ray was a wonderful listener and a sympathetic critic, someone who gave students a great deal of freedom in what they studied while setting a high standard for whatever work they chose to do. Religious history was not a familiar topic to the "Francophile" group that had gathered around the Tillys, and at the time historians of France in the United States had often looked away from or dismissed the millions of French who went on pilgrimages to Lourdes and other shrines, where they sought healings for their personal ills or, when France was threatened by enemies, God's intervention. Ray's support helped me gain the confidence to argue for the weight and significance of religious movements in modern France.

Beyond such professional reasons, however, and perhaps with the benefit of hindsight, I now see my dissertation as an exploration of the fundamental religious questions that I was grappling with as I moved away from Catholic ·practice. What is the relationship between God and man? Does God intervene in this world in response to prayer and supplication? How can belief in the miraculous and the power of prayer be reconciled with an acceptance of modern science? How does the Catholic Church serve both its members and its own interests in acting as an intermediary between God and man? I don't recall this period as one of personal religious crisis, but looking again at *Miracles and Prophecies,* it does strike me that I was working out a view on God and the miraculous that combined skepticism about the reality of divine intervention with sympathy toward those who sought it. Similarly, I saw the Church and the clergy as genuinely sensitive to people in their appeals for help but also manipulative in how they responded to these needs. Although I realize it sounds like special pleading for one's own specialty, it strikes me that the history of Catholic devotions in nineteenth-century France provides an invaluable historical case for thinking about religion and religious change in the modern world. I have been gratified to see that other historians of France agree, to judge by Ruth Harris's book on Lourdes and Ray Jonas's study of the cult of the Sacred Heart and the construction of the Sacré Coeur in Paris.

I first went to France in the spring of 1974, where I worked mostly in Paris, on the famous F19 series on religion in the Archives nationales and on pamphlets in the Bibliothèque nationale. But as with Ann Arbor, it is impossible for me to recall this first trip only in intellectual terms. I went with my wife Claudia, who was doing research for her dissertation on French family law in the Third Republic. We had little money, the exchange rate was awful, we lived in small and uncomfortable rooms, the work was at times alienating and frustrating (due in part to our weak spoken French)—and we had a wonderful time. I had been to Europe once before, for a summer program in Florence, but our trip to France in 1974 (only four months, alas) put us on our own, as we engaged in the *"rites de passage"* familiar to many American scholars: finding housing, constantly monitoring the exchange rate, struggling to find and read documents for a project that we feared might never end. By the end of our stay, Claudia and I had established our credentials as French historians, but we were not yet rooted in France, a process that took some time.

In moving to Notre Dame in South Bend, Indiana, I was moving back into a Catholic milieu that I knew from my childhood and adolescence. But Notre Dame under the leadership of Father Hesburgh was (as it continues to be) intellectually ambitious as well as vigorously Catholic, and I was hired primarily because my colleagues in the history department were interested in someone from the University of Michigan who applied the fashionable methods of social history to religious phenomena. Given its constituency, it is not surprising that Notre Dame's sports teams are known as the Fighting Irish, but, as the name suggests, Notre Dame was originally a French institution, founded by Père Sorin, of the Congregation of Holy Cross, in 1842. Sorin made dozens of trips back to France throughout the nineteenth century and established Notre Dame as a bridgehead for French Catholicism in the United States. For a number of years, for example, Notre Dame had a monopoly on the distribution of water from the fountain at Lourdes to American Catholics, and a shrine modeled on the grotto of Lourdes has drawn thousands of students for over a century. When the French government expelled thirty thousand priests, brothers, and sisters in 1905, the president of Notre Dame at the time, Father Zahm, was the only American religious leader to travel to France, where he helped arrange havens for those forced to flee. The French connection I found at Notre Dame suggests to me a larger point, that French Catholicism has played a major but largely unstudied role in the development of American Catholicism. Because Italian, Polish, and Irish Catholic immigrants were so numerous, and those from France so few, American Catholics have not realized the profound impact that French missionary congregations, such as the Holy Cross fathers and brothers of Notre Dame, have had in creating institutions and importing devotions, such as Our Lady of Lourdes and the Sacred Heart.

Notre Dame's connection with France has continued through its program at the Institut Catholique de l'Ouest in Angers, in western France. Since the 1960s Notre Dame has sent about 1,500 of its students for either a semester or longer to Stage Université Notre Dame en France. The "stage" is directed by a Notre Dame faculty member, and from the time I arrived at the university I was encouraged to think about spending a year or two in Angers. I defined my next project on beliefs and practices surrounding death to include a focus on Anjou, the region surrounding Angers that included both a pious western region and a less devout area in the east, bordering the Paris basin.

As with my work on miracles, studying the history of death made professional sense, for the topic had provoked great interest among historians of France, most notably Michel Vovelle and Philippe Ariès, who wrote me a brief but encouraging note shortly before he died. Vovelle, however, was a specialist in the eighteenth century, and Ariès's wonderful synthesis *The Hour of Our Death* dealt extensively with the nineteenth century but moved at a high level of generalization. I hoped that a book including a case study based on Anjou, with its rich archives and religious diversity, would be a useful contribution to a developing field. But as I wrote in the preface to *Death and the Afterlife in Modern France,* "death is not a topic that can be viewed impersonally." The questions in the background of *Miracles and Prophecies* focused on the relationship of God and man and on the mediating role of the Church. In *Death and the Afterlife* I was concerned with questions about our ultimate fate, about how we deal with death, what we believe happens to us after we die, and the relationship between the living and the dead. For me, thinking about such questions is only possible by placing them in a particular time and place and then seeing how the answers change over time. In doing my research for *Death and the Afterlife* I was drawn especially to Courbet's masterpiece *The Burial at Ornans,* which dominates its room in the Musée d'Orsay; it captures for me the tensions that the French experienced as they struggled with religious doubt while still depending on Catholicism for its rituals mediating between the living and the dead.

In the fall of 1982 I made a second research trip to France, spending a month in Paris and a month in Angers. At this point I was a French historian, but still an outsider with regard to France as a place and as a culture. But during this stay I began to feel a different connection forming. The director of the Notre Dame program in Angers at that time, Charles Parnell, was perhaps the most blatant Francophile I had ever met. Charles and his wife Simone introduced me to their friends over meals where I was forced to speak my miserable French, which gradually became less so. During this stay as well I managed to talk my way into the diocesan archives of Angers, protected at the time by Père Pouplard, who combined a gruff exterior with a genuine desire to help. I spent a lot of my time in October 1982 deciphering manuscript sermons from the early nineteenth century, gaining confidence in my ability to read French scrawl, and establishing a connection with Angers.

Angers became home for me and my family for two years, from 1984 to 1986. With the help of a grant, I spent the first year doing research on the history of death in France. In 1985–1986 Claudia and I were co-directors of the Notre Dame program. These two years were not always an easy period for us, especially the first, when we lived in a one-bedroom apartment and slowly began to make friends. But our lives in Angers rooted us in the city, and in France, through friends, work, and contact with the French state bureaucracy. When I think of this period, I think of my research, of course, but the most vivid memories are personal and familial, for these are the source of the strongest bonds that tie me to France.

We arrived in Angers in July, with two small boys (Daniel, 8, and Joseph, 4) and with Claudia seven months pregnant. The boys spoke no French, and our command of the spoken language was still limited. Nonetheless, we managed to buy a used car, find a summer camp for the boys, arrange for their schooling in the fall, and locate an obstetrician. We were of course apprehensive about having a baby in France, and Daniel and Joseph were nervous about school. (Dan burst into tears when I first announced that we were moving to France for two years!) But there is probably no better way to find out quickly how a social system works at the ground level than through hospitals and schools. With both institutions, Claudia and I were puzzled at times, but in general we were deeply impressed with the level of care and concern. In the case of Julie's birth, Claudia spent five days in the Clinique Saint-Louis, pampered by a large and friendly staff. Soon afterwards, we were contacted by a social worker who wanted to make sure we knew about our rights as parents. Because Claudia was studying the history of French family law, she took up the suggestion that we apply for the *allocation familiale,* the state subsidy paid by the French government to all parents. Given the fact that we were not French citizens, we never expected to receive any funds, despite the assurances of the social worker that this was irrelevant. But at the end of our first year, after finally receiving our residency permits, we were sent a surprisingly healthy check, apparently because Julie was our third child, thus qualifying us as a "large family" (*famille nombreuse*). Our French friends tease us about this "aid to underdeveloped nations," but in our experience it was just one more illustration of the family-friendly policies that we profited from during our time in Angers. We also took advantage of the public nursery school system, which accepts students free of charge starting at the age of two, and the municipal system of day care, which provides very reasonable short-term baby-sitting. Remembering all of this, it is easy for Claudia and me to understand why so many French are concerned about the current fragility of their welfare state, which offers families so much more than the services available in the United States.

Our most gratifying experiences in France, however, came as a result of our growing confidence in our French and therefore in our ability to make friends with our neighbors and colleagues. It was also humbling to realize, at some point, that Claudia and I would always be foreign speakers, far from bilingual. By our second year in Angers, Dan and Joe, whose French by then was unaccented and colloquial, were embarrassed at times by our American inflections. My French will never be as good as I would like, but the two years in Angers gave me the confidence to inflict it on any French person in the general vicinity. My family jokes about my French radar, my ability to detect French speakers in American airports and restaurants, and my almost craven desire to engage them in conversation. But in virtually every case I have found (and my family is forced to agree) that those I accost are pleased to chat in their native language about what they're doing and where they're going. Speaking French has of course also made it possible for me to develop friendly relations with colleagues in France, who are still by and large monolingual. Since 1986, I've been in France at least a dozen times for research and pleasure. Perhaps Claudia and I will return to Angers for another turn at the Notre Dame program, but even if we don't, our time there was a turning point in our lives, the basis for a relationship with France and with the French that has become essential to our identities.

Studying France has become for me a way of exploring religious questions in a context that offers both common ground with my own past and a contrasting case that provides a kind of protective distance. Questions about the relationship of God to man and the role of churches in society can be personally painful and politically contentious, as is clear in the current debates in the

United States about abortion, school prayer, faith-based initiatives, and a range of other issues. I find it helpful in thinking about such questions to consider the personal and social religious dilemmas faced by the French a century ago as a way of lowering the emotional level that can color discussions, and sometimes distort them, making it harder to find a resolution. At the same time, the bitterness of current debates in the United States has helped me to feel some of the passions at work in nineteenth-century France.

This fascination with religion and French history is clearly at play as well in my current interest in Jewish-Catholic relations, religions conversion, and complex religious identities. When I married Claudia in 1973, I married into a Jewish family. Claudia's parents, Max and Marianne Scheck, fled central Europe in the 1930s as refugees from the Nazi regime, and although they were not intensely devout, the Schecks still had a strong Jewish identity. Both my Catholic family and Claudia's Jewish parents welcomed our marriage, which is not so surprising if one abandons the idea that strong religious and ethnic identities are always accompanied by intolerance. My mother, who set the religious tone for the family, was convinced that children needed some religious education ("they should have something" was the way she put it), but her Catholicism was open-hearted, even as it was deeply felt and believed. Our three children were raised as Jews and have gone through the ritual of *bar* and *bat mitzvah* in a reform congregation, with both sides of the family present and supportive. Personal bonds tie me both to Catholicism and to Judaism, but this situation has not left me torn between the two. Instead, I see myself standing outside of both, while also somehow still attached to them.

I have begun to wonder how the freedom that I have, to live on the borderlands of Catholicism, Judaism, and disbelief, became possible, and as with other questions that I have asked (how does God work in the world, what happens to us when we die), I think about this question through an investigation of the religious history of France. Jews and Catholics in France, as elsewhere in Europe, have had a deeply troubled and at times catastrophic relationship. The origins and development of this animosity constitute an enormously significant historical question, one made more relevant in the current context of religious and political tensions surrounding the growth of the Muslim population in Europe. In my view, the first half of the nineteenth century in France is a particularly telling moment in Catholic-Jewish relations, for it followed the granting of civil rights to the Jews in France by the Revolutionary government of 1791. In practice, however, Jews continued to suffer from discrimination, to be regarded as venal, grasping, and hostile to all gentiles; Catholics generally continued to disparage Jews for stubbornly resisting the truths of Christianity and for holding instead to a legalistic and shallow religion. The various social and religious strains of anti-Semitism could take on any number of combinations, but there was counter-pressure as well from the legal gains that survived the Revolution, gains that included granting Jews the right to practice their religion on equal terms with all other French people. The newly acquired religious liberty in France created tensions both within and between religious communities. Some Catholics made a renewed and intensive effort to convert Jews, a movement that was led for the most part by Jewish converts.

In one case that became famous at the time, Alphonse Ratisbonne, a Jewish banker from Strasbourg, claimed in 1842 to have been instantaneously converted through an apparition of the Virgin Mary to him in the church San Andrea della Frate in Rome. A close look at the Ratisbonne family, however, provides a fascinating glimpse of how Jews adjusted to the formal right of religious liberty as a small minority within a culture that was itself divided over the status of Catholicism. Some family members, including his fiancée, reacted at first with horror to Alphonse's conversion, seeing it as a betrayal of the community and, given the equal rights that Jews now enjoyed, unnecessary. But eventually most of his family reconciled with Alphonse, without themselves converting. The Ratisbonnes and families like them provide a microcosm that I hope will allow me to explore how religious liberty was experienced in France in its earliest phase. The Ratisbonnes were operating along a religious boundary with which I am familiar, though their own sense of it was certainly different from my own. The willingness of Alphonse and others to cross a religious border revealed and exacerbated tensions between religious communities, which nonetheless were forced to accept a heightened level of individualism and voluntarism as the basis of religious identity. The relative ease with which Claudia and I were able to marry, raise children, and remain on friendly terms with our families suggests how powerful these forces have become, at least in some cases. The current pressures for religious conformity among many French Muslims recall the similar tensions faced by Catholics and Jews in the early nineteenth century. My personal experience with religious liberty has thus led me to consider how and when such rights emerged in France in the period just after the Revolution, the psychological and social tensions they produced, both within individuals and their families, and the resonance of this issue in the troubled religious atmosphere surrounding Islam in the contemporary world.

Over the past few years it has become a commonplace for journalists to comment on the sharp contrast between religious United States and secular Europe, with France frequently serving as the prime example of a society that rejects any intrusion of religion into the public sphere. My French friends, even those who are part of the small minority of practicing Catholics (less than 10 percent), have difficulty grasping the role that conservative Christianity plays in American politics. At the same time, however, the French state policy toward religion known as *laïcité*, which seeks to restrict religious expression to the private sphere, has come under pressure, particularly from Muslims who have defended the right of young women to wear headscarves, the infamous *foulards*, in French schools. The French law prohibiting students from wearing ostentatious religious symbols while in school has also been defended by some Muslim women who are claiming the right to make their own religious choices. France is a more secular society than the United States, but questions about religious belief and identity, about the tensions these foster between individuals and families, and about the relationship between religious communities and the French nation are at the center of some of the most important debates in contemporary France. Although I have no particular expertise on current events in France, I can't help but look at them through the lens of nineteenth-century French religious history. This perspective in turn has been shaped by my religious experience, which includes American Catholicism, Reform Judaism, and religious skepticism. Studying France has been for me an opportunity to move between the personal and the professional, the past and the present, France and the United States. While the results have been personally enriching, I hope as well that my particular perspective illuminates a religious dimension of the past that has always struck me as fascinating in its own terms and of central significance in the history of France.

CHAPTER 9

✤ Europe without Personal Angst

Jan Goldstein

I never set out to become a historian of France. Even after I decided to go to graduate school in history, I had no intention of devoting my energies to the Hexagon. In fact, even after I had spent over a year doing dissertation research in Paris in 1973–1974, I still thought of myself as a modern European intellectual historian whose first project happened to be about France but whose subsequent projects would no doubt focus on other countries. So fluid was my professional self-definition at the end of that year that I was actually taken aback to learn that one of my graduate advisors had recommended me for a teaching position in modern French history. But, despite these personal expectations of omnipotentiality, my dissertation on nineteenth-century French psychiatry did, in the end, define me professionally. The requirement to transform the dissertation into a book led me to return to Paris several times for additional research while I was an assistant professor at the University of Chicago, and during one of those return visits I realized that I was hooked. My long stint of dissertation research had, I now perceived, given me something that could be construed as expertise. Moreover, this little nugget of expertise had a way of generating new problems that I wanted to investigate. And, finally, I loved being in Paris, moving with increasing agility and self-confidence through its streets, and having, by dint of professional commitment, a tie to the place that transcended tourism. Hearing colleagues back home speak of the hardships of research in less hospitable settings—for example, the Soviet Union—vindicated my choice, made me feel a bit smug, and generally reaffirmed my self-identification as a historian of France.

If, then, over the short term, I more or less fell into my so-called vocation, what, over the long term, made such an outcome possible? Why did I gravitate to historical investigation to begin with, and why, when called upon to frame a dissertation topic, did I situate it in France?

An unanticipated byproduct of becoming a historian is that one gradually trains the historian's eye on one's own biography. As someone who has long had a scholarly interest in the role of institutions in propagating and normalizing systems of ideas, it was probably inevitable that I would one day realize the extent to which I myself had been shaped by the ideologically laden curriculum of the New York City public schools of the 1950s. My grade school acculturation occurred at P.S. 8, in the northwest corner of the Bronx. The fragility of the world could not escape us—we practiced taking cover under our desks and wore dog tags in preparation for a nuclear attack—but the basic message we received from our teachers was nonetheless one of great geopolitical good fortune. Our identities as Americans and as New Yorkers were constantly drummed into us ("Hear ye, hear ye, know your city!" said the bell-ringing town crier who opened one of the educational radio programs I vividly remember), and the two went hand in hand. New York City, we learned, had originally been Dutch but had early on been taken over by the English; present-day New York, we learned, was notable for the enriching influence of immigrants from many foreign countries: it was therefore essential, for example, to know the location in Manhattan of the neighborhoods dominated by Germans, Chinese, Italians, east European Jews, and other groups. Virtually all the students in my grade school classes were either the grandchildren of immigrants (as in my case), the children of immigrants, or foreign-born themselves; virtually all were either Catholic or Jewish. In such an ideological climate, foreignness carried a positive valence. It was a source of pride and excitement for me at the age of six or seven to have one classmate from Hungary and another from Estonia. I was in my twenties before I learned about derogatory "Polish jokes"; I had previously associated Poland only with the exquisite piano music of Frédéric Chopin.

But if our immigrant backgrounds and immigrant sympathies as New Yorkers were everywhere in evidence, they were fully balanced by our identities as Americans. The Pilgrims, hounded out of England for their unorthodox religious beliefs, were *our* ancestors, we were taught. The disparity between these metaphorical or honorary Anglo-Saxon ancestors and our real, much more recently arrived, and non–English-speaking ancestors was never confronted or even articulated. I can now see that it produced in me an unspoken confusion that powerfully affected my intellectual development. It helped to determine both my choice of a college major and my eventual dissatisfaction with that choice; it undergirded my decision to become a historian of continental Europe and, within the continent, made France an especially congenial option.

My single most important adolescent intellectual experience was an Advanced Placement English course during my senior year at the Bronx High School of Science in the early 1960s. There a certain fiercely intellectual Dr. Isabel Gordon initiated my classmates and me into the mysteries of the New Criticism, the then prevailing school of literary interpretation that treated the text as an autonomous, self-referential artifact and concentrated on its strictly verbal features. We spent two or three months reading *Hamlet,* pondering the shimmering meanings of its individual lines, and I concluded that all worthwhile knowledge could be obtained from the close textual analysis of great literary works. Persuaded by Dr. Gordon that no one could hope to read adequately in a language other than one's mother tongue—a person's linguistic antennae had, after all, to pick up the seven types of ambiguity made famous by the English critic William Empson—I took no foreign language at all in college. (I had taken French in junior high and high school and, on the basis of a college proficiency test administered upon arrival, placed out of the requirement for additional foreign language instruction.) I majored in the combined field of history and literature at Harvard and, as a confirmed Anglophone and metaphorical descendent of the Pilgrims, automatically picked England as my country of specialization. It never crossed my mind to use my supple English to study American history and literature. American history, then narrated as a straightforward success story, seemed bland and uninteresting, and American literature seemed a pale shadow of its English progenitor. I wrote my honors thesis on the decline of allegory as a mode of literary expression in the late sixteenth century, studying the poetry of the allegorist Edmund Spenser and the anti-allegorist Philip Sidney for the purpose.

My education at Bronx Science had prepared me to tackle Harvard academically, but that renowned Ivy League institution baffled me sociologically. I had grown up in a social milieu that would have pleased Rousseau and the *sans-culottes:* everyone was of about equal fortune (we clustered toward the lower end of the middle class), and luxury was unknown. Moreover, at that historical moment, the ethos of my Bronx neighborhood was reinforced by that of the country as a whole: during the decades immediately following World War II, the income gap between rich and poor was at an all-time low in the United States. Within this egalitarian culture, the rigorously meritocratic New York City school system—with its special high schools, like Bronx

Science, available to anyone who passed the entrance exam—provided a legitimate outlet for the desire to distinguish oneself as well as the obvious means of upward social mobility. It was this institutional apparatus that had brought me to Harvard with both a full scholarship and an unshakable sense of my right to be there. Imagine my surprise, then, when I realized that the population of my college dormitory was far from socially homogeneous. In Cambridge, Massachusetts, I lived next door to a Rockefeller, the crown princess of Sweden was on another floor, and the daughter of the curator of the Museum of Modern Art had a room down the corridor. I felt uneasy in such company, but, utterly lacking in social categories (my New Dealer parents were not leftists and the New York City public school curriculum had recognized no social classes), I could not put my finger on the source of my discomfort.

It is against this backdrop that a vivid memory from sophomore year of college falls into place. That memory is of learning, in Samuel Beer's Soc Sci 2, about the Weberian concepts of rationalization and bureaucratization as they applied to medieval English society. Unrelated to the content of this justly celebrated "General Education" course, which influenced me intellectually in myriad ways, I had a sudden epiphany: the English peasants on the twelfth-century manors were not my ancestors. They were instead genealogically linked to those well-to-do Anglo-Saxon Protestants whose novel presence in my immediate environment since the fall of 1963 was the cause of my pervasive sense of unease. This insight did not, to be sure, weaken my resolve to use the tools of my mother tongue to study English history and literature. But it was, I think, the first breach of my New York City public school ideology— that is, my first recognition that the heritage of the West belonged to me in different ways and to different degrees; that the categories of personal ancestors and cultural ancestors did not always overlap.

After graduation I spent two years working in publishing in New York and pondering my future. Having lighted on intellectual history as a way to combine the separate disciplines of history and literature that had made up my college major, I entered graduate school in history at Columbia University in 1969. I picked up where I had left off—in the early modern field that had been my college specialty—but I soon found myself drawn to the modern period and to the European continent rather than England. There was, I can see with hindsight, a kind of muted identity politics behind this evolution. I came from a family of adamantly non-practicing Jews (Russian on my mother's side, Lithuanian on my father's) with a strong, if unfocused, sense of their Jewishness. It would never have occurred to me to study Jewish history: in the early 1970s such a blatant quest for roots would have seemed to me parochial and self-indulgent, lacking in the broader and disinterested perspective that I associated with scholarship. Still, I found it oddly self-affirming to learn that Jews, so absent from the English history I had studied in college, actually figured in modern continental European history, even if largely as the butt of anti-Semitism. How pleasant it was to discover that the Dreyfus Affair played a significant role in Jacques Barzun's course on fin-de-siècle European cultural history or to learn from Arthur Hertzberg that Voltaire's attitude toward the Jews was a topic of considerable scholarly debate. The continent, it appeared, engaged my being more than the British Isles did.

To study it would, of course, mean doing research in a foreign language, which Dr. Gordon had expressly forbidden. The subject of language was fraught for other reasons as well. My grandparents spoke fluent Yiddish and halting English, making work in a foreign language a way to identify with them. From my family's viewpoint, however, such identification was not an entirely good thing. The whole purpose of coming to America, after all, had been to forget "the old country," to leave it decisively behind and make a totally fresh start. (The similarity between this temporal manipulation and that of the French after their Revolutionary rupture only struck me much later, leading me to suspect that my whole biography had prepared me to sympathize with the French Revolutionaries.) My relatives mentioned the old country so infrequently and in such withering tones that, during my childhood, I imagined Europe as a place where everyone was lined up at the docks, waiting for a boat to America. In short, to study continental Europe, to put features on that eerily blank canvas, was for me a covert, circuitous way of reappropriating my European Jewish heritage, just as studying England had been a covert, circuitous way of insisting on my unmitigated Americanness.

But why study history at all, especially since I had started out as such a zealous student of literature? In my case, the New Criticism—which enjoined the reader to bracket the context of a literary work and to seek meaning solely through the complex interplay of the words employed—had turned out to be a self-limiting passion. I felt that a clever enough New Critical reader could make a case for just about any interpretation and hence that the method readily disguised cheating. If, for example, the text turned up something completely contrary to the interpretation you were pushing, you could easily neutralize and incorporate the offending bit of evidence by alleging that the author had presented it in the ironic voice. I was myself a very clever and resourceful New Critical reader, and I began to crave something extra-textual off of which I could bounce possible interpretations and test their plausibility. That extra-textual something was the data of political, social, institutional, and economic history.

While I initially experienced my need for history in an entirely intellectual register, I later began to hypothesize that the need had a large personal component as well. As I have already suggested, my family constructed a peculiarly ahistorical or even anti-historical narrative of itself. Pre-emigration life in Russia or Lithuania was rarely alluded to, and certainly never thickly described. It existed merely as the antitype (although, as a city kid who had encountered farm animals only in the Bronx Zoo, I secretly coveted the goats in the Russian backyard of a great-aunt who had once sewn for the local nobility). Our underlying assumption was that life, time, and history had begun when the family reached American shores and, furthermore, that the history inaugurated at that point would be one of neverending progress, with each generation outdistancing the previous ones in terms of accomplishment. After a thoroughgoing childhood indoctrination into this view of the world, I seem as a young adult to have wanted to fill in the glaring lacuna that was history. This hypothesis was later borne out when I read Philip Roth's family memoir, *Patrimony* (1991), and was moved to tears by his recognition that "the real work, the invisible huge job that . . . that whole generation of Jews did was making themselves American." For me Roth's remark principally evoked the ruthless blotting out of a pre-American past that this cultural work had entailed.

But if I was going to study continental Europe and embrace a foreign language for research, what language would it be? Relying once again on my junior high and high school instruction, I had passed the French reading exam at Columbia and had then embarked upon the requisite acquisition of German reading ability. My courses in European intellectual history with Leonard Krieger and Fritz Stern, as well as the historically oriented lectures of the visiting Heidelberg philosopher Dieter Henrich—in successive years he traced the development from Kant to Hegel to Marx and Kierkegaard in the domains of epistemology and moral philosophy—had turned my interests toward Germany. Hegel seemed to me the Mount Everest of the intellectual historian, the challenging peak that had to be scaled because it was there. Hence, the summer after passing my orals (I had done two German fields, one British, and one French), I went to a Goethe Institut in the Bavarian Alps outside Munich to improve my German language skills in preparation for my scholarly career.

I had visited Europe for the first time after my junior year of college in 1966, but this was my first trip to Germany. I returned home convinced that I could not possibly get my German up to speed and therefore had to abandon my plans for a dissertation using German sources. One of my teachers at Columbia, Geoffrey Field, then an assistant professor of modern German history, suspected that linguistic incompetence was merely a convenient alibi and that my deeper reason for changing my plans had been a distaste for Germany itself.

While I protested loudly against his theory, it now strikes me as correct. Never in my life had I been so self-conscious about being a Jew as during my two months in Munich and its Alpine surrounds in the summer of 1972. Upon hearing my last name (or spotting it and my New York address on my luggage tag), Germans would sometimes ask point-blank, "*Sind Sie Jude, Fräulein?*" The question was bone-chilling, all the more so because, having recently seen Max Ophuls's documentary *The Sorrow and the Pity,* I was palpably aware that most of the adult Germans in my midst had lived through the Nazi era. Lacking the verbal facility to probe my questioners' motivations—did they have an oven that they wanted to send me to?—I would merely say yes. This answer resulted either in an even more bone-chilling inquiry about whether my parents were German—wouldn't they have likely perished in the camps or endured some harrowing near-death experience if they had been?—or in rambling monologues about the speaker's personal experiences during the war. Having lost no relatives in the Holocaust, or at least none that I knew of, I had, perhaps naïvely, expected a visit to Germany to carry no special emotional charge. I was startled at how uncomfortable it felt to be on German soil, or, rather, how uncomfortable the obtuse and tactless queries of the Germans, who were no doubt only trying clumsily to come to terms with their own terrible history, made me feel.

Then, too, I was uncomfortable about my relationship to the German language. As I learned more of it, I would sometimes ask my parents, passable speakers of Yiddish, about how certain things were said in Yiddish so I could compare them to the German. Finding out that my mother's variant of Yiddish did not always agree with my father's made me aware of the nonstandardized nature of that language as a dialect of German. I found myself thinking proudly that I was learning a "pure" German as opposed to the "impure" form to which my shtetl ancestors had been consigned. This thought, in turn, made me feel guilty and ashamed.

And so it was with no small relief that I came to the conclusion in the fall of 1972 that I would have to do dissertation research in and on France. France was my default option; it was Europe without the personal angst. French, the "serious" language that I had chosen in junior high school above the Spanish that was already being promoted for its urban practicality, now recommended itself above all as a neutral language: one lacking direct entanglement with my personal history.

That is how I ended up in Paris in the summer of 1973 on a yearlong fellowship to study Freudianism in twentieth-century France, a topic that soon moved backwards in time and evolved into a study of the professionalization of a home-grown French psychiatry during the nineteenth century. I was not especially interested in France per se, although the presence on the Columbia faculty of two excellent professors of French history, Robert Paxton and Isser Woloch, certainly facilitated my decision to make it my field of concentration. I was interested (intellectually) in understanding how social and political factors shaped the kinds of scientific conceptions of the human personality that could take root in a given culture; and I was interested (psychologically) in getting closer to the Europe of my family origins. France was my case study, neither more nor less. Had I done research in Germany, I would have studied a comparable subject there.

During my first trip to Europe in the summer of 1966, I had spent about ten days in Paris. At that time, I found the city much more beautiful than London (or New York), but I hardly fell in love with it. Its prickly, arrogant side stood out. The taxi driver made me pronounce the address of my hotel correctly before he would deign to drive me there. The man in the ticket booth at the railroad station pretended not to recognize the city name "Bordeaux" when the college boyfriend with whom I was traveling pronounced the second syllable, impeccably to my ears, as "dough."

My dissertation year gave me ample time to contemplate this linguistic perfectionism and other less-than-lovable features of life in Paris. At the libraries and archives where I spent the bulk of my time, my American accent in French often caused the faces of librarians and archivists to scrunch up in apparent pain on those rare occasions when I asked a question. With time, I realized that this response was likely a defense against the difficulty of the questions I posed. For miraculously, the acknowledged king of Paris librarians, the gaunt and mustachioed man stationed in the catalogue room of the old Bibliothèque nationale, understood me perfectly; and on many days, his zest in helping me solve my bibliographical puzzles gave me the courage to go on. The manner of the general run of French library personnel came as a profound shock to me: accustomed to American "friendliness" and can-do optimism, the faint disdain of the French functionaries to whom I turned for help and their readiness to declare a problem—my problem—utterly insoluble struck me as a cultural defect. I would come home exhausted from a day of doing battle, convinced of the superiority of American civilization.

But, however unpleasant, this experience of the libraries and archives was also a kind of ethnographic fieldwork: it helped me to recognize the bureaucratic nature of France—something that I had read about in Tocqueville but that earlier had been only an abstraction. The extreme reluctance of the staff to apologize for delays and errors had, I eventually saw, its own cultural logic: the library, integrated into the state bureaucracy, was an emanation of the French state, and the grandeur of the state precluded apology. The hierarchical micro-dynamics of the bureaucracy also gradually revealed themselves to me: the unwelcoming functionaries whom I encountered were merely passing on to me the frosty and disparaging attitudes of their superiors.

These experiential discoveries contributed to my scholarship. In my work on psychiatry, I became intent on unearthing the bureaucratic connections of the nascent psychiatric profession, both under the Old Regime and after the passage of the asylum law of 1838. More generally, I began to see institutionalization within the centralized bureaucracy as the concrete prize sought by proponents of vying intellectual currents in modern France, and I continued to pursue this theme in subsequent work. In addition, my firsthand sensitivity to France's bureaucratic underpinnings made me especially receptive to Michel Foucault's writings in the 1970s about the "disciplinary" mode of power in modern society. Foucault's refusal to ascribe power to specific individuals in the modern era, his correlation of modern individuality with powerlessness, and his contention that "it is the apparatus [of surveillance] as a whole that produces 'power'" all gain in credibility when one's point of reference is the vast machine-like network of the French state bureaucracy churning out dossiers full of empirical data (medical, educational, judicial) that endow lowly people with particular life stories.

Once I had grown accustomed to "official" French unfriendliness and acquired an intellectual comprehension of French bureaucracy, I ceased to take the host of daily slights personally. At that point, the positive pole of my love-hate relationship with the country I had chosen to study was allowed to flourish. Or, to change the metaphor, what had begun as a marriage of scholarly convenience blossomed into something akin to an on-again, off-again love affair. Familiarity with Paris had only intensified my initial, college student's perception of the city as beautiful. After living there for a year and making repeated return trips, I found it a place of remarkable, even superfluous visual beauty. To walk across the Pont des Arts and see the spires of Sainte-Chapelle and Notre-Dame rising out of a cluster of trees on the Île de la Cité regularly tugged at my heartstrings and could even provoke lyrical (if slightly morbid) longings that my ashes might one day be sprinkled in the Seine. The perfect architectural proportions of the *cour carrée* of the Louvre and of the place des Vosges soothed my spirits. I derived aesthetic pleasure from even the small visual details: the ornately carved wooden doorways of old apartment buildings, the exuberant displays in shop windows, the meats arrayed on the butcher's counter. Perhaps above all, as a native New Yorker accustomed to Manhattan's vast manmade canyons, the intimate scale of Paris entranced me. I had not yet read Walter Benjamin on the nineteenth-century Parisian arcades when I was struck by the way the streets of the old center city were not exactly outside but, because one could always duck under an awning or into a cafe to avoid a sudden shower, a kind of utterly original hybrid between outside and inside. I felt protected by these streets, at home on them on some primordial level.

When I was not preoccupied with railing against French haughtiness and bureaucratic sclerosis, Paris offered me still more sensuous pleasure. Even on a graduate student's budget, one could in the 1970s dine in restaurants that seemed exquisite to me, coming as I did from a country that had just begun to replace Wonder Bread with Pepperidge Farm. A simple and inexpensive lunch of *steak-frites* followed by a dessert of *fromage blanc, crème anglaise* and *sauce caramel*—the standard fare at a little hole-in-the-wall restaurant on the rue Louvois across from the old Bibliothèque nationale—could have been ambrosia. Like food, clothing appeared, during my Francophilic phases, much better in Paris than at home. While still a graduate student, I mostly looked at it in the streets and shop windows and felt enormous admiration for the uncanny ability of Frenchwomen to drape their silk scarves. Once I was gainfully employed, I sallied forth into the boutiques and department stores. While I was regarded as on the small side at home, my height and weight were those of the average Frenchwoman (were the French my "real" people?), and the clothes fit me well. Dressed in my French garments, I might even be mistaken for a Frenchwoman—until I uttered my first syllables in French.

Shopping for clothing in Paris was, like struggling with the library bureaucracy, a form of ethnographic fieldwork. My native impulse was to buy something that did not cling too tightly. But French saleswomen almost always urged me to choose a smaller size or a more revealing neckline. While I took their advice with a grain of salt, their unabashed belief in the value of displaying the female body made me aware of the strong Puritanical streak in American culture and its corresponding absence in French culture. So, too, did my experience of the Paris streets and cafés, where people sized one another up with a frank interest and curiosity that was not deemed impolite. I began to see French and American culture as complementary, each supplying the lacks of the other. The United States had achieved an easy informality in social relations at the expense of purging them of erotic connotations; on the other hand, the order imposed by France's strict formalisms, bureaucratic and otherwise, opened up a delicious sphere of sophisticated and playful eroticism in everyday life.

Given the complementarity of the two countries, the opportunity to dip regularly into French culture, to possess a rudimentary French cultural identity that can serve as a foil for my more robust American one, has over the years seemed to me one of the great, unexpected boons of a career as a historian of France. France has proven, in Claude Lévi-Strauss's useful phrase, good to think—and, in my case, perhaps nowhere more so than in the realm of politics, where it has served as a touchstone in the formulation of my political views.

As democratic republics born in late eighteenth-century revolutions, the French and American polities share many features. That situation of basic similarity has the effect of highlighting their differences and providing a ground from which to contemplate them. As the United States has, during my adulthood, drifted farther and farther from the political culture of my childhood and become more nakedly individualistic, more worshipful at the altar of the laissez-faire market—and as these traits have, under the name "globalization," come increasingly to characterize the world at large—my attachment to aspects of French political culture has deepened. Indeed, it is fair to say that in the ethos of French republican solidarity, given classic expression by Jean-Jacques Rousseau and Emile Durkheim and still vital today, I have recovered something akin to my Ur-political position: the democratic egalitarianism inculcated in the New York City public schools of the 1950s, with its faintly socialist belief (never labeled as such) in the necessity of government-funded institutions—public schools, public libraries, public hospitals, public transportation—to supply what the average family could not on its own provide to its members.

That ethos of republican solidarity came through, for example, in the contrast between the American and French public advertising campaigns for AIDS awareness in the early 1990s. A poster in the Chicago buses portrayed a man who confessed his initial fear of being tested for HIV but had subsequently realized that marshaling the personal strength to face the truth was in his best interest. The underlying ideal was individual courage. A poster in the Paris Métro, by contrast, depicted two people, one of them wondering, "If I told you I had AIDS, would you still love me?" That poster portrayed AIDS as a problem in social solidarity; its underlying ideal was the obligation of the community to support its members in distress. The concern for the collectivity that pervades French republican thought and culture, the suspicion that individualism is too often tantamount to egoism, is of course not always heeded in actual practice. I think of the heat wave of the summer of 2003, when it was reported that vacationing Parisians became resentful upon learning of the health authorities' request that they return to the city to take charge of the burial of frail, elderly relatives who had died in sweltering apartments. But holding up social solidarity as a goal seems to me infinitely preferable to the current situation in the United States, where political discourse has moved so far to the right that such a goal is often deemed politically un-American and mutual aid is relegated to the private sector. And I frankly wonder which is my own country when I remember the times when I have sought emergency medical assistance in Paris and have received it immediately and without question and, by contrast, the time when I was on leave in California and presented myself at the local urgent care facility, only to be left waiting for a good fifteen minutes while the staff checked up on my health insurance policy.

The controversy over Muslim girls' wearing of headscarves in the French public schools has likewise proven good to think. It is a controversy in which I find it hard to take sides, replicating as it does the dilemma of hyphenated Americanness in my own life history. But, even if my decision to study France resulted from my perception of the inadequacy, for me, of being simply American, I have considerable sympathy with the official French position. I know through personal experience the advantages of the public school as an essentially neutral space, where children come together on the basis of the human traits they all share and where ethnic and religious difference, while acknowledged and valued, is, at least in that space, deliberately deemphasized. The French belief, grounded in the Enlightenment and Revolution, in a universal, unmarked humanity, seems to me to contain more political wisdom than the exaggerated forms of American identity politics that put a single facet of one's particularities first. That we all possess many identities—some combination of gender, race, class, religion, ethnicity, occupation, and sexual orientation—seems to me an empirical fact; but among those identities should figure the purely abstract one of the universal subject. For the sake of human comity, we should all have access to a level of consciousness or a subject position in which we are simply human beings, equal to our fellows and obliged to treat them with the respect and fairness that we ourselves require—a level of consciousness in which (as one French proponent of the headscarf ban put it) we can be different from our difference. Or as Daniel Defert, the French AIDS activist, once remarked to me when expressing incredulity about American gay identity politics, "Why would people want to be homosexuals if they could be universal subjects?" If French universalism has tended to err on the side of effacing particular difference, it has made a signal contribution by emphasizing and defending that universal level of consciousness, which only becomes more indispensable in an increasingly multicultural, globalized world.

I suspect that it is French universalism that has, over the long haul, made my choice of France as a country to study at once so satisfactory and satisfying. When I felt most happy in Paris as a student or a young adult, the description of my situation that most often came to mind was that of a *citoyenne du monde*. France has, moreover, afforded me that lack of self-consciousness about being Jewish that I am accustomed to as an American and that I unconsciously sought when I decided not to do dissertation research in Germany.

After my German experience of the summer of 1972, a small interchange in Paris in the fall of 1973 was particularly reassuring. The apartment I had rented used a space heater reliant on a fuel called Primagaz that came in industrial-sized containers. The blue-smocked French workman who carried my first container up four flights of stairs and delivered it to my door mused on the customer's name marked on the order slip. "Goldstein," he said smiling, "I know a plumber named Goldstein."

CHAPTER 10

🕏 France, a Political Romance

Edward Berenson

I wish I could say that I had nothing but deep intellectual motivations for studying France, but the truth is: there was this girl. She was a young woman, of course, a brilliant fellow Princeton undergraduate who became my wife and later my ex. She spoke beautiful French and knew French history, writing a senior thesis on the nationalism of Maurice Barrès. I had never learned or even uttered a word of French, but Cheryl wanted to study in Paris and I went along for the ride.

It was the winter of 1973, and I had just been freed from the draft. Military conscription had been a sword of Damocles hanging over my head since the Selective Service lottery of December 1969, the middle of my junior year. Going to Paris seemed an ideal way to celebrate my newfound liberation—and not just to indulge a youthful romance. As a student radical I had also been smitten by the romance of May '68, by images of young people nearly toppling a retrograde regime. These French events had resonated deeply with my opposition to the war in Vietnam and interested me in France's long colonial involvement there and, ultimately, in history itself. It wasn't enough to oppose the war; I wanted to know—needed to know—how and why it had come about.

As with any life, mine is a tangle of conscious perceptions and unconscious designs, of feelings, intentions and drives, all shaped by my successive environments and jostled together by the happenstances of time and place. Without the seven months I spent in Paris, from January to July 1973, I likely would not have become a historian of France. But then again, I probably wouldn't have been attracted to the woman who drew me there if I hadn't already developed some emotional and intellectual connection to that country. Looking back, it's clear that this original stay in Paris became a turning point in my life, creating new possibilities and allowing earlier proclivities to blossom into fresh understandings, ambitions, and goals. It was my first trip outside North America and only the third time I'd been on a plane. I had grown up in Levittown, Pennsylvania, and my horizons didn't extend very far. In 1973, going almost anywhere would have been exciting; Paris opened a whole new world.

We had no friends or acquaintances there and had to live on modest savings from my two years of post-college employment. A former roommate had recommended a fleabag hotel off the rue Dauphine that cost the equivalent of five dollars a night. The Hotel de Nesle, we soon learned, was an entry-level *maison de passe,* with rooms rented by the hour. The *toilettes* were down the hall, and I remember distinctly that the "windows" were open holes innocent of any glass. None of that mattered. The hotel put us close to the Seine and Notre-Dame and in a lively neighborhood not nearly as gentrified as it would become. I soon discovered the Luxembourg Gardens, where sitting on the grass was *"interdit,"* and you had to pay to park yourself on one of those green metal chairs. None of that mattered either. The Luxembourg was the best place to run I had ever seen.

After two weeks at the Hotel de Nesle, we lucked into a terrific fifth-floor walkup just across from the old École Polytechnique. We became friendly with our landlord, a chemistry professor at Jussieu who would rent us the same apartment on our second stay in Paris in 1977. From my vantage point on the rue Monge, I witnessed the long afterlife of May '68, marked by frequent and sometimes violent demonstrations in the Quartier Latin and the regular presence in my neighborhood of paramilitary CRS troops. It often felt like we were living in an occupied zone. The Salle de la Mutualité sat directly behind our building, and the political meetings there often drew even larger contingents of CRS. Such a heavy paramilitary presence would have been unimaginable in New York or Los Angeles, even with the recent history of riots and demonstrations. Even so, I persisted in seeing France as a healthier democracy than the United States.

In the early and mid-1970s, I felt extremely alienated from my own country, angry over the war in Vietnam, the corruption of the Nixon administration, and the sorry state of American urban life. Once in Paris, I was dazzled by the widespread refusal to accept the status quo. The Socialist Party had recently achieved its resurrection, and the Communists still received more than 20 percent of the vote. Now formally allied, the two parties seemed to represent a force for change unimaginable in the United States. I became totally hooked by French politics.

My sympathies lay with the Socialists, though I was enormously encouraged by Eurocommunism. I believed that the Communist Party had moved further away from the Soviet Union than was actually the case. In any event, the political scene in France appeared not only more encouraging than in the United States but far more interesting too. In 1973, dramatic political change seemed possible, even likely, and I harbored the hope that France was capable of a political revolution at once peaceful and democratic. It's true that the blasé French reaction to Watergate gave me pause, but I explained away this disappointing indifference as the result of too much sophistication, not of too little democratic culture.

I would have loved to discuss Watergate and French politics with native Parisians, but my inability to speak the language kept me mute. Whenever I tried to say a word in French, it was German, the language I had studied in high school and college, that popped out. My abject ignorance of French produced some embarrassing guffaws. A pharmacist doubled over in laughter after I asked for *"papier hygiénique,"* the translation my ancient Larousse gave for "toilet paper." He handed me a box of Kotex. The first time we invited new French friends for dinner, I asked if they wanted their whisky *"sur les rochers."* More guffaws greeted this image of Johnny Walker cascading over a high shelf of rock. "On ze rocks" would be something I'd never forget.

My French needed some serious attention. The solution, I found, was to avoid Americans as much as possible and take classes from morning until night. So, every morning I attended the *Cours de civilisation française* at the Sorbonne; afternoons an intensive conversation course at the Alliance française. The one gave me grammar and vocabulary, the latter a safe place to sound out words without making people laugh. In six months I learned a huge amount of French, thanks in large part to Laurent Gouze, my teacher at the Alliance. Laurent improved my awful pronunciation by having me speak with a pencil balanced between my nose and upper lip.

The two of us became good friends. When we got together, Laurent patiently waited for me to stammer out sentences and gently corrected the most grievous mistakes. He cared not a whit for politics, my overriding passion; he was interested in two things above all else: Victor Hugo, none of whose works I had read at the time, and American movies, especially the classic westerns of the 1940s and 1950s. When Laurent spoke English, he did so with a western American twang, learned from watching the films of Howard Hawks and John Ford dozens of times. Laurent dismissed my interest in Godard and Truffaut, scornfully amused at my insistence that European films were weightier and more "artistic" than those from my own country. It was, in fact, from this French friend that I learned to appreciate the greatness of American cinema. Laurent also taught me about Jerry Lewis, convinced that I would finally understand his hero's comic genius if I experienced him in a French setting. But even after seeing Jerry Lewis live at the Olympia, I didn't get the joke.

Laurent introduced me to his cousin Jean-Christophe Mitterrand, François Mitterrand's son, a young man so rowdy at age twenty-five that our concierge threatened to eject him from the premises. This was many years before he fell afoul of the law and earned the nickname "Papamadit" (Daddy told me) from his African associates. I came to know Christophe fairly well and got to visit his father's beautifully restored house on the rue de Bièvre, just around the corner from where I lived. Mitterrand, then leader of the Socialist Party, would walk around the neighborhood, crossing the place Maubert or venturing toward Notre-Dame, an unmarked police car following discreetly behind.

My limited French made me shy away from any political involvement in France, but I felt exhilarated by the growing strength of France's democratic left. By 1973, I had evolved from the New Deal liberalism to which my parents were attached to being a fellow traveler of the New Left. My parents had supported Adlai Stevenson and President Kennedy but became disillusioned with LBJ. They opposed the war in Vietnam early on, and my father had played a role in the integration of Levittown, whose builder, William Levitt, had refused to sell his mass-produced homes to blacks. When the first African-American family moved in, my father helped protect the house from hostile neighbors who wanted to vandalize the property and intimidate the new owners. Neither of my parents had ever so much as flirted with communism, but some distant relatives considered themselves Marxists. As a high school student, I argued with a great-uncle over why we had gone into Vietnam. He said it was to capture vital markets in Hue. I didn't know why we had invaded Vietnam, but it didn't seem about money.

When I got to college, the War loomed so large that it soon colored almost everything I did. Thinking about Vietnam deepened my interest in politics and turned me into a student activist. I never joined the Students for a Democratic Society, the era's main radical group, partly because they seemed too enamored of violence, at least rhetorically, and sometimes in practice. A history Ph.D. candidate I knew told me he had learned to shoot a rifle in preparation for the revolution to come. Student radicals talked a great deal about "the Revolution" in the late 1960s, but even then I was skeptical that such an upheaval could take place in a country without a revolutionary tradition and no history of strong revolutionary movements. But I thought France might be different; perhaps it was a place where revolutions could succeed?

I hadn't yet studied the French Revolution in a serious way, but what little I had learned made it appear an extraordinary achievement—far more so than the American Revolution because the French had gone further toward political liberty and social equality. Or so I believed at the time. And then, at the end of my freshman year in college, France erupted in what seemed to be a new revolution, the events of May 1968. The shockwaves of these events pulsated across the Atlantic and into the halls of American academe.

Little had happened yet at sleepy, conservative Princeton, but the building occupations at Columbia just fifty miles away provided a local taste of what was taking place on a much grander scale in France. There, in the home country of western revolution, students had led a national upheaval, promising, "All Power to the Imagination" and chanting, "It is forbidden to forbid." The more radical I became, the more I found myself swept up in the romanticism of May '68. So even before going to France for the first time, I had come to admire the country from afar, both for its revolutionary tradition, realized anew in May '68, and for its leaders' opposition to the American war in Vietnam. I knew, of course, that France had fought in Vietnam before we did, and that dim knowledge made it increasingly clear to me that I couldn't understand contemporary problems without a deep knowledge of their historical roots. I had majored in sociology in the naïve belief that doing so would equip me to solve social ills. But for many of the sociology courses I took, "historical perspective" meant going back to 1945 and no further. To understand the war in Vietnam, I would have to study history. It was thus Vietnam that turned me toward the discipline, and May '68 that attuned me to France.

But I didn't yet think to focus on that country, and my interest remained too subconscious and unformed to move me to take French courses or to consider, say, a junior year abroad. Still, the Events of May sunk in, percolating in my gray matter where they would later interact with the mental and emotional effects of an early romantic relationship and my student activism, intellectual mentors, draft anxieties, and first sojourn in France. May '68 plunged me into a current in which I wanted to swim. Or at least wade.

That summer I went to the Democratic convention in Chicago, not to demonstrate in the streets with the Yippies and SDS but to root for Gene McCarthy from inside the International Amphitheater. Once in Chicago, I found myself as drawn to the street demonstrations as to the surreal party ritual rapidly eluding Mayor Daley's grasp. I could witness the two faces of Chicago because I had not yet become so radical as to forbid myself the experience of the convention itself. On the streets and in the environs of Lincoln Park, I sniffed plenty of tear gas but stayed well back from the front lines of demonstrators most vulnerable to the police force's attack. I escaped unharmed but not unchanged. Chicago would be the first of a great many antiwar demonstrations I would join over the next several years. But I would never fully shed the "clean-for-Gene" liberalism that always leavened my radicalism with a measure of ambivalence and doubt.

Back at Princeton in the fall of 1968, I found the calm and tranquility of the place a soothing respite from the violence of Chicago a few weeks earlier. 1968 had been a momentous, extraordinary year: the Tet Offensive, the assassinations of Martin Luther King and Robert Kennedy, student rebellions, the Soviet invasion of Prague, the Chinese Cultural Revolution, the Democratic Convention, the election of Richard Nixon. It is small wonder that so many university students became politicized. Though politics played a central role in my undergraduate life, it wasn't everything. I actually took some courses and read a fair number of books.

I learned European history from wonderful scholars like Steve Cohen, Arno Mayer, and Carl Schorske, who exposed me to the dazzling world of fin-de-siècle Vienna. It's extraordinary how much reading Mayer assigned and even more extraordinary how much we were willing to do. Each week, there was a massive book—Isaac Deutscher's thick biography of Stalin, Churchill's *The Gathering Storm,* Mayer's own phonebook-sized *Politics of Diplomacy and Peacemaking*—and I remember reading them cover to cover, often at the expense of work in other courses. Mayer and Schorske took an interest in activist students who had some intellectual proclivities; getting to know them heightened my interest in becoming a historian. Mayer, in particular, spoke to my nascent radicalism. He was himself sympathetic to France's revolutionary tradition, and his courses gave me my first exposure to French history.

Meanwhile, the War continued needlessly to claim American and Vietnamese lives. Adding immeasurably to Vietnam's urgency for me was the looming danger of the draft. In 1969, the year I became eligible for military conscription, the Selective Service had reinstituted a lottery system for the first time since 1942. I drew the number 15 out of 366; on graduation, I would be among the first in my age cohort ordered to Vietnam. I had resolved not to go, even if it meant leaving the United States for good. In the summer of 1972, Cheryl and I took what she later called a "reconnaissance mission" to Quebec in case we needed to move there in flight from the draft. We began in Montreal and drove down the St. Lawrence River to Quebec City and eventually around the stunning Gaspé Peninsula, where we boiled and ate fresh lobster on the beach. This excursion marked my first exposure to French language and culture, and it gave me a foretaste of France.

As it turned out, the Quebec trip served not as a prelude to exile but to my crucial first stay in France. Shortly after returning home, I received an official letter that granted me a nirvana of relief. The Selective Service had dubbed me a conscientious objector. Then, in December 1972, I won a class-action suit that released me altogether from the draft. These astonishing developments— I had applied for conscientious objector status as a tactic of delay—meant that in January 1973, I traveled voluntarily and as a free man to Paris, instead of fleeing unwillingly to Montreal. I thus experienced my first stay in Paris as a liberation from the worries that had plagued me as a younger man. From then on, France and things French would hold deep emotional resonance for me as a land of freedom, a *lieu de mémoire* where I resumed control over my fate. These emotions became key ingredients in my decision to study French history; they thickened the strands of personal and political interest and inclination that had already opened me to the study of France.

❦

In the fall of 1974, I began graduate work in history at the University of Rochester. The department had high standing, a leftish tint, and considerable strength in French history. Rochester, New York, was then a prosperous company town, the headquarters of both Kodak and Xerox, whose anti-union paternalism had long deterred organized labor from operating anywhere in the city. When a brash new hospital workers' union (Local 1199) burst into town, I joined a group of students in supporting a successful effort to organize the university's medical center. Some of the faculty had become involved as well, and the union drive heightened the excitement of an enormously stimulating department. I served as a teaching assistant for Eugene Genovese, one of the best lecturers I've ever seen, and I first read Durkheim in Christopher Lasch's seminar on the history of the family. Elizabeth Fox-Genovese gave me a solid grounding in early modern France along with a brilliant introduction to the *Annales*. I studied nineteenth- and twentieth-century France with Sanford Elwitt, a specialist in the early Third Republic. Orthodox Marxist that he was, Elwitt criticized the new American social history for downplaying class conflict and for neglecting its surrounding political and ideological disputes. His unhappiness with American work moved him to assign French historians instead. These readings did much to improve my knowledge of French and exposed me to many of best works of socioeconomic history: Ernest Labrousse, Albert Soboul, Georges Lefebvre, Michel Vovelle, and the like. It was thanks to Elwitt that I discovered the work of Maurice Agulhon. I first read *La République au village* in 1975, and that book more than any other determined the direction my own dissertation research would take.

At the time, I saw Agulhon as a French version of E. P. Thompson, the

British historian of working-class politics and culture. Like the maverick English Marxist, Agulhon impressed me as more interested in the ideas and attitudes of ordinary people than the social structures that supposedly confined them. One of the things that made him different from Thompson was his emphasis on peasants and rural society. Agulhon had brought anthropology into the picture, analyzing peasant cultural expressions like the *charivari* and informal institutions like the rural *chambrée,* a sort of social club for peasants of the Midi. What I found most significant about Agulhon's work was the convincing way he demonstrated the independence of the "superstructure" from the "base." He showed how political and cultural phenomena not only stood on their own but could serve as determinants themselves. Thanks to him, I now possessed the *problématique* that would underlie my first scholarly work.

Secular republican that he is, Agulhon did not, it seemed to me, perceive the religious elements of the rural culture he had otherwise analyzed so well. Once I began working in the Archives nationales and the Archives départementales, these elements seemed to jump out of the documents I came across. Without Agulhon, I would have been less sensitive to the cultural aspects of rural politics in the nineteenth century, but his own political and cultural orientation left largely unexplored the study of popular religion I undertook. Agulhon was extraordinarily helpful to me when I returned to France in the fall of 1977 to begin my dissertation research. He received me in his attic office in the Sorbonne, completely tolerant of my still inadequate French. He gave me things to read, told me what archives to visit, and most important, invited me to attend his seminar at the École Normale Supérieure.

Fortified by my initial meeting with Agulhon, I went to the Archives nationales. Working there was a trial by fire, and I remember feeling intimidated by the *président de salle,* perched up high behind a huge elevated desk like a judge presiding over his court. Even when my French became decent, the effort to ask even the simplest questions left my tongue tied up in knots. From the start, I understood that readers could request up to six cartons of documents a day; what I failed to comprehend was that you had to ask for them one at a time. So, on my first visit to the Archives nationales, I deposited six green call slips with their attached green stubs in the slot by the president's desk. About fifteen minutes later, the Man himself strode up to my desk and slapped all six stubs down in front of me: *"Vous demanderez,"* he said through clenched teeth, *"les documents UN PAR UN!"*

❦

Thanks to a fellowship and Cheryl's well-paying job for NBC News, we were able to live in Paris for nearly three years (1977 to 1980). The long stay enabled me to research and write the entire dissertation in France. I composed my chapters in the library of the Maison des sciences de l'homme, working by hand on yellow legal pads. After typing them on the Smith-Corona portable I had received for high school graduation, I gave them to my friend and future colleague Debby Silverman, who offered some of the best friendly criticism I've ever received. I didn't, in fact, know how to structure a dissertation chapter, and this is one of the many things Debby has taught me over the years.

While working on my dissertation, I remained glued to the French political scene. My interest was excessively partisan, and I overlooked a great many things. I was so exhilarated over Mitterrand's near presidential victory in 1974 and the Union of the Left's chances for a parliamentary majority four years later that I dismissed the crucial French debate over totalitarianism taking place at about the same time. The debate had stemmed from the translation of Solzhenitsyn's work and the belated acknowledgment of Stalin-era crimes in some quarters of the French left. I also failed to notice the extent to which key intellectuals had begun to distance themselves from the organized political left that would come to power in 1981. And I didn't think about whether the widespread nationalizations proposed by the Socialist-Communist Common Program and eventually undertaken by Mitterrand made economic sense. I wasn't alone in these forms of naïveté, but it is painful to remember how profound they were. Even so, I continue to believe that Mitterrand's victory in 1981 stands as a high point in recent French history, and I'm sorry I wasn't there to witness the event.

In some ways, my own first scholarly work bore the influence of the 1970s Union of the Left. Though I was primarily interested in the role of popular religion in politicizing workers and peasants before and during the revolution of 1848, the protagonists of my story were a kind of union of the left. The *parti démocrate-socialiste,* or *démoc-socs,* represented the alliance of two groups, republicans and "utopian" socialists, that had opposed each other before 1848. After the repression of the June Days, the two groups came together, creating a kind of common program and agreeing to wage electoral campaigns as a united front. The *démoc-socs* never came to power, of course, and the socialists of the mid–nineteenth century had little in common with the Communists of the 1970s. But the post-1848 coalition did manage to win significant victories in 1849 and 1850, creating a precedent for other leftist alliances to come.

I finished my dissertation in September 1980, just as I was beginning my first teaching job at UCLA. I had been hired for a position in social history, not French history, during a year in which Eugen Weber was on leave. Several months earlier I had published a long critique of Weber's *Peasants into Frenchmen,* challenging its reliance on modernization theory and arguing, among other things, that Weber had misconstrued the Revolution of 1848.

The eruption of democratic politics at midcentury did not fit his modernization model, which denied that peasants could become politicized in the absence of other, supposedly more fundamental elements of modern life. Weber's
book was one of those extremely important but highly controversial works
that stimulate healthy intellectual debate. In publishing my own response, I
had no idea Weber would soon be my senior colleague.

Granted tenure in 1985, I was firmly ensconced in an adult American life
six thousand miles from Paris; it was that U.S. context, far more than any
French one, that would shape my new scholarly work. Besides, France seemed
far less attractive than it had a few years earlier. Its leftist dream of the 1970s
had turned into a bitter reality of economic failure and political retreat. In Los
Angeles, I joined the movement for a nuclear freeze, but its politics became irrelevant as the Cold War wound to a close. Like most people I knew, I intensely disliked the Reagan administration and the depressing political culture
it had spawned, but I can't say I tried to do very much about it. It's not that I
consciously turned my back on political activism but rather that I gradually allowed a combination of personal and professional responsibilities to claim the
lion's share of my time. The radicalism of my twenties had subsided, no longer
nurtured by either the Vietnam War or the hope that France could provide a
new political model, a socialist democracy, to which others could aspire.

As a young faculty member at UCLA, I found my job immensely satisfying. I had gotten over a difficult divorce and met the woman, Catherine Johnson, who would become my second wife and life partner. Although Cheryl had
been crucial to my early interest in France, Catherine has helped me develop
that interest into a much more mature set of reflections, ones linked to newer
forms of politics and social life. Catherine had earned a Ph.D. in film studies
and had read far more French Theory than I. She didn't much like postmodernist writers and ultimately abandoned her corner of academia to escape their
dominance. But I profited enormously from what she had learned (and rejected) and even more from her gifts as a writer. I also found myself deeply influenced by her acute psychological insight, feminism, and sensitivity to the
meaning and importance of gender, around which my new work would turn.

I had developed a vague interest in the French Radical Party but didn't
know where I wanted it to go, except perhaps in the direction of microhistory.
After reading Jean-Claude Allain's masterful two-volume biography of Joseph Caillaux, I decided to write a book on the strange case of his wife Henri-
ette Caillaux, who shot and killed her lover in 1913. My study would focus on
gender, thanks not only to Catherine's influence but to the example of feminist historians like Karen Offen, Bonnie Smith, and Joan Scott. In *The Trial of
Madame Caillaux,* I tried to show how *Belle Époque* conceptions of femininity

and masculinity shaped the understanding and outcome of the case. Madame Caillaux, I concluded, convinced the jury to acquit her of murder charges by presenting herself as a "real woman" swept away by emotions beyond her control. Hers was a "crime of passion" for which she should be absolved.

The new book required several trips to France, and before our first child was born in 1987, Catherine and I traveled there as often as we could. Les Gobelins became our neighborhood thanks to Marie-Laurence and Jean Netter, close friends who allowed us to stay in their apartment while on vacation and have continued to offer me hospitality far beyond anything I could ever repay. I had met Marie-Laurence in the early 1980s when she helped direct François Furet's seminar. Through her and Arno Mayer, who was Furet's close friend, I came to know the author of *Penser la Révolution française*. I invited Furet to spend two weeks at UCLA as a distinguished lecturer, and there he spoke mainly about Tocqueville. Furet had not yet taken up his position at the University of Chicago, but it was already clear that he enjoyed spending time in the United States and that, like Tocqueville, he used the United States as one of his intellectual frames for thinking about France. I first read *Penser la Révolution française* in 1981, and it changed my understanding of the Revolution forever. Until then I had accepted what Furet called the Jacobin-Marxist interpretation, and I had downplayed the dangers of Revolutionary excess. I was doubtless overly swayed by the intelligence and originality of Furet's book, and I later came to agree with those who argued that he had diverted Revolutionary historiography too far from social and economic history. But Furet confirmed for me, as no other historian had, the problems associated with partisan readings of the Revolution, especially those that explained away its illiberal effects. If France's socialism and Eurocommunism no longer offered a model to follow, its newfound liberalism, especially political liberalism, looked more promising.

❦

Everyone's life changes when children come into the world; ours changed perhaps a little more than average. In 1991, when our son Jimmy turned four, two UCLA specialists diagnosed him with autism. We had known for a long time that something was wrong, and the diagnosis confirmed our worst fears. Jimmy's language had stopped developing at age two, and he became extremely difficult. He couldn't sleep at night, and neither could we. He threw tantrums constantly, became aggressive, and could never, ever sit still. The prospect of an eleven-hour plane flight (Los Angeles to Paris) became unimaginable. So did the idea of one of us caring for him alone. With research trips to France now impossible, I had to change the kind of work I did. I labored for several years on a textbook, wrote review essays and historiographical pieces, and began to do administrative work.

In 1994, my wife gave birth to twins. One of the twins was diagnosed with autism. The geneticist we had talked to beforehand told us the chances of having a second autistic child were next to nil. We have since learned that families with one son or daughter with autism have a 25 percent possibility of having another. Even if we had known that statistic, we would likely have gone ahead and had another child. It hasn't been easy raising two autistic children, but they're both wonderful kids (so is our "neurotypical" son), and I couldn't imagine life without them. But unable to travel, I lost direct contact with France for nearly a decade. I didn't stop reading French history, of course, but being so far away and unable to do research in France made it seem a very distant place.

All that changed dramatically when I moved to New York University in 1998 and became director of its venerable Institute of French Studies. Suddenly, I found myself once again at the center of things French, only more so now than ever before. One IFS alumna, the historian Alice Conklin, has called the IFS "the most French place in the United States." She's right, I think, and being at the IFS has put me in intellectual contact with many of the most important scholars in France—and not just historians. Now that my children are older and more manageable, I've resumed traveling to France, taking on new research projects, teaching there, and, with Nancy Green, organizing a huge Franco-American conference at the Bibliothèque nationale de France.

In many ways, I have come full circle, renewing the intense relationship with France I had begun in the 1970s. Only, I have changed, and so has France. Outwardly, the Hexagon has become more like the United States, thanks to globalization, the European Union, and the rise of competitive political parties. In fact, the two countries remain miles apart—on foreign policy, public welfare, religion and secularism, and many other things. No longer do I see France as superior politically and socially to the United States, though I continue to admire its vibrant intellectual life and its widespread belief in a "social model" of public welfare, even if the model's current form cannot be sustained.

I also admire France's freewheeling debate over the legacy of its colonial empire and its willingness to stare revelations about Algerian torture in the face. The discussion of empire is largely new, and it has spawned an interest not only in studying colonialism and immigration but also in linking the colonial past to a general French history that has mainly ignored it until now. We Americans have our own reasons for studying empire and for examining what imperialism does to people and institutions both overseas and at home. Though American historians have long studied the British Empire, we have only recently turned to "*La Plus Grande France.*" With a new project on empire and the popular press, I have joined a growing group of Americans drawn to French colonial history. This book-in-progress strikes out in new directions, especially as I bring in comparisons with Britain's colonial past. It also renews my longstanding concerns, with its emphasis on journalism and public representations of political events.

What does this new work say about me and my politics and my relationship to France? It suggests that, like many historians, my intellectual work shows the influence of contemporary events and, perhaps, that I've changed somewhat less than I had thought. The war in Vietnam, with its imperial overtones, helped spark my original interest in history. And now, America's imperial ambitions—and their limits—have stimulated my historical interest once again, this time directly for the colonial past. France is the country whose history I know best, so it makes sense that I would study the French empire and not, say, the American role in the Philippines or Cuba. But I've been drawn to the troubled, contentious Franco-British relationship of the late nineteenth century, a rivalry that bears some resemblance to the postcolonial Franco-American relationship of today. The flareup between Washington and Paris over Iraq echoes aspects of the Belle Époque hostility between Britain and France over Egypt, Fashoda, and the Boer War. If the United States has replaced Great Britain as the world's imperial superpower, France has retained its place as the bête noire of Anglo-American hegemonic designs. The motives of French leaders are no purer now than they were a century ago, but there is something commendable, or at least interesting, about their unwillingness to accept the diminutive, conformist role the Hexagon has been assigned. I admire this stubborn refusal to give in, though not as much as I once admired the dream of a democratic and socialist France.

My thanks to Steven Englund, Cheryl Gould, and Debora Silverman for their insightful comments on various drafts of this essay.

CHAPTER 11

ಐ Choosing History, Discovering France

Herrick Chapman

Just what possessed me to give Robespierre's final speech before his appointment with the guillotine in my high school's annual oratorical contest I cannot say for sure. "The defenders of liberty will be but outlaws so long as a horde of knaves shall rule!"—lines like these first uttered by a man with a checkered reputation were hardly calculated to win over the faculty jury, much less my fellow students in Denver's East High School auditorium. We amateur orators knew full well that courtroom speeches by Clarence Darrow usually brought down the house in these contests (as one did again that year). But something drew me to the challenge of bringing Robespierre's ironic martyrdom into this annual school event. Was it simply the mystique of the French Revolution? Perhaps it was the speech itself, so otherworldly but still compelling in its plea for justice and its disdain for narrowminded self-interest. Decades later, I now recognize that this way of seeing the French past—as speaking poignantly to my own world and yet removed from it in some exotic way—accounts as much as anything for why I have derived such pleasure from my work as a French historian. I had no inkling at age seventeen where I was headed. But I see now in this episode something similar to what continues to motivate me as an American historian of modern France: a desire to venture into a distant place and time, one not too different from our own, and bring back something that my compatriots (and, I would hope, even a few French readers) might find useful for understanding our own condition and the wider human experience.

It took a while to come to this vocation. Only late in my college years at Princeton did I figure out what a historian really was, and it took several years beyond that to discover France as the place where I could fruitfully explore what interested me. Not that I lacked for early sources of inspiration. I grew up in a household that valued books, art, and music, and my first real exposure to European history took the form of reading Opal Wheeler's biographies of the great classical composers for elementary school children. Beethoven, Mozart, and Bach were my first serious cultural heroes; I had naïve aspirations at age nine or ten of becoming a composer. As a teenager my reading often turned to the past. *A Tale of Two Cities* was the first adult book I remember galloping through in a state of lost abandon.

Travel, too, figured hugely in my young life, and I wrote voluminous diary accounts of what I saw when I traveled. Tourism ran deep in the family. My paternal grandparents had met in 1905 when young Lillian Herrick went on a properly chaperoned trip to Europe under the auspices of the "Chapman Private Vacation Tours," my grandfather's one-man tour guide business, which he invented to fill the summer months when he wasn't working as the chaplain of the Elmira State Reformatory in upstate New York. Once married, my grandparents continued to lead summer European tours until 1914. My father then followed in their footsteps after college by taking a job with the American Express Company, back when it was a travel business. By the time I was born, in 1949, it had sent him to manage the regional office in Denver. My physician mother was also an avid traveler and even on occasion tried her hand at freelance travel writing. Europe figured prominently on my parent's mental maps: they and their friends spoke of London, Paris, Rome as meccas and of the Alps as a Valhalla even more glorious than our local Rockies. If years later in college I would learn that World War II had brought an end to the age of European predominance, it was scarcely noticeable in my family, in which the coronation of Queen Elizabeth, my first major TV memory, was observed with reverence.

As for my own travel life, it really began in earnest after my parents divorced when I was seven. My sister and I spent much of every subsequent August visiting my father and stepmother wherever American Express had relocated them—Cincinnati, Milwaukee, Pittsburgh, Boston. I learned from my father, a railroad enthusiast with a keen interest in business, how these cities worked as manufacturing and transportation centers, how steel got made in Pittsburgh—the stuff of economic and social history, as I would later think of it. Traveling with my mother had a more historical and cultural flavor: to drive with her through Spain was to be transported into the world of El Greco, Murillo, and Goya and to imagine the pilgrimage to Santiago de

Compostella. By the time I had finished high school I had seen a great deal of the United States, and, because my older sister was on her way to becoming a specialist in Spanish and Latin American literature, we'd also visited Spain, Portugal, Mexico and been all over South America. Still, for all this early exposure to history and travel, as germinal as I may see it now, it hadn't occurred to me to become a professional historian. When I set off for college at Princeton in 1967, my ambitions ran more toward government and public service.

My sense of direction became less clear once I encountered the political upheavals of the late 1960s. I had come to Princeton with little understanding of the rapidly escalating Vietnam War, though I did have firm, liberal convictions about race relations based on my experiences in Denver's integrated schools. But nothing was quite the same after 1968, with the Tet Offensive, the assassinations of Kennedy and King, the student protests in Paris, Mexico City, and Prague, and the Democratic convention in Chicago. Princeton was hardly a bastion of radical politics like Berkeley or Columbia. Among the many images of the immense march on Washington against the war in 1969, few got as much attention as the large parade banner that read "Even Princeton." By my sophomore year I had become involved in the antiwar movement and engaged in projects to respond to the sharpening of racial divisions on and off the campus. I worked for the campaign to elect Kenneth Gibson as the first black mayor of Newark and spent a summer teaching in a storefront school for dropouts in that same city. When Nixon invaded Cambodia in April 1970, I threw myself fully into the strike at Princeton, as did many of my friends and a new acquaintance, Liz Cohen, who in 1977 became my wife and eventually an American historian. Amid all this activism, my politics had moved leftward, well shy of the revolutionary margins but far enough to question the assumptions of the liberal mainstream with which I had identified.

This political education inevitably informed my studies. I majored in public and international affairs at Princeton's Woodrow Wilson School and went on to complete a master's degree in that field. Educational policy interested me most. But I also grew frustrated with policy studies. Courses in economics were strong on theory but weak on explaining where economic institutions came from or why people made the economic choices they did beyond some abstract notion of "maximizing utility." Most of my policy courses ignored the longer-term causes of the problems we examined. Happily, the Wilson School program left plenty of room for history, which did more to explain why liberal societies in Europe and North America could, despite their virtues, produce poverty, urban blight, racism, and colonial wars. Historians seemed to me to be best equipped to speak to my political discontent. Russian historian James Billington, although a conservative, shared with us "lefties" a despair about technocratic management on campus and in Washington and offered courses on the revolutionary tradition that respected every student's point of view. When he let me read some of the draft chapters of what years later became *Fire in the Minds of Men,* I got a clearer picture of history as a writer's craft that combined a freewheeling life of discovery with the application of moral conviction. I got this sense, too, from the two teachers I came to regard as mentors—Arno Mayer, who was working out his ideas about the domestic origins of foreign policy in Europe and was an especially eloquent critic of American foreign policy, and Carl Schorske, who was writing about the crisis of liberalism in fin-de-siècle Vienna and its effects on art, literature, and urban design. These teachers saw the big picture across large swathes of time and territory, and this kind of knowledge made it easier to imagine social change and think intelligently about it.

During the summer of 1971, while in London on an internship working on issues of race relations and educational policy, and then traveling across the continent, I began to think seriously about pursuing doctoral studies in European history. I had been gaining confidence as a writer, and now that I was in Europe I saw how fascinating that terrain could be for exploring my questions about urban life and social conflict. After interviewing West Indian activists in London about schooling in their neighborhoods, I wanted to learn more about how race relations evolved in London and Paris, where colonialism and slavery had left a rather different legacy than I was used to in the United States. Class, too, seemed to be expressed differently, and much more explicitly, in Britain—in the strength of the unions, in the acute attention paid to language and manners, in the continuing attachment of the British left to notions of working-class emancipation that seemed much less far-fetched in Europe than in the United States of the early 1970s. European history, then, seemed to me to offer a larger and more variegated landscape for writing about my core interests in politics, policy, and society. After returning to Princeton in September, I wrote a paper for Schorske on the novelist Émile Zola's response to the rebuilding of central Paris in the 1860s, a paper which, despite its shortcomings, confirmed my conviction that working on Europe was what I wanted to do.

How did I then find my way to France? Arriving at Berkeley in 1975 to begin my graduate studies, I had no firm commitment to a national specialty. I briefly toyed with the idea of doing comparative history after reading Charles Maier's *Recasting Bourgeois Europe,* a hefty comparison of how Germans, French, and Italians stabilized their societies and refurbished their economies after the bloodletting of World War I and the revolutionary upheavals that followed. I admired the explanatory ambition of the book, its effort to account for why capitalism survived war and revolution and why the Germans and

Italians took the fascist path and the French did not. I was drawn, too, to the model it provided for integrating social, economic, and political history by focusing not just on the major political actors in the story but also on businesspeople, trade unionists, bureaucrats, journalists, and intellectuals. I likewise admired the sweeping scope the "big" books Europeanists were reading then —Perry Anderson's *Rise of the Absolutist State,* Immanuel Wallerstein's *Modern World System,* Theda Skocpol's *States and Revolutions.* For me, these studies spoke indirectly to the worrisome political conditions we seemed to be experiencing during the Carter era, a moment when the left-wing possibilities of the early seventies seemed to be narrowing, though not closing down altogether. The times called for rethinking big structures and tracking down the hidden sources of power.

Still, several considerations kept steering me toward France. One, simply, was language. Because I only began to study German when I came to Berkeley, I had a suitable working knowledge solely of French when I began to write my research papers. More important were the advantages I began to see in working mainly on one country. What had attracted me to history were the opportunities it offered to contextualize events thickly and track complicated processes of change over time—to see the manifold ways in which a city plan, a welfare policy, or a decision to go to war was shaped not only by circumstance but also by institutions, habits of thinking, and patterns of social relations. That meant working close to the terrain and learning it well.

By the mid-1970s, moreover, budding historians felt the full blast of the social history revolution that had started in the 1960s, the commitment to history "from below" with a special premium placed on examining social movements, workers, women, and ethnic and racial minorities. Although it wasn't inherent in the logic of social history to specialize in a single country, it made sense to do so, since most social historians studied carefully defined groups in specific locales or industries. Like most young modern Europeanists, I took statistics to facilitate quantitative analysis, read the cultural anthropologists Clifford Geertz and Victor Turner, and devoured E. P. Thompson's *The Making of the English Working Class* and big chunks of the French *Annales* school histories of rural France in the Old Regime. *Annales* founder and French resistance martyr Marc Bloch became something of an idol for me (as he has for so many historians), though less for his magisterial work on feudal society than for his searing analysis of France's defeat in 1940, a work that deeply affected my thinking because it pointed to a multitude of problems one could study in interwar France. But at the end of the day it was the new social history coming out of Germany that made the biggest impression on me. Historians such as Hans-Ulrich Wehler and Jürgen Kocka kept questions about state power and public policy at the center of their studies, but they anchored their work in richly textured analyses of interest groups, social movements, and economic change—asking the kinds of questions I had found so compelling in Charles Maier's work. Most of the young American historians who were taking up modern France in the 1970s were concentrating on the Revolution or the nineteenth century. It struck me that twentieth-century France offered a wide-open area in which to work, especially if I brought to it the kind of questions being asked in German history.

France had another appeal as well. As an advanced capitalist country with a longstanding democratic tradition (like the United States), it seemed better suited than Germany for studying the promises and shortcomings of a liberal society. The same could be said of Britain, of course, but having lived in London I found Britain too familiar and too lacking in cultural distance from the United States. Unlike Britain, moreover, France had an astonishing history of political regimes. For a historian interested in thinking about the relationship between capitalist development and the making and unmaking of democratic institutions, France seemed like a better bet.

And then there was the sheer excitement of the contemporary French scene. France had emerged by the 1970s as a leading economic power, second to none in Europe in aviation, medicine, cuisine, fashion, cinema, and much else. At the same time, the French Left, after years of factionalism, had hammered out a Common Program and appeared poised to mount a serious challenge to the Gaullist establishment. Ideas about "self-management" reanimated the trade union movement. Even the French Communist Party, that most Stalinist of western Marxist parties, stood at the brink of reform (or so we thought) through the liberalizing trend of what came to be called Eurocommunism, as distinct from the still-doctrinaire Soviet communism. I followed these political developments with great intensity, as I began to recognize that if I were to become a specialist on France I could help cast light on the French present with what I was learning about its past. My first published articles, in fact, were a lengthy feature in the *Daily Californian,* the Berkeley student paper, on the resurgence of the French left in the 1970s and an op-ed piece in the *New York Times* on Mitterrand's nationalizations in 1981. Indeed, by the early 1980s I came to feel as invested in French policy debates as in American ones, and I hoped that my historical work might make these debates more understandable on both sides of the Atlantic.

For my own dissertation research, I set out to look for the early twentieth-century origins of the kind of working-class radicalism and volatile labor relations that set postwar France apart from most other countries in Europe. I decided to write a social history of the French aircraft industry during the

1930s and 1940s. Aircraft workers had been in the forefront of the great strike wave of 1936 and had remained key supporters of the communist trade union movement thereafter. Léon Blum's Popular Front government made aviation an early experiment in nationalization, and the industry figured prominently in all the major stories about business life in the era of World War II—the desperate struggle to rearm the country, the collaboration with Germany during the Occupation, and the controversies over the Marshall Plan. Although it was customary to write either about the interwar years or the Occupation, I hoped that by limiting my subject to a single industry I could bridge both periods to learn how the French experienced life in an industry from the Great Depression to the Cold War.

To carry out this research, I finally went to France in the summer 1978 and again for over a year in 1979–1980, when Liz and I set up a household in Paris. Before these trips, I had only spent four days in the country back in college, yet here I was claiming the right to write its history. How I envy my own graduate students of today, nearly all of whom begin their doctoral studies at NYU with a year or two in France behind them. My rocky experience practicing spoken French in evening classes or tutorials while working by day in archives and libraries and interviewing workers, engineers, and generals was like building a roadster while driving it on the thruway. Still, I benefited from lots of advice—especially from Charles Tilly, whom I had met at the Bibliothèque nationale and whose *Strikes in France* had influenced my thinking as much as any book on labor, and Patrick Fridenson, a distinguished labor and business historian in Paris who like a sherpa helped me (as he has so many other foreign scholars) plot a path through the many archives and interviews my subject required.

As it turned out, the aircraft industry had a big impact on the way I became acquainted with France. Because the national archives had only a portion of what I needed for my thesis, I had to go directly to factories, trade union locals, business associations, and the homes and offices of retired people in all walks of life related to the industry to track down records and conduct interviews. One day I would tour a factory in Bourges as an engineer explained to me how assembly methods had changed in the industry. Another day I would spend scribbling away in the back offices of a trade union headquarters, copying old meeting minutes or newspaper articles while overhearing people in the room next door arguing about union strategy. I spent a good deal of time reading documents at the union offices for the leading aircraft engine company, where an aging activist would share with me his theory that the British and the Americans had bombed French aircraft factories during the Occupation to get a leg up on the airplane market after the war. When I interviewed top businessmen or engineers I often found myself in the posh sixteenth *arrondissement,* where on one unforgettable morning my interviewee instinctively poured himself (and me) a nerve-calming Scotch whenever I brought our conversation back to his role as a government official during Vichy. All of this took considerable time, but I can see now how much of a sociological introduction it gave me to France, an exposure to people and homes and workplaces that an exclusive diet of reading could not have provided. It also gave me a deep appreciation for the French appetite for history and reflective, exploratory conversation, shared by workers and top officials alike.

Not that everything in my research went so smoothly. While nearly everyone I asked to interview proved remarkably welcoming to a young American daring to inquire into their past, I was also often disappointed in my efforts to scare up business and labor archives. France is a notoriously difficult terrain for historians in this respect. And government archives could be hit or miss. In Toulouse, I had some initial luck obtaining permission from the prefect to consult a terrific collection of closely guarded police-spy records about the local aircraft unions in the 1930s. As I read these precious records, I couldn't help but notice the agitation of some of the archive personnel. After a couple of days, I made the mistake of asking for a few photocopies, only to be told a little while later that my permission to read these records had been revoked. In my outrage at this misfortune, I realized how deeply invested emotionally I had become in my work. I understood, too, what it was like to feel divided, as so many people are in France, over the uses of state authority. One minute one admires the extraordinary public train service, the next minute one feels abused, as did I that day in Toulouse, by an arbitrary and wounding assertion of anonymous authority. I spent the next two years, to no avail, seeking permission to see those sensitive files again.

≶

What of the France I encountered outside my research? When I arrived in Paris in the summer of 1978, a young historian at Mount Holyoke, Susanna Barrows, was looking for someone to occupy the extra room in the apartment she had rented just south of the Luxembourg Gardens. I signed on, little knowing that she would introduce me to friends and a vast world of Parisian neighborhoods, hidden bistros, offbeat museums, tiny shops, architectural gems, and gastronomic treats that would have taken me years to discover. With Susanna, I learned to notice small, revealing traces of the past—the fading framed ordinances on the café wall that confirmed the state's right to shut the place down if it became a meeting ground for insurrectionaries, the aging prostitutes down the street whose clients were sometimes aging Germans they had met during the war. "Don't just be an archive rat," Susanna warned. An assiduous researcher in her own right, she nonetheless believed that we historians had a duty to learn not only by reading the documents but also by letting everyday France get under our skin. I found this an effortless lesson to absorb. Living in a foreign country, where everything was in a different language and refracted through an unfamiliar history, sparked my interest in things I'd normally ignore at home—shop windows, street names, vapid television programs, chattering fellow travelers on the Métro. The constant sensation of oscillating between the foreign and the familiar, whether I was struggling with French plumbing or reading legal documents in the archives, intensified my curiosity and hence my feelings of attachment to France.

During the year Liz and I lived in Paris, we built a network of friendships and emotional connections to France that have remained the foundation of my engagement with the place ever since. Liz became involved with the small but passionately committed community of French scholars who studied the United States, historians like Marianne Débouzy and Catherine Collomp, who were as eager to think about French-American comparisons as we were but from the opposite side of the looking glass. By attending the monthly Saturday seminar in social and economic history presided over, in the classic mandarin tradition, by Jean Bouvier, Maurice Lévy Leboyer, and François Caron, I met up-and-coming French historians who were working on their dissertations in business, labor, and financial history. And then there was an American world in Paris that sustained us as well—long-term expat journalists, to whom Susanna had introduced us, and fellow young historians.

As a counterpoint to this Paris-centered experience, Liz and I also made a big effort to travel in the provinces, first to the cities I needed to go to for my aircraft industry research—Marseille, Bourges, Nantes, Bordeaux, and especially Toulouse—and then to other regions for the pure pleasure of eating and drinking the local fare, puttering around tourist sites and bookshops, and thinking about what new odd mixture of the French present and past was being worked out before our very eyes. Our copy of Waverly Root's *Food of France,* with its splendid blend of cultural and gastronomic history, was practically in tatters at the end of the year. Ever since, Liz and my daughters have been willing to indulge my own geographical fetish of trying to see as much of the country and its overseas departments as I can, an obsession that I suspect is fueled not only by the pleasures of travel but also by a need to acquire additional authorial authority by visiting the places I read and write about. What emerged, too, out of the intensity of the Franco-American network Liz and I had haphazardly created was the beginning of a permanent conversation within the family about France and the United States. Liz and I had each already become the most important reader and critic for the other. But the comparative perspective I had always wanted to be a part of my work became something we automatically sustained by living under the same roof.

Since writing my thesis and the subsequent book on the aircraft industry, my relationship to France has only deepened and widened further. New research projects have taken me into the history of France's steel towns, welfare policies, gender and family issues, shopkeeper politics, political commemorations, and various aspects of industrial renovation and economic policy in the twentieth century. I have also returned to questions of immigration and race that had initially intrigued me as an undergraduate but that I had set aside to do my aircraft industry study. At the heart of most of this work has been a sustaining fascination with the French state, its changing role in economic and social life, and the way different groups have construed and resisted its authority. If in the 1970s the vitality of the French left played a key role in steering my attention to labor history, the protracted struggle that began in the 1980s over whether and how much to dismantle the *dirigiste* state of the 1940s and 1950s has reinforced my desire to write about the history of state interventionism across a number of policy areas.

My teaching has played no less a role than my research in shaping my relationship to France. Because Liz and I faced the challenge of establishing two careers in history, I have had a rather complicated professional itinerary that has had a salutary effect on how I work on France. While Liz was doing her doctoral work at Berkeley, I took up my first teaching job at Stanford, where the history department's traditional curriculum built around lecture courses in national histories helped consolidate my sense of identity as a French historian. After a year of writing some forty-odd lectures on France from the French Revolution to the Mitterrand presidency, I finally had a basic command of the material ranging beyond what I had acquired as a graduate student. When Liz and I were both given the opportunity to teach at Carnegie Mellon University a few years later, we moved to Pittsburgh, where a thematically organized curriculum, a strong community of social historians, my teaching in comparative history, and an immersion in the history of Pittsburgh all encouraged me to situate my thinking about France in a wider European and transatlantic context.

With yet another dual career move in 1992, this time to New York University, my work in the history department and at the Institute of French Studies had the effect of recentering my teaching around France. Life at the Institute brought me into a remarkable multidisciplinary community of graduate students, colleagues, and visiting professors from France who were working at the cutting edge of French studies, the wider Francophone world, and French-American relations. My connections to France became even denser after 1999 when the journal *French Politics, Culture, and Society,* founded in 1984 at Harvard by Stanley Hoffmann and George Ross, became a joint undertaking of Harvard's Center for European Studies and our institute. As its editor, I have sought to take the journal into the terrain where some of the best new work is being done on France—on immigration and empire, on linkages between culture and politics, on France's relationship to Europe and the United States, and on issues of religion and Islam. I have sought, too, to encourage scholarly dialogue—back and forth across the Atlantic and the English Channel, between historians and specialists of contemporary France, and between thinkers of differing points of view.

❧

France thus plays a greater role in my daily life than I could have imagined when I began my career. I often feel, as Robert Paxton once remarked, that we specialists on France have more in common with our French colleagues than we do with many of our own compatriots. Yet, I know how much I remain an *American* historian of France, working at the crossroads of two cultures. The strangeness of France continues to inspire my research. How startled I was not long ago, for example, when I first learned about the intensity with which French tax inspectors worked their small districts, knowing their turf like small-town doctors, in contrast to the anonymous IRS agent who audited my taxes in Pittsburgh—a discovery that led me to look more closely at how changes in the inspection system helped fuel the great tax revolt in southern France in the mid-1950s.

Inexhaustible though France still feels to me as a place to study, some historians do question whether the nation-state is a suitable focus for research, given how much more alert we are today to the transnational movement of people, money, and ideas in the past and present. Transnational processes rightly deserve the historian's keen attention. But despite globalization, the nation-state remains the prevailing framework for governance, military power, and economic regulation, and it is still a key wellspring of collective identity. For me the key question is not whether to abandon national history but how to practice it so as to broaden the context in which we think about a country like France, and thus better understand the two-way flows across its borders that shape its history. This effort requires immersion in the country and explorations beyond it. In this respect my own unplanned and peripatetic career has been a blessing. My years at Stanford and NYU threw me headlong into

France, whereas Berkeley and Carnegie Mellon and a life shared with an Americanist pushed me outward beyond the Hexagon. The balance, I like to think, has made me a better historian of France.

The value I place on having a comparative and transnational perspective on France also makes me especially hostile to the facile use of clichés about the French that pass for analysis in the press and at the politician's rostrum. For centuries the Americans and the French have traded insults in the form of cultural stereotypes to forge their respective national identities. The frenzy of France-bashing during the first months of the Iraq War—from "freedom fries" in the Congressional cafeteria to columnist Thomas Friedman's outburst in the *New York Times* that "France is becoming our enemy"—is only the latest chapter in a long history of Francophobia. To make a political point, critics of French policy too often resort to old-fashioned notions of national character. The French people become bearers of an unchanging Frenchness.

I try in my work to combat this way of thinking by complicating the picture—exploring the French in their astonishing variety, making internal French comparisons as well as international ones, and observing how porous the boundaries of France have been with Europe, the Mediterranean, the United States, and the rest of the world. What moves me is hardly Francophilia. I consider the dark chapters in the French twentieth century, and they are legion, as important to write as the brighter ones. But we live in a global age where the price of ignorance about other countries and their histories is too high. The French, like peoples everywhere, are too implicated in our common future to leave to pundits and politicians the job of defining "the French" for the rest of us.

CHAPTER 12

An African American in Paris

Tyler Stovall

"Welcome to graduate school! So, what do you plan to write your dissertation about?"

"Well, I don't know, something to do with modern European history."

"That's a very broad field. What country in Europe do you plan to study?"

"Um, I don't really know."

"All right, so what European languages do you read?"

"French, and a little German."

"Good, then you'll study French history."

So occurred the rather inarticulate birth of a French historian. The above passage more or less recapitulates my first meeting with my graduate advisor, Harvey Goldberg, when I began my studies for a doctorate in European history at the University of Wisconsin, Madison. I start this essay with it in order to make the point that my choice of French history as a profession was very much a matter of happenstance. When this conversation occurred I had only been to France once in my life, for a few weeks the previous summer, and while I had studied French for a year in college, I had never felt particularly drawn to French culture. I was very interested in studying European history, in large part as a counterpoint to the American experience, but that did not necessarily mean France. Had I chosen another graduate school or another advisor, I could easily have ended up as a historian of modern Germany.

So, what does my experience reveal about American historians of France? Not all of us are Francophiles, at least not originally so, and many different factors have led us to devote our lives to French history. Moreover, we bring a diversity of American experiences to the study of France. Few people would probably have expected someone like me, a young black man from *l'Amérique profonde* (Columbus, Ohio), to choose French history (or any kind of history) as a profession. As one aunt reacted when I told my family about my decision to pursue a Ph.D., "History! I always wanted to study history. But I had to earn a living." At the same time, whatever our reasons for choosing our field, we have all had to deal with certain basic questions confronting those who study the history and culture of another nation. What can we bring to the study of a society not our own, and what can we learn from it? Can we ever really understand people who speak a foreign language and whose cultural markers differ in so many ways from ours? Does our interest in another people's history constitute a flight from our own, and what does it reveal about us as Americans and about our own country?

Most American historians of France would probably agree that our position carries both advantages and disadvantages. While we will probably never have the same kind of understanding of France possessed by those born and raised there, we can offer an outsider's perspective, with any luck bringing new insights to issues that the French themselves at times take for granted. In addition, I would argue that American historians of France both challenge and reaffirm the idea of national history. We have dedicated our careers to the study of one nation, defining ourselves with its boundaries. At the same time, our very existence complicates the idea of national histories, demonstrating that the very idea of the nation is a matter of transnational production and consumption. I hope that the experiences of one historian can shed light not only on how we see the history of France but also on what it means to be American today.

❧

The mystically inclined might argue that the circumstances of my birth predestined me for a career in French history. I was born on September 4, the anniversary of the founding of the Third Republic, and to this day I take a little pride in the fact that streets throughout France, and a Parisian Métro stop, bear the name of my birthday. Perhaps more momentously, I was born in a small town named Gallipolis, which is in Ohio on the banks of the Ohio River. Anyone who has read Harriet Beecher Stowe's *Uncle Tom's Cabin* or Toni Morrison's *Beloved* will immediately realize the symbolic significance of a black couple traveling north across the Ohio River, traditional boundary between slavery and freedom, to give birth to their first child. Yet, as I only learned many years later, the name *Gallipolis,* city of the Gauls, was no accident. In fact, Gallipolis was created at the end of the eighteenth century by émigrés from the French Revolution, tricked by land swindlers into believing that a Rousseauian paradise awaited them on the Ohio frontier. French doctors founded the hospital where I was born. Thus, the two histories that would shape my life already circled around me during my first days on earth.

None of this, of course, had any discernable impact on my fairly ordinary childhood in Columbus from the late 1950s to the early 1970s. Other factors prompted my desire to study history by the time I entered college. When I was very young, my parents would read stories to me at night, ranging from traditional children's tales to simplified versions of Greek myths (even, at one point, a comic book version of *The Odyssey*). These constituted my introduction to the study of history, which has remained for me in essence a series of exciting stories. As I grew older, my interest in the study of the past merged with an engagement in the exciting political issues of the time. Growing up in the era of the civil rights movement, Black Power, and the war in Vietnam gave me a deep and abiding interest in the study of social change, how it happens, how people make it happen. This gave my interest in history a new dimension, more focused and more politically engaged. In high school I mostly studied American history (more often, "social studies") in the standard range of required courses. These courses, often taught by various athletics coaches, were generally lackluster at best in quality, leaving me with the (most erroneous) impression that American history was boring. Yet instead of leading me away from history in general, this conclusion turned me toward the study of another region of the world, Europe. Coming of age at a time when the histories of Africa, Asia, and Latin America scarcely existed in American high school curricula, Europe represented the only practical alternative to American history. I had enjoyed my class in Western Civilization, so I went off to college intrigued with the possibility of becoming a historian of modern Europe.

If my childhood gave me a strong interest in history, college and graduate school trained me to be a social historian. As an undergraduate at Harvard I began to learn about Marxism and to wrestle with theoretical explanations of social change. Yet I quickly concluded that abstract theory, while important, interested me less than how individuals and groups had attempted to apply theories to better their world. A class in British labor history and my first reading of E. P. Thompson's *Making of the English Working Class* brought me to the study of European labor history, which I viewed as the key historical context out of which Marxism and many other radical systems of thought arose. Therefore, when I began my graduate studies at the University of Wisconsin in the fall of 1976, it was with the intention of following in the path laid out by Thompson and others.

Most professional historians are intimately familiar with the powerful role played in one's academic life by one's dissertation advisor, and I was no exception. Harvey Goldberg was a larger-than-life figure not only for me but for many others in Madison, both within and outside of the university. A joke at the time put it this way: "If this university ever gets rid of Harvey Goldberg there will be a revolution! Yes, and it will be the French Revolution!" Harvey was not only the person who introduced me to French history, he was also a man firmly committed to both the historical study and contemporary advocacy of social change. By the time I met him, Harvey devoted less time to publishing and more to teaching and activism. An immensely talented and compelling lecturer, he mesmerized generations of students with his accounts of the French Revolution, the Paris Commune, and other historical events far removed from the daily life of the American midwest. Thanks to Harvey, the study of France's history became an intimate part of Madison's large community of New Left activists. At one point the head of the Madison Federation of Labor, the local branch of the AFL-CIO, was a graduate student in French history. During the 1970s and 1980s the nineteenth-century idea of France as the land of revolution was alive and well in this small corner of the upper midwest. This gave me a far more profound interest in France than I had ever had before, one that meshed well with my own political interests. Both my subsequent research and my sojourns in France would reinforce this as I struggled to build a career as a French historian.

Harvey Goldberg had a tremendous professional and political impact on my life. At the same time, like many other graduate students, I found that a key part of my education consisted in challenging his ideas and charting my own path toward the study of history. In particular, this revolved around our different ideas of social history. For Harvey, social history was essentially socialist history, above all the history of great socialist men. His study of Jean Jaurès showcased his talents as a historical biographer of one of the great political leaders of modern France. While I shared his interest in the history of the left, I viewed social history as the recuperation of the neglected voices of the past. The new social history of the 1960s and 1970s had shifted interest in popular movements from the study of organized unions and parties to a broader grasp of working-class lives in general, a trajectory with which I identified fully. Inspired by the historical sociology of Charles Tilly, I wished to explore how ordinary men and women had conceptualized progressive politics. Consequently, when it came time to choose a topic for my dissertation, I decided to consider not unions or political parties but rather the politics of community life in one Parisian suburb, Bobigny, after 1900.

My decision to study the Paris suburbs represented a departure from the
norm in more than one respect. Harvey did not oppose my decision, in fact he
suggested Bobigny as the suburb with one of the strongest Communist voting
records. Yet he probably would not have proposed a social history of suburban
Paris as a dissertation topic: it lacked the glamour of the Paris Commune, the
rich historiography of the Revolution, the Popular Front, or the Resistance.
My choice also deviated from standard research in French social history in two
respects. First, most historians writing French social history in this period, in
both France and America, concentrated on the nineteenth century, the era of
industrialization and the formation of the working class. This was true for a
variety of reasons, ranging from the desire to engage Marxist theory critically
to the greater accessibility of sources. The twentieth century, even the period
before 1945, was still too recent to merit much attention. From this flowed a
second difference, the lack of attention to the Paris suburbs. The great works
of French social history, by scholars like Charles Tilly, Rolande Trempé, Joan
Scott, and Maurice Agulhon, took provincial communities, both rural and urban, as their areas of study in order to counterbalance the traditional Paris-
centrism of French life. If Paris, for once, received less attention, the Paris
suburbs got almost none. Ungainly *enfants maudits* of the twentieth century,
they possessed little of the charm that attracted so many Americans to France.
Indeed, they seemed more like the parts of America that some of its citizens
hope to escape. For these and other reasons, my research into the social history
of the Paris suburbs in the early twentieth century forced me to think about
French history in new ways.

In the summer of 1981, I left Madison to spend a year in Paris researching
my dissertation. Although I had traveled to France briefly a few years earlier,
this was my first sustained encounter with a country and people I had now
been studying for several years. A highly romanticized mythology surrounds
the life of Americans in Paris, the product of novels and memoirs ranging
from Ernest Hemingway's *Moveable Feast* to Diane Johnson's *Le Divorce*. The
expatriate experience supposedly represents a rejection of bourgeois America
in favor of the more aesthetically and personally enriching way of life found
in the French capital. This corresponded to neither my desires nor my experience. I had never dreamed of living in Paris, and I felt that living abroad,
while fascinating in many respects, also involved abandoning political struggles in my own country. Most important, for me life in Paris was primarily a
means to an end, getting a doctorate in French history, rather than an end in
itself. Incredible pressure surrounds a graduate student's year of field research:
one is well aware that one is doing the work that will not only earn one's doctorate but also determine if one gets a job (and eventually tenure). As a result,
I developed a kind of tunnel vision while in France, focusing overwhelmingly

on my archival research and no doubt missing out on many experiences that might have given me a more profound understanding of French people and culture. At one point I even turned down the opportunity to go drinking with the celebrated African-American author James Baldwin in favor of returning to my "real work."

And yet I did not turn into a total archive rat; Paris forced me to come to terms with French life, giving a whole new dimension to the abstract knowledge gleaned from historical texts. It was an exciting time in France. I arrived in Paris a few months after the "Rose Revolution" that brought François Mitterrand and the Socialists to power and witnessed both the triumphs of the new administration and its difficulties in coping with the neoliberal global pressures of the Reagan-Thatcher era. Jack Lang's cultural policies had a particular impact on me: I listened to the new *radios libres* and dutifully played my harmonica in celebration of the first *Fête de la Musique.* I also witnessed the historic shift of French intellectual political culture from left to right and observed the debates over Euromissiles and environmentalism. I avidly read French newspapers, especially *Le Monde* and *Libération,* both to improve my reading knowledge of French and to understand better the ways in which the French viewed both themselves and the world around them. I remember reading *Libération*'s groundbreaking article on the twentieth anniversary of the October 17, 1961, massacre of Algerian demonstrators in Paris, an event that has only recently begun to receive the attention it deserves.

This much-contested time had a decisive impact on my views of France, politics, and the relationship between the two. The beginning of the Mitterrand era in France was also the start of the Reagan era in the United States: for those with progressive inclinations it was easy to sympathize with Paris rather than with Washington, even to rejoice in having landed in the more tolerant nation and culture. While in France I helped to organize a group of American dissidents abroad who protested American foreign and domestic policies in a number of venues, including street demonstrations. Given that I went to France on a Fulbright scholarship, and was thus in a sense a representative of the American government, I sometimes found myself in delicate situations. I remember spending one evening at a reception hosted by Nancy Reagan (even getting to shake her hand!) after spending the morning distributing leaflets protesting American foreign policy. Yet life in France also gave me a much better sense of the political conflicts within French society, in ways that prevented any facile celebration of French politics. I did not support all the actions of the Mitterrand administration, for example, nor did I agree with the positions of many French people on questions like disarmament and the environment. Both my agreements and disagreements with the political currents in Paris during the early 1980s increased my interest in that nation, giving me a far more sophisticated and global vision of politics, one made in France.

Finally, I began to develop an appreciation of France beyond current events. I learned to drink red wine; to eat omelettes, French bread, and cheese; and to go shopping for vegetables in the market. Most significantly, I got to know people, both French and American, in a few cases creating some of the most enduring friendships of my life. I sat in on seminars at the University of Paris, worked with Jacques Girault, author of important studies of the Paris suburbs, and met scholars like Patrick Fridenson, Annie Fourcaut, and others. The Centre d'études historiques sur les mouvements sociaux et syndicalistes at the University of Paris 1 became my intellectual home away from home. At times in spite of myself, that year in Paris gave me the beginnings of an appreciation of French life; far beyond my archival research, it turned me into a historian of France.

I returned to Madison in 1982 and spent the next two years writing my dissertation, "The Urbanization of Bobigny," later published as *The Rise of the Paris Red Belt,* which reviewed the history of one Parisian suburb from the start of the twentieth century to World War II, concentrating on the development of Communist political culture. Bobigny was an excellent choice for this study, since it had voted for the PCF (French Communist Party) for nearly sixty years without a break. When I began my research, I looked for the roots of politicization in the labor process, following the lead of social historians of the nineteenth century. I soon discovered, however, that this explanation would not work: unlike provincial factory towns or more industrialized suburbs like Saint-Denis, Bobigny in the early twentieth century was essentially a bedroom community with few workplaces or unions. Further research forced me to revise my ideas about the reasons for Communist political power, coming to focus instead upon community issues and the process of urbanization. A small town until 1900, Bobigny grew explosively in the decade after World War I, as hundreds of thousands of working-class Parisians and provincials moved into the Paris suburbs in search of better housing. What they found instead were the *lotissements,* shantytowns hastily erected by unscrupulous land dealers, the housing quality of which was often worse than the Paris slums many had left behind. The PCF, many of whose members lived in the *lotissements,* took the lead in organizing to improve the urban infrastructure, in the process creating an enduring political tradition.

My study of Bobigny taught me a great deal about working-class urban life in France and, more broadly, about twentieth century French history. From it I concluded that working-class life was more than the labor process, that everyday concerns of housing and "leisure" also had their political dimension. It also taught me about the importance of community life and politics in understanding modern history. In rewriting my dissertation I supplemented my readings in social history by considering sociological and anthropological approaches to the study of community. This scholarly literature has both advantages and disadvantages: it permits an in-depth study of local relationships and individuals but can also become so embedded in minutiae that it loses sight of the broader picture. My own work reflected the merits as well as demerits, yet I also learned that in studying suburbia one had to address both the dynamics of individual communities and the broader urban context of the metropolitan area as a whole.

Finally, my work gave me important insights into the politics of modern consumerism. In France, as in the United States, bourgeois social reformers had long regarded suburbanization and individual home ownership as ways of de-radicalizing the working class and integrating workers into bourgeois morality and politics. In Bobigny, however, this approach boomeranged: rather than creating a new conservative constituency, the difficulties of suburbanization turned it and many other Paris suburbs into centers of Communist political power. From this I have concluded that those who regard modern consumer culture as de-politicizing and driven by capitalist imperatives are missing out on another important dimension of consumerism, its power to motivate radical social change.

Such themes certainly had relevance beyond France. However, both my dissertation research and my life in Paris had taught me that they could only be understood in the context of local and national cultures, more particularly that not only were people in places like Bobigny intensely French, they had their own ideas about the meaning of France as a whole. Spending several months working in Bobigny's Hôtel de Ville and observing French Communist municipal culture up close had made that clear to me. Thus my growing appreciation for life in France was reinforced by the conviction that, if I really believed in the importance of comparing social movements across national frontiers, I had to develop a profound understanding of the national cultures that shaped those who made those movements. For reasons of both political interest and personal experience, I chose France.

I left Madison in 1984, having been fortunate enough to receive a postdoctoral fellowship at the University of California, Berkeley. During these years social history was challenged, and to an important extent ultimately superseded, by another approach that took the name of the new cultural history. As fate would have it, Berkeley's history department, which I now entered as a postdoctoral fellow, was one of the epicenters of the movement. Philosopher

Michel Foucault visited the campus several times between 1980 and 1983, building up a substantial following among faculty and graduate students. The anthropologist Paul Rabinow became a leading exponent of postmodern theories. The literary critic Stephen Greenblatt turned the interdisciplinary journal *Representations* into a leading tribune of the New Historicism. Among historians, a talented group of young professors, including Lynn Hunt, Susanna Barrows, and Thomas Laqueur, gathered around themselves an impressive group of graduate students and made the department a center of cultural approaches to the past.

My encounter with the new cultural history came as a shock; nothing during my years in Madison had prepared me for it. For years as a graduate student I had struggled to master social history, without much help from my advisor. Now I found that what I had viewed as the latest word in historical methodology was increasingly called into question, indeed viewed as old hat. Feeling that I had a lot of catching up to do, I spent my two years as a postdoctoral fellow in Berkeley reading not only the new cultural historians, but also the theorists from whom they drew inspiration, including Foucault and Jacques Derrida, Mikhail Bakhtin and Michel de Certeau. The new cultural history's emphasis on *différence* in general and the study of race in particular would spur my own research for many years to come. However, I was disappointed by the new cultural history's tendency to downplay or reject class analysis and neglect the study of working people. For this reason in particular, while I valued many of its insights, I continued to identify as a social historian.

Negotiating this new methodological terrain consumed much of my energy as a historian during the next several years. I left Berkeley in 1986 to take my first job at Ohio State University. This was a rich and productive time, yet I only stayed at Ohio State for two years. From there I moved on to the University of California, Santa Cruz, where in 1990 I won the grand prize of American academia—tenure. I would remain there for another decade.

During those years at Santa Cruz I began working on a new, very different research project. For some time I had toyed with the idea of writing a book about black American expatriates in Paris, and once I got tenure I decided to proceed with it. The project intrigued me for several reasons. For one thing, it spoke to my own personal history. My grandfather, Otha Fuller, had served as a soldier in France in World War I. For years, according to my mother, he would try to trump any argument with my grandmother by exclaiming, "Well, Pearl, she ain't seen nothing, but I've been to Paris!" At the same time, over the years I had become very interested in questions of immigration, ethnicity, and race. The new project reflected my continued interest in neglected aspects of the history of Paris.

The most compelling reasons for my new project, however, derived from my relationship to both French history and the world of American academia. I had long been aware that I was one of the very few African Americans studying and teaching French history—at times it seemed like the only one. While this did not strike me as much of an issue in graduate school, it loomed larger as I settled permanently into the world of French history. Race remains a major concern for most American history departments and most American universities in general. Not only are black historians significantly underrepresented in American academia, but most are concentrated in one field, African-American history. Both blacks and whites tend to react with surprise at the prospect of a black scholar studying any history other than his or her own. My choice of French history and the segregation of the American historical profession tended to split my life neatly into irreconcilable halves, ensuring that my family and my black friends would have little to do with my professional world. Many blacks in particular view French and European history as white history, something that has little to say to their lives. To the experience of bridging two worlds, which is common to all American historians of France, I added my own experience of trying to bridge America's racial chasm.

Paris Noir: African Americans in the City of Light thus challenged both the segregation of the American historical profession and my own bifurcated existence. In considering the history of black Americans who moved to Paris during the twentieth century, I sought to write a book that would appeal both to French historians and to a broader African-American public: as I put it to one audience, a book that would attract readers of both *French Historical Studies* and *Ebony*. This was a tall order indeed, and trying to achieve it meant changing how I thought of and wrote history. I intentionally wrote *Paris Noir* for a popular audience, abjuring footnotes and historiographical discussion and choosing not to work with a university press. (In contrast to France, most American history professors publish with university presses, whose books are for the most part read by other professors and graduate students).

Writing this book also meant rethinking what I considered to be French history. Others before me had chronicled the history of African-American expatriates in France, notably the great French biographer of Richard Wright, Michel Fabre. For the most part, they had viewed this topic as a part of African-American history. Without rejecting that perspective, I also considered the story of black Americans in Paris to be a part of French history. From this standpoint, the history of France embraced all those who lived in France, whether or not they enjoyed French citizenship or even intended to stay there permanently. This approach also reflected my continued commitment to the study of France: rather than using this topic to move into other fields of study,

I continue to insist than French history offers numerous possibilities for asking questions about blackness, race, and difference in general.

My studies reaffirmed this sense of commitment to France. I undertook the research for this project in very different conditions from those surrounding my dissertation work. In contrast to my work on Bobigny, I did not spend a full year living in France, making short trips there over the course of several summers instead. Far more than before, my research in France involved not only visits to the archives but also oral interviews and meetings with individuals. It meant getting to know the members of the African-American community in contemporary Paris as a way of understanding that group's history. The personal nature of this research was borne out by the coincidence that the very first person I interviewed for my study was named Stovall—Tannie Stovall, then as now a key figure among black Americans in Paris. More generally, I found myself gradually being adopted as not just a chronicler of this community but also as a member. More than my earlier experiences in France, researching *Paris Noir* made me feel at home in Paris, now that the varied communities that made up life in France included at least one to which I belonged.

The publication of *Paris Noir* in 1996 coincided with (and I hope contributed to) two major intellectual trends. First, American historians of France began addressing the nation's colonial past to a much greater extent. When I was in graduate school, most French historians regarded the study of colonial Africa, North Africa, Indochina, and the Caribbean as an entirely separate field. I turned down my advisor's suggestion to study the history of the Réunion island, fearing (correctly) that I would not be marketable as a professor of French history since few colonial specialists could get jobs as historians of France. How things have changed! In the fall of 2005 I taught for the first time a graduate seminar on the history of French colonialism. Some students even told me that they wanted to take the course to increase their chances on the job market. Starting in the early 1990s, a number of graduate students began reassessing France's colonial past. Inspired by scholars like Edward Said and Ann L. Stoler, they began considering the ways in which the colonies and metropolitan France were both shaped by the colonial encounter. This trend has continued to the point that today roughly half the graduate students of French history in American universities are studying colonial topics. Accompanying this explosion has been a new interest in postcolonial France. Once the appanage of anthropologists and literary theorists, the study of communities of colonial origin in France has entered the realm of history as the twentieth century fades into the past. This has combined with greater interest in questions of immigration and race to suggest important new ways of conceptualizing what it means to be French.

At the same time, the field of African-American studies was experiencing its own conceptual shifts. Until the 1980s black history and studies in the United States had overwhelmingly emphasized the domestic experience, whether slavery or emancipation. Starting in the 1970s and 1980s, however, a group of black British scholars of Caribbean descent, including Stuart Hall, Hazel Carby, and Paul Gilroy, began challenging this orientation. Embracing the methodology of cultural studies, they rejected Black Nationalism as essentialist and argued instead that the key to modern blackness was the experience of diaspora. Their successful challenge to the prevailing orthodoxy of African-American studies dramatically reoriented the field toward an interest in the experiences of black communities outside the United States and of black intellectuals who had lived overseas and whose lives had transcended the limits of the nation-state. By the 1990s black studies departments all over the United States were adding the words "diaspora" or "diasporic" to their titles, encouraging scholars to view blackness as shaped by African heritage and the history of the Atlantic slave trade and, at the same time, as endlessly diverse in terms of geography, gender, class, and sexual preference.

These new approaches to French and to African-American history shared a common feature: they questioned the importance of the nation-state and of national histories. For example, does the tale of an immigrant's life belong to the history of the country of origin, the country of settlement, both, or neither? Is globalization merely a phenomenon of the present or does it have a history—and if so, how can one approach that history? In writing a book about Americans in France, one that not only considered the relationship between the two countries in general but also implicitly addressed my personal history and view of France, I hoped to write a history of France that was at the same time local and global.

Some might object that writing a study of African Americans in Paris is less about expanding the idea of French history than about inserting the author (myself) into the story of another nation. Both views are true. Moreover, any historian ultimately shapes the history she or he writes according to his or her own personal tastes, desires, and convictions. Likewise, the histories of France we write inevitably respond to the interests of our students and our colleagues in other fields of history and to the broader publishing industry and market for scholarly books here at home. That more and more American historians of France are writing books addressing Franco-American relations reflects both a certain inward turn in American life, and at the same time our desire to emphasize the importance of the French experience for both our own lives and for America as a whole.

Since publishing *Paris Noir* I have coedited two books on race in France. The question of race has become a hot-button topic in French historiography since the mid-1990s, and the subject illustrates some of the contrasts between the field as practiced in France and in the United States. American historians live in a society in which racial questions are paramount in public life; many of us are old enough to remember the civil rights movement, and most of us have confronted the issue of affirmative action in our colleges and universities. Moreover, the historiography of the United States frequently views racial difference as central to American history. In contrast, French public culture rests in large part upon ideas of republican universalism that view the drawing of racial categories as irrelevant at best, racist and pernicious at worst. The rise of large nonwhite populations (and of powerful racist movements like the National Front) in contemporary France has placed these different perspectives on the front burner. Some French scholars accuse American historians who write about race in France of trying to impose American historical categories on a different situation. I would respond by defending the importance of race as a category in French history and by insisting that different international perspectives on a nation's history constitute a strength, not a weakness. Such disputes will, I believe, only increase our understanding of the French past.

When I started graduate school I had just turned twenty-two; I am now fifty years old. The study of France has thus shaped my life for the majority of my time on earth, enabling me to achieve my most cherished professional goal, a professorship of history. I still travel to France as often as I can, and I find that some of my best friends live there. Because American academics tend to move around a lot, we often develop some of our deepest friendships where we do our research rather than where we live, and I am fortunate to have known friends in France long enough to watch their children grow from infancy to adulthood. The community of French historians in America, organized in its three main national organizations, has provided another source of camaraderie. Like Thomas Jefferson, I often feel that I have two homelands, my own and France. During the years of transatlantic tension over the Iraq War, I proudly proclaimed that the French were right and happily asserted my continued commitment to "freedom studies." In short, I feel extremely lucky to have become a historian of France. While trying to understand another nation's past still seems at times an exercise in limited vision, the exercise has enriched my life immeasurably. Above all, I am grateful to the people of France for their toleration and encouragement of this foreign historian. Over the years my initial curiosity and incomprehension toward them and their history have matured into feelings of sympathy, respect, and, finally, love.

I am very grateful to my wife Denise Herd, my mentor Susanna Barrows, and my colleague Michael Vann for their support and encouragement during the writing of this article.

CHAPTER 13

Writing at the Margins

Leonard V. Smith

The French army archives at the Château de Vincennes, where I did most of the research for my doctoral dissertation, was the most agreeable place I have ever worked. They were much less frequented in the mid-1980s than today, still less frequently by researchers not working on genealogy or Napoleon. It was easy for me to become a curiosity for the staff, which comprised a few civilians and some military personnel, including the *petits militaires* who actually fetched the cartons. Their concern for my welfare and their indulgence (particularly with the photocopy machine) did much to belie the stereotype of French archivists as capricious and unhelpful. In retrospect, I think their interest in me was largely explained by bafflement and a certain bemusement as to just what I was doing there, asking for carton after carton about the 5e Division d'Infanterie during the Great War of 1914–1918. Numberless times I was asked why I was studying the French army and not the American. One of my favorite archivists asked me one day whether I had ever served in the military. More than usually puzzled that I had not, she posited that surely I would be called up in the event of a general mobilization. I resisted the urge to tell her that as I lived in New York City at the time, I would be an atomic shadow on a wall long before anyone could issue me a rifle. Not that I could have done much for national security with one anyway. I have worked on the margins of military history, and to some extent on the margins of French history. I have found the margins largely a pleasurable place from which to write.

For better or worse, I have a multi-generational disconnection from things military. My grandfather on my mother's side was drafted at the end of the Great War, but the Armistice was signed by the time he reached the railroad station (in Syracuse, New York, I believe) to depart for training. My father was a bit too young for World War II and was supporting his mother and hence exempted from military service in the Korean War. I was too young for the Vietnam War, though I did wonder as a child how I was going to avoid being sent there if it continued until I became eighteen years old, as it showed every sign of doing. That war remained a dark, if distant, cloud as I began to become aware of the broader world in the late 1960s. As it happened, I turned eighteen in 1976, the first year registration for the Selective Service was no longer required. By the time eighteen- and nineteen-year-olds had to register again, I was twenty-three. Some Frenchmen my age (forty-seven at this writing) served in the army during the Great War, but military service for me at this juncture seems a remote possibility. Georges Clemenceau said that war had become too important to leave to the generals. Likewise, I believe the history of war is too important to leave to military people.

Nothing in my background marked me for a career in academia, let alone one in which my research specialized in the history of the French at war. My forebears came primarily from the British Isles sometime in the late eighteenth or early nineteenth century, though I really have no idea just when or where. I descend from economically marginal family farmers from central upstate New York, who became economically marginal industrial workers, who became economically marginal postindustrial workers. We grew up not with the hopes of immigrants but with the disappointments and low expectations of a long-settled rural population. I have no family connection to France apart from an uncle by marriage, who I believe landed in Normandy on D-Day. I did, however, have the good fortune of being a child in the early 1960s, a time of great optimism and opportunity. It never occurred to me that I would not go to college, a state of mind fostered by a succession of talented elementary school teachers.

I had a real if unfocused interest in history, and now that I think about it, in the history of war specifically. But my real intellectual passions as a child were first dinosaurs and then space travel, these being the heroic days of the Gemini and Apollo programs. The film *Patton* came out in 1970, and I remember doing an eighth-grade report on him. Then came a succession of high school courses in "social studies," which seemed to go out of their way to extinguish any interest in history. I did take four years of high school French, considered at the time in Schenectady, New York, to be a less marginal language than Spanish. The teachers were not the best, and I responded in kind.

It never occurred to me throughout high school that I might one day connect French and history.

In one way or another, the history department at Oberlin College has loomed large over my entire adult life. It was as a student at Oberlin that I acquired what I can only refer to as a love for the study of history. Sarah Fishman (herself now a distinguished French historian) had been a high school girlfriend and was a sophomore at Oberlin when I arrived in 1976. At her advice, I took the yearlong survey course in European history from Robert E. Neil. He was a complex figure, about whom even today I have divided sentiments. As a presence in the classroom, he was brilliant, a term I use neither lightly nor often. Because of Neil, I came to love European history. But he published practically nothing, and never gave students much of an idea of what historians actually do. As one of my present colleagues once put it, he cared about teaching, but not about students.

Entranced by what I thought Neil thought historians did, I wrote an honors thesis under his direction, on de Gaulle's European policy from 1961–1966. It provided, let us say, a somewhat romanticized account of the subject, heavily influenced by de Gaulle's own world view. At the time, I found his nineteenth-century nationalism in a twentieth-century world quite heroic. But whatever the shortcomings of the thesis, writing it proved one of the few things I did in college that directly prepared me for the graduate study of history. Neil provided next to no direction, which compelled me to acclimate myself to the uncertainty and tedium of research. I learned that I needed independence and resilience more than I needed an advisor.

I graduated from college in 1980, certain that I had bid farewell both to the study of history and to the state of Ohio. I entered the masters program at the School of International Affairs at Columbia University, mostly because I was certain that doctors of philosophy in European history would end up starving in the streets. But living in New York taught me how little it took actually to get on in the world. I decided that upon completion of my present program I would migrate to history, provided I could get someone else to pay for it in the form of a fellowship. This proved forthcoming at Columbia, perhaps despite my rather vague claim in my application that I wanted to continue my research on de Gaulle as a dissertation topic.

Yet I remained curiously on the margins of history as a profession. I began the program at Columbia as a young volunteer might join the army—interested, somehow drawn to the lifestyle but not yet appreciating the level of commitment just undertaken. The first year thus came as a kind of a basic training, with standards of critical thinking and writing well beyond anything I had been accustomed to. I had a kind of adolescent rebellion toward Neil, by whom I felt let down. Only later did I appreciate his ability to foster the affective attachment scholars have for their subjects. This, in turn, lay at the heart of my persistence, which I remain convinced is the single most important quality for an academic career.

Somehow, I managed to survive the purge of first-year graduate students for which Columbia was famous at that time, and along the way to write a serviceable master's essay on the city of Nantes during the events of May 1968. This proved to be my major encounter with issues of center and periphery in French history. I became intrigued by the odd and situational collaboration in Nantes among conservative farmers, discontented aviation workers, and enraged students against the backdrop of the temporary disintegration of central authority in Paris. In retrospect, my master's essay gave rise to an interest in the different paths liberal democracy took in France and the United States, though it took me years (and a good bit of Tocqueville) to appreciate it. I became fascinated by the myriad ways that the French, for all their effervescence in 1968, ultimately depended on the monarchical republic. Like many Americans, I am still surprised when the French seek freedom not from the state but through it.

Why did I undertake the study of French history at all? I think that in my early years, the process of elimination played a distressingly large role. United States history was never an option. American historians seemed too likely to bring their psychological preoccupations front and center. I prefer writing about "them" to writing about "us," even though "we" always lurk in there somewhere. In the early 1980s, Britain, Germany, and France still dominated the study of European history at Columbia. My ethnic roots notwithstanding, I found British history an insular field, still in the shadow of Louis Namier or E. P. Thompson. I have never warmed to the German language, which no doubt contributed to my need to take the doctoral language exam four times in order to pass it. Spain, Italy, and Eastern Europe, while on the ascent even then, seemed out of the mainstream, and I had no experience in the relevant languages at all. More than one historian has been drawn to France because this proved the path of least linguistic resistance.

In my first year at graduate school, my teachers broadened the horizons of what I thought of as "military history," beyond troop movements and technical explanations for victories and defeats, to the history of armies as social institutions. I can date my interest in this kind of military history very precisely—the spring of 1983, when I did a presentation on Jean Paul Bertaud's *La Révolution armée* (1979). There I found the moral passion of a historian who believed in the Revolution and its democratic legacy combined with the expert practice of social history. Bertaud's soldiers sought freedom not just through the emerging Revolutionary state but through taking up arms as its exemplars.

I see social history as having two broad sets of roots—Marxist-inspired labor history and the *Annales* school, with its focus on geography, structures, and temporalities. I have nothing in the world against labor history, but for my own research, it was a nonstarter for a simple, brutal, reason. I had grown up thinking of the working class as something to leave, and I could muster little interest in returning to that aspect of my roots. I also found tedious the endless debates of the day about what class was. The *Annales* offered more promise, although I had limited patience for tracking landholding patterns over the centuries, for divining just how far north olive cultivation reached. Soldiers, of course, came from society; indeed, that fed a good bit of my initial interest in them. But they created their own society once in uniform. That was the society I set out to study as I looked for a dissertation topic.

My advisor at Columbia was Robert O. Paxton, whom I knew to be interested in military history, as he had written his first book on the Vichy officer corps. For some time, I felt that he was not very interested in me, though I eventually figured out that this was not the case. Graduates of liberal arts colleges often trundle off to graduate school as though it were an episode of *Star Wars*. I expected my advisor to be Obi-Wan Kenobi, training his young Padawan to become a Jedi knight. This was not how Paxton saw it. Never, I think, did I have such an important relationship remain so unspoken. It was all about the establishment of proper boundaries. There were certain practical things Paxton could do for me, as he could for any of his students. He could be my advocate in the byzantine competition for resources at Columbia, he could read my work quickly and well, and he could write letters that hiring committees would take seriously. But he could not teach me the Ways of the Force, professionally speaking. Those things were my problem. From the beginning, responsibility for my career was primarily my own. He never took on students in order to reproduce himself. He had become well integrated into communities of historians in France, and subtly expected his students to do likewise. In time, I came to appreciate Paxton as not just a good teacher of graduate students, but a great one.

This was not to say that Paxton never gave advice. Indeed, it was he who steered me toward World War I, albeit indirectly. In what I think was our only general conversation about a dissertation topic, he suggested I not do what he did, that is, study a topic recent enough that access to archives would be a problem. Once I decided to accept this sage counsel, the matter resolved itself simply. I knew I wanted to study France and I knew I wanted to study war. The

Great War of 1914–1918 was the latest period for which I knew I would not have serious problems getting into archives. I wish that I could say I had a more exalted reason for choosing the research area in which I have toiled for more than twenty years. But once this was settled, I hit on what I think was a genuine innovation. I would try a French social history–style local study of one military unit for the duration of the war. So began my dissertation, and with it my extended period of happy research in the military archives at Vincennes.

Whatever the combination of circumstances that landed me in French history in the first place, I decided to remain there amidst the challenges faced by any graduate student and young scholar. Bit by bit, and not altogether knowingly, I became seriously committed to my profession and my subject. My relationship to France has always been more complicated than my relationship to my profession, though it has grown less so with time. I have never been a true Francophile, and I vaguely distrust Francophilia in others, particularly in American historians of France. I have always associated Francophilia with seeing what one wants to see in France and the French, and nothing else. I have also wondered whether Francophilia involves wanting at some level to become French. I love the things one is supposed to love about France—the food, the wine, the architecture, the sense of style. But I have a very poor sense of smell and was never going to make much of a wine connoisseur; in any event I seem to lack the sensibilities of a *bon vivant*. In my experience, work and play do not easily coexist in France. And I have never wanted to become French, nor did I see the point of writing French history as though one were anything but a foreigner. All of my French friends are patriots in one way or another, but none, I think, is a Francophile. Moreover, the French to me seem a people who love paradox, doubt, and ferocious individualism. All of these seem inconsistent with Francophilia. One of my personal paradoxes is that I began to make friends in France only when I stopped trying to fit in, and embraced instead a certain alterity to France and Frenchness. But what could be more French than that?

It is not easy to look back on one's first book. A common reaction is to feel as though someone else wrote it. And someone else did. The surprisingly frank preface makes me recall all the personal relationships and dramas behind it, as well as the great distance between now and then. I realize now that the psychological preoccupation that drove the book was my father's illness and death in 1975 and my attempt to make an uncontrollable situation controllable through rational calculus. Looking at the book now, I am surprised at how much I once knew about things like French conscription law, military organization, and tactics. It is always a sobering experience to look at page after page of one's own prose, with only the most vague memory of ever having written it.

Between Mutiny and Obedience operated at the margins of two fields, social history and military history. It also touched upon emerging issues of cultural history. I made a point of identifying myself as an "assistant professor of European social history" on the cover and maintained in the preface that soldiers and even generals have a social history because they remain part of society. This now seems like not much of an explanation, however. The book certainly bore traces of prior practices. I carefully situated the Fifth Division in its prewar environs in Normandy, around Rouen. There were a great many numbers in it—casualties, replacements, even some calculations of casualties per kilometer of ground gained. But I think I persisted in thinking of it primarily as social history because it was about resistance, its focal point being the mutinies of 1917. The mutinies, I argued, were about military matters and about the political symbiosis in French republicanism between the citizen and the soldier. They were to no significant degree about class. I saw in the book my chance to study resistance minus the ideological tangles of labor history as they had evolved by the late 1980s.

Military history in its more conventional forms always seemed to me the history of military efficiency, of why wars are won or lost. In this sense, I was never a military historian and never wanted to become one. But one could hardly write about soldiers without engaging military history, and military historians were always a readership I wanted to take my work seriously. Military historians come in many shapes and sizes. Some are simply great historians who happen to write about things military. Others are excellent practitioners within the paradigm of military efficiency who remain open to different ways of thinking. These two groups proved an excellent audience for the book. Indeed, they engaged it much more thoughtfully than social or cultural historians—or for that matter, French historians in the United States, who at times have seemed just a bit oblivious to the ways war has made and remade France. There are also stiff-necked and resentful military historians who have blamed their largely self-imposed marginalization first on left-wing academic politics, then on feminism, then on a conveniently amorphous "political correctness." I never tried very hard to win them over.

The gestation period of *Between Mutiny and Obedience* coincided with the rise of "cultural history," which many Americans in the profession these days take to mean history directed by literary and critical theory. I still remember the first time I was clubbed over the head with cultural history in this sense, when Dominick LaCapra interviewed for a job at Columbia in the spring of

1988. He gave a talk on Paul de Man, and I remember understanding very little of what he said. But during the questions, he said something about the prospect of reading an inquisition record as though it were a literary text. The idea, frankly, had never occurred to me before, and it helped provoke an interest in narrative that has stuck with me ever since.

Like rappers, though much more amicably, French historians in the United States of my generation could be broadly divided into West Coast and East Coast camps. The West was the domain of Berkeley and Michel Foucault. I sometimes wonder how my career might have taken a different course had Foucault been a visiting professor at Columbia instead of Berkeley. In the 1980s and 1990s, Berkeley students seemed to mine discourse out of the California hills like gold in 1849. As a group, I found them genial, bright people, formidable competitors on the job market and now valued colleagues. But I was never one of them, and they seemed to far outnumber us. The East, rather than the West, was then the lawless land in French history. Easterners had no particular paradigm to join as social history gave way to cultural history, and perhaps we poached from several alternatives. Some Easterners became Westerners, with varying degrees of plausibility. I think I have been not so much marginal among French historians in the United States as an affirmed Easterner.

Professional good fortune descended on me in 1990, in the form of a tenure-track job at Oberlin. As one of only three European historians, I was expected to teach European history rather than French history. I would be hard-pressed now to offer a survey course in French history, not that there is much unfulfilled demand for such these days among American undergraduates. I have come to consider myself more a European historian who works on the Great War in France than a French historian. It does seem that teaching at a liberal arts college rather than a university can lead to a somewhat bifurcated career. I believe I have become a voice to be reckoned with among historians of France and the Great War, in France as well as in the Anglophone world. It is a fiction that teaching at a liberal arts college in itself precludes much of a research career. But I am not terribly well read outside my research field, beyond what is needed to teach undergraduates.

To my surprise, I grew much closer to France and the French in my professional adulthood than I ever expected to. Part of this was situational, in that my coming of age coincided with a reawakening of interest in the Great War, particularly in Europe. I had met the foremost senior specialists in France, Jean-Jacques Becker, Guy Pedroncini, and Antoine Prost, during my dissertation research. But unbeknownst to me, there was also a new generation of scholars who would later become my primary intellectual community beyond

Oberlin. In the early 1990s, these people came together as the guiding spirit of the Historial de la Grande Guerre in Péronne, in the battlefields of the Somme. There now existed a whole cohort of French scholars about my age such as Stéphane Audoin-Rouzeau, Annette Becker, and Christophe Prochasson, who were comfortable reading English and keenly interested in the work of Anglophone scholars. They drew in other foreigners such as Jay Winter, John Horne, and Gerd Krumeich. Without really realizing it, I had relocated an important part of my professional life to Europe.

This strategy proved unintentionally shrewd, given the pronounced decline of interest in European history in the United States. French history has especially suffered, with the unseating of French in favor of Spanish as the predominant first foreign language as well as the gradual shift of American economic and geopolitical concerns away from Europe. More generally, I believe that nothing in the twentieth century fed American self-absorption as much as the end of the Cold War—not even the end of the Great War. To be sure, plenty of students remain interested in European history as long as it is not sold to them as a canonical part of "Our Shared Western Heritage." But from a scholarly perspective, if you want to go duck hunting, you go where the ducks are. Péronne has been a lovely pond.

It is difficult for Americans to appreciate what the Great War means in French history, as a past that will not become the past. Americans have the Civil War, though we as a nation have often found it convenient to overlay the genuinely dire nature of that conflict with a comforting but misleading mythology of a "war among brothers." The French tried to invent a comforting mythology of "victory" in 1918, though the unsettled nature of the outcome of the Great War, from the time of the Armistice to the bitter tribulations of the interwar years, led to the literal deconstruction of that mythology well before the German breakthrough at Sedan in 1940. Some of the passions still aroused by the Great War predate it—such as a reflexive antimilitarism on the left that is much stronger in France than in the United States. But the United States since the Civil War has never suffered a national trauma remotely on the scale of the Great War in France. National traumas are tricky and largely pointless to compare. But we could do so with the Great War for France and the Vietnam War for the United States. As a percent of the total population, the 1.3 million French dead of 1914–1918 would have to correspond to nearly 6 million Americans dead in Vietnam (as opposed to some 55,000 who actually died).

As a foreigner, I found it easier than I might have thought to take part in the ongoing conversation in France about the long-term meaning of the Great War. Certainly, academics in the United States have not returned the favor in

taking seriously the work of foreign Americanists, on the Civil War or anything else. Perhaps the participation of Robert Paxton in the national debates
about Vichy helped pave the way for subsequent generations, alongside the
general opening up of French academia. I have found it helpful in France to
preserve a certain distance from old debates and learn from all the protagonists I could, be they on the left, right, or center. New debates, I think, found
me more than I found them.

Péronne historians have been associated with grand concepts, such as *culture de guerre, consentement,* and *brutalisation. Culture de guerre* comprises
nothing less than the totality of all the systems of representation of the war.
Consentement revolves around the myriad discursive means through which
Europeans persuaded themselves to fight so hard for so long. *Brutalisation*
seeks, paradoxically, to restore violence to the study of war by taking account
of just what sorts of things human beings are willing to do to each other in extreme circumstances.

The Historial has drawn opposition, particularly in France. To my mind
somewhat unfairly, critics have sometimes tagged Péronne historians as reactionary, as though failing to condemn the Great War obsessively means
somehow affirming it. *Consentement* has proven particularly controversial,
considered by some historians as right-wing patriotism under another pernicious name. *Brutalisation* has likewise drawn criticism by those convinced that
the vast majority of men at war kill only under duress. At the onset of this
mini–culture war, both sides made use of my work, and each side saw very
different things in it. To Péronne historians, my book affirmed consent. Their
critics saw in it the traces of the influence of social history—the fact of resistance to military discipline as conventionally conceived. Because my work
seemed to mean different things to different people, I was able to operate for
a time with the dispensation of a foreigner on the margins of debates around
Péronne historians.

That time came to an end in 2003, when I published a survey of France and
the Great War written with Stéphane Audoin-Rouzeau and Annette Becker.
Specifically written for an Anglophone audience, the book is unlikely to be
translated or to attract much attention in France. But to those in France aware
of the book, its publication simply made clear that I had been a Péronne historian all along. Collaboration among historians seems to work best when no
one pretends the labor is divided equally. My coauthors duly wrote their assigned sections and deferred to me thereafter. They provided more than their
share of the content, but the final prose was nearly all mine. Reworking the
text, I felt like Ferdinand Foch in 1918, commanding the generous reserves
provided by their previous work in the forward advance of our narrative. For

myself, writing the book made me understand one reason that narrative history has proven so resilient—it's so much fun. I loved telling the stories: Sarah Bernhardt rising to stand on one leg (the other having been amputated) in order to exhort her compatriots in 1915, Georges Clemenceau accepting the presidency of the Council of Ministers in 1917. I found narrative a seductive art and became impressed anew by how thoroughly historians can control understanding through choosing which stories to tell and which not.

My extended collaboration with colleagues in France does not mean that I never disagree with them or that I consider us one voice writing on different topics. Péronne historians have been monumentally productive, but I wonder whether that productivity has taken its toll. Cultural history, like cultural theory, is a messy business. As written these days, cultural history requires a sustained engagement with difficult concepts that lead in unpredictable directions. I also wonder whether we have written too much for ourselves and have not concerned ourselves enough with what cultural history is or ought to be. The grand issues that have preoccupied Péronne historians may have unintentionally undermined the task of making the Great War a field of study in its own right rather than one long prelude to World War II. The more I teach both world wars, the more convinced I become that what separates them matters as much as what they have in common.

Safely tenured, I have found it a long trek between my first monograph and my second, which is only now completed. I make no apologies for this. Various shorter-term projects intervened, as did the legitimate requirements of having a family and a life more generally. Intellectually, I grappled with cultural history primarily through narrative. A question came to intrigue me as I finished *Between Mutiny and Obedience*. If soldiers really did learn to manipulate military authority in significant ways, how did we come to understand experience in the trenches as simple victimization? This led me to investigate how war stories become war stories, and how experience becomes experience through narrative. This, I think, will be the last book I have in me on French soldiers of the Great War. I have become interested in diplomacy—like military history a field long considered somewhat on the margins of the historical profession. I expect I will always write about France in one way or another. It is no longer, really, a question of affective attachments to the *grande nation* or even personal and intellectual attachments to my friends there. France, corny as it sounds, has become a part of me.

I have come to believe along the way that the margins of history may have become too large. Marginality can be a pose, one that I have tried to write about, mostly playfully, in this essay. Writing on the margins implies exclusion, but it also implies not needing to feel implicated in what goes on in the mainstream. I have found that my need to establish a distance from the mainstream has diminished with time. Conference panels at large conventions can seem populated entirely by the marginalized. I have heard gender and women's historians, cultural historians, political historians, labor historians, environmental historians, military historians, Africanists, Asianists, and a great many French historians all complain of marginalization. History has always been an undisciplined discipline, which helps explain why many of us still squirm just a bit when we are referred to as "social scientists." The confusion over the disciplinary and geographic boundaries of history has, perhaps, helped confuse all of us as to just where its margins are. The pleasures of the margins and the pleasures of the mainstream may well be the same thing.

CHAPTER 14

It's Not About France

Ken Alder

> I never had the Latin for the judging. . . . I managed to get through
> the mining exams [though]. They're not very rigorous; they only ask
> you one question. They say "Who are you?" and I got seventy-five per-
> cent on that.
>
> PETER COOK, "The Coal-Miner Skit," *Beyond the Fringe*

Stick a pin into the geographic center of France and it will poke through near
Bruère-Allichamps, some forty-five kilometers south of the cathedral town of
Bourges. Or at least that was the location of France's center as calculated in
1799, soon after Jean-Baptiste-Joseph Delambre and Pierre-François-André
Méchain completed their seven-year survey of the French meridian to establish the length of the meter as one ten-millionth of the distance from the North
Pole to the equator. There have, of course, been other contenders for the nation's balancing-point in the past two hundred years. As France's fortunes have
shifted, so has its center: with the incorporation of Nice, Savoy, and Corsica;
with the gain and loss of empire; with the loss and gain of Alsace-Lorraine;
not to mention with the calculator's attitude toward France's colonial holdings
and *départements d'outre-mer* in Algeria, sub-Saharan Africa, southeast Asia,
and tropical islands around the globe. Even to answer so simpleminded a question as the location of France's geographical center—the balancing-point of *le*

patrimoine—depends on a political calculus, one that has altered with the years and with the allegiance of the balancer. All the more telling, then, that historical precedent has persistently awarded the crown to Bruère.

I was biking through Bruère in August 1999, researching my book on the Revolutionary survey of 1792–1799, zigzagging my way down the meridian on the trail of Delambre and Méchain and, like them, navigating by way of the great Cassini map of France (which an archivist at the University of Chicago had kindly let me photocopy), when I began to see notices spray-painted on the surface of the road: "*Course d'âne, 5km,*" "*Course d'âne, 4km,*" "*Course d'âne, 3km.*" At first I was not sure what this meant. A donkey race, presumably. But literally?

It was a sweltering August afternoon, and I was feeling groggy and not at all literal-minded. I had been cycling hard since leaving Bourges, having come the long way around after a night in a cheap hotel not far from the inn used by Delambre in 1796, itself not far from the inn used by the cartographer Cassini III in 1740 (their respective distances calculated geodetically by Delambre in his expedition logbook, which an archivist at the Observatory of Paris had grudgingly let me photocopy). Delambre had been trapped in Bourges for an entire summer while the hyperinflation of the year III doubled and redoubled the price of rented horses. Even his tip for the stable boys had gone up by a factor of ten. (I had an account book to prove it.) For my part, I had been obliged to spend an extra night in Bourges because my Kryptonite lock had rusted tight around my front wheel, and I had been forced to carry my bike from the damp hotel cellar to the motorcycle shop down the street, mentally planning, as I went, the laborious explanations I would have to make: that I wasn't stealing the bike, and that I would prefer to avoid going to the police station to fill out a report, et cetera. But the stocky mechanic in the blue smock shrugged off my explanations and cut the lock off for free.

That left me the afternoon to climb the tower of the Bourges cathedral and visit its pelican weathervane, which Delambre had used as one of his sighting targets. The view from the top was magnificent: a corrugated terrain of green and yellow fields dotted with distant spires, two of which were Delambre's stations to the south—and my immediate destination. From this vantage point it was easy to feel yourself at France's center.

There are many lines one may draw across the terrain. Fortified lines mortared with the blood of millions of young men. Political lines drawn for administrative convenience. Lines that encircle. Lines that divide.

You will not find the line of the meridian recommended in any Michelin guide; it's not the sort of circuit that leads you efficiently past three-star cathedrals and two-star panoramas. Tourists don't have the leisure to travel in a straight line. Nor is the meridian likely to become the route of a future Tour de France. Lance Armstrong and company are not interested in a stage so hyperrational it leaves out grueling *hors catégorie* climbs. Nor is the meridian the sort of route followed by penitent pilgrims, itinerant *compagnons,* or contemporary gastronomes—though it transects all of these.

The meridian line is not a route, but an ideal: a line carved in the scientific imagination. No one has ever traveled this meridian; what they have done repeatedly over the centuries is *triangulate* it, inferring its trajectory by measurements taken from one side, then the other. It has served as the spine of cartographic France, as evidence for the shape of the earth and as the fount of the world's standard of measurement. And I had set out to cycle the route taken by Delambre and Méchain not in hopes of re-enactment but in the spirit of scientific dissection. It would be, I imagined, like taking a random cut of the national tissue. How had these universal claims been extracted from the lumpy surface of the French countryside? How had the ancient heterogeneity that had gone into the making of France—its former linguistic, customary, and marketplace diversity—been effaced by the spread of a national (and global) market, itself abetted in no small part by the Revolutionary creation of the metric system?

Not that I cared about the metric system itself, one way or the other. Was there any subject more calculated to make an American's eyes glaze over with boredom? I remembered being told by my fifth-grade teacher to learn the metric system, as its use would soon become obligatory in America. Having waited in vain for this scientific future to arrive, I had turned to the topic in graduate school with a feeling of vengeance, seeing in the history of the meter a way to unmask the political, and hence contingent, character of science's foundational unit, as well as its most touted contribution to global commerce. The prospect of this unmasking gave me that "Ah-ha!" feeling which is the cheap thrill that keeps many a historian of science going. This adolescent delight was intensified when I discovered manuscripts in the Observatory of Paris indicating that one of the two savants had committed an error in his observations and hidden this fact from his colleague until after the meter had been promulgated, and that this error had been replicated in every subsequent definition of the meter, including our current meter, based on the distance traveled by light in a vacuum in one 299,792,458th of a second. So not only was the universal measure I had so dutifully learned in elementary school wrong; it didn't even *matter* that it was wrong because the meter was whatever scientists said it was. The meter was, after all, a social convention.

But surely Delambre and Méchain understood this. So why had they spent seven years during one of the most unsettled periods in modern history trav-

eling some seven thousand kilometers—including the inevitable backtrack-
ing—to measure a one-thousand-kilometer stretch of the meridian with
quixotic accuracy? Closing in on the halfway point, sweat dripping off the end
of my nose, I was beginning to wonder if I was on a *course d'âne* of my own.

❧

The answer to the question of why I became a historian of science, and then
focused my research interests on eighteenth-century France—like the answer
to any historical question—is at once hopelessly overdetermined and irre-
deemably fortuitous. Hence, the art of making the identified explanandum appear plausible lies in selecting the proper details and arranging them in such
as way as to make the inevitable outcome appear to be as freely chosen, if unanticipated, as it does to the participant(s). For my part, a research expedition
down the meridian of France was certainly *not* what I would have anticipated
for myself at the age of twelve, or eighteen, or even twenty-six, inevitable as it
may seem in retrospect.

I well remember the day (I must have been about twenty-six) when my dissertation advisor casually asked me what my parents did for a living, and I answered that my father was a scientist and my mother taught French, and he
said, "Oh, so that explains it." And with as much ingenuousness as I could
summon, I said, "Explains what?"

Yes, my father was a physicist; to be specific, a Jewish-German refugee, an
industrial chemist's son who had left the Rhineland for Switzerland in 1933 at
the age of eight, and Switzerland for Berkeley, California, in 1941 at the age
of sixteen. He had been a chemistry student at U.C. Berkeley when he was
drafted into the U.S. Navy.; And he had been stationed in the Philippines,
preparing for the invasion of Japan when the atomic bomb was dropped.
Then, after the war, while a graduate student at Cal Tech, he helped develop
new methods of computational analysis to model the behavior of matter under extreme conditions and was hired to bring those skills to Lawrence Liv-
ermore Labs, where the first hydrogen bombs were being designed. One
characteristic of the physicists of that generation is that they found all the other
professions trivial in comparison, what with the Bomb on their c.v. and all.
"Physics envy" was the term for it. Physics had produced the most foundational theories and the biggest bang. My father was determined that his firstborn son become a physicist, especially if he showed any mathematical
aptitude, which I did. But to my father's disappointment, I had spurned the
secular-Jewish priesthood.

And yes, my mother taught French; to be specific, she had grown up speaking Yiddish in Toronto, learned English when she went to kindergarten,

French from Scottish-Canadian harridans of a certain age. But I never learned more than a word or two of French from her, perhaps because she started off by reading me *Babar*—even at six I found the book distressing. So my parents had nothing to do with my chosen career—except, of course, that they had everything to do with it.

To define oneself in contrarian terms is to live within bounds defined by others. Which is to say, cultural capital is not easily chucked aside. My father insisted that I become a scientist. My mother taught French. I wanted to be a novelist. Therefore I became a historian of French science.

This much I know, if only by subtraction. . . . I was conceived under the sign of Sputnik at Bell Labs in Murray Hills, New Jersey, during the year my father was there on sabbatical and AT&T helped launch America's first orbital sphere in response to the Soviet challenge. One academic year later I was born in Berkeley: nine pounds, eleven ounces, a big boy, a hard delivery, thirty-six hours culminating in forceps—or so my mother likes to remind me. I attended public school in a nearby East Bay suburb, learned the New Math and the metric system, practiced bomb drills and earthquake drills, and became part of the first generation to be educated entirely in interracial schools. Although the student protests of the 1960s took place only five miles from my home, they hardly registered on my childhood consciousness except as a series of local aftershocks: Black Power, the drug culture, environmentalism, a vague sense that the future might be different from the past. Not necessarily better, mind you, but different.

Then, when I was twelve, my father took my younger siblings and me on sabbatical to Europe in the early 1970s. We spent the first half of the year in Amsterdam, where I attended the American school and first became aware of history, meaning World War II. This was understandable, since the Holocaust had claimed a large portion of my family, and just around the corner was the house of Anne Frank, who might as well have been a kissing cousin. Yet it was the story of those who fought back that gave me goosebumps. That fall I read all five volumes of Winston Churchill's *The Second World War*. As if further proof were needed that I was a nerdy child, it was the original memoranda I found most fascinating. I remember the sensual pleasure I took in poring over their dates, their bureaucratic headings, and, above all, the extraneous content that was their gauge of authenticity. Of course, if I had not gone on to study history, this memory would not provide the jolt of retrospective predestination and be hardly worth recalling. But I do recall it.

The second half of the year we lived in Paris, where I attended the École Bilingue. I wore a school uniform, memorized the anatomy of the mollusk, learned to cross my 7s, and became a Métro-rat. With a pack of classmates I cheated my way past the *mutilés de guerre* who punched the tickets, snuck onto the first-class car, and dropped firecrackers onto the tracks. Or at least I wanted to do those things; it wasn't easy for me to be bad. So I practiced on my family. Like most secular Jews (refugee edition) we seemed to be doing endless penance to European high culture, as if *we* had somehow betrayed *it*. We must have visited a thousand churches, and I said I hated them all. We must have visited a hundred museums, though I did develop a secret crush on the Winged Victory of Thrace. I was miserable in the usual thirteen-year-old way. Parisian high fashion that year seemed to involve tall slender women wearing American cub scout uniforms tight across the breasts. I was a former scout and this somehow heightened my misery.

Only in retrospect did that year have much importance. In some ways, it gave me an outsider's eye for America. We returned home to the Watergate hearings, the oil shock, the era of global limits. Suddenly American cars seemed gargantuan; American consumption, grotesque; American suburbia, a prison. In other words, it was as if the year had never happened. I promptly forgot my French. Besides, Gothic cathedrals and the Winged Victory hardly seemed relevant at a high school that was three-quarters African-American. Nor was physics, for that matter, though my father was still determined that I should be a physicist and attend MIT, Cal Tech, or Berkeley, preferably Berkeley, where I could live at home. A German-Jewish father's expectations for his firstborn son are not easily set aside.

The strange truth was, I found physics simultaneously irrelevant and politically suspect. How could science, a form of knowledge about nature, be politically suspect? Surely it had more to with mushroom clouds than my father's insistence that I become a physicist? Because there was something else, a complication. Though I found physics irrelevant and suspect, I also admired its rigor and radicalism, the way it submitted its speculations to the constraints of logic and evidence, the way its practitioners were willing to follow that logic and evidence to their utmost conclusion. So again, how could science, a form of knowledge about nature, be politically suspect? That is the question I have spent my life answering.

I will always be grateful that I was admitted to Harvard because not even my father could turn down the prestige. As a condition of letting me go, however, he obliged me to major in physics and pay my own tuition. This was a price I was willing to pay. I managed it by using my science training to take summer jobs in environmental protection (which my father, to his credit, helped me find), thereby putting my physics to less suspect uses and my money in Harvard's purse. This also gave me the autonomy to plot my escape. As a first step I switched my major from physics to "physics and chemistry." You might think that my father would see this as a sign of my deepening commitment to science. But you would be wrong. He saw, correctly, that I was losing focus and giving science the slip. This prompted him to write the only letter he has ever written me: a threat to make me withdraw from university. In the end, it was easier to switch my major back to physics and take half of my classes in the arts and humanities. This included a course on fiction-writing in which I wrote my first short story, a thinly disguised tale of my dreadful adolescent year in France. I had decided that I wanted to be a novelist, even though I understood this to mean that I would have to live off of technical jobs for the foreseeable future. The strange thing was, at the time I considered myself a rebel.

So after graduation I took a job as a technical consultant to pay off my debts. Most of my work was devoted to radiation protection in a uranium mine near Moab, Utah. Unfortunately, these were the early years of the Reagan administration, and funding for environmental research was being shifted to military research. I got into bitter arguments with my senior co-workers about this. One of our new contracts included work on chemical warfare agents, which they justified as a defensive measure against those agents. I refused to work on the project. It was frightening to see how easily you could slip across the Cold War mirror if you had a useful skill. So I got a Fulbright to work on radiation protection in Lausanne, Switzerland. One might as well ask: Why Switzerland? In part because I had Swiss citizenship through my father and so could get a work permit on the side. But mainly because it was the most dutiful escape I could think of. Neutrality anyone? Once there, I ended up designing computer models for solar energy and my free time carousing in bars, practicing my fiction, relearning French, and riding my bike up and down the hills.

It was a bottom-of-the-line Motobécane, a venerable French brand, though mostly assembled out of imported parts. A friend taught me how to strip it down to the ball bearings and reassemble it. That summer I set out across France along the Geneva–Saint-Malo line, the supposed boundary between the northern France of literate industrial modernity and the southern France of illiterate reactionary peasantry. Not that I knew anything about this particular fault line at the time. I was just looking for a plausible goal, and the Atlantic seemed within reach.

So, in the summer of 1983, as the temperatures soared, I set out west from Lausanne. Nights, I slept in a tent in private woods off the side of the road. One day I ate nothing but meringues. I remember being as happy as I had ever been: pedaling past the creamery-yellow pastures of the Jura, the flickering forests of the Morvan, the presumptuous *châteaux* of the Loire, out for the final alluvial approach, then an about-face to Paris to return to Switzerland in a final three-day burst.

In fact, I spent those three weeks plotting out a novel about a white fifteen-year-old kid who goes to a predominantly African-American high school near Berkeley in the 1970s and wishes he were black. It was to be a semi-autobiographical book, like many a first novel: my fictionalized family, my fictionalized high school, my fictionalized self. Not that I had ever dared wish I were black, exactly. If anything, it was a year in the relative racial homogeneity of Switzerland and France that inspired me to tell that story—that and a James Baldwin essay I had been reading about his desultory life in a Swiss village not far away. Which goes to show that being contrarian can be the shortest route home. I finished the book the next year while living off my savings in New York, and it was published a few years later as *The White Bus* (1987). The day it was accepted for publication was the most euphoric day of my life.

In the interim I decided to return to Harvard for a doctorate in the history of science. I intended this as a plausible cover story while I worked on my next novel about a scientist who, almost as a joke, starts a radical world revolution in physics and then changes his mind and tries to take it all back. I suppose this would have to be considered another semi-autobiographical book—or species of wish-fulfillment, as if there's any difference. I thought a few years of graduate study might teach me something valuable along those lines. What made this such a plausible cover story was that I had applied to study the Weimar origins of quantum mechanics, and it's hard to get more sober-young-man than that. At least the grant officers at the NSF and Mellon saw it that way.

The problem with delayed gratification, though, is that it can become a habit. I did write the novel, but you know what they say about grad school: it's monkey see, monkey do, monkey climb.

To avoid stepping on my own fictional toes, I deliberately chose a dissertation topic that did not concern America, the twentieth century, or modern physics. So I really wasn't being entirely disingenuous when I told my dissertation adviser that my parents had nothing to do with my prospective project. For all that, my chosen subject—the rise of engineering rationality in eighteenth-century France and its (hidden) role in the politics of the French Revolution—can certainly be read as still another semi-autobiographical project. The resulting work, *Engineering the Revolution* (1997) is most emphatically a Cold War book, a history of the origins of the military-industrial-research triangle. It interprets the vituperative late Old Regime debate over Gribeauval's new artillery system in light of the debate over Reagan's "Star Wars" satellite-guided missile defense program—that is, as a debate over military hardware standing in for a debate over geopolitical strategy standing in for a debate over the national character. The general claim of the book, that artifacts have political qualities, is an outgrowth of an environmental politics that sees distinct forms of political life embedded in the design of technology. And the specific argument of the book, that the engineers' embrace of a particular sort of meritocratic culture served to cover their ideological agenda, is a direct out-growth of my own commitment to affirmative action and racial politics in America.

Put like this, the book sounds tendentious, even anachronistic. But I did everything in my power to write from the point of view of its protagonists: about France, not America; about the late eighteenth century, not the late twentieth; about muskets and artillery ballistics, not satellites and nuclear weapons. The book may have been composed with self-consciously political and filial *motives*, but I was determined to make its persuasiveness depend on identifying the turn to modern techno-science in a strain of Enlightenment thought and the social and intellectual mobilization that occurred under the flag of the French Revolution. Given that the book was written against the sort of Whiggish account that takes the trajectory of science as leading inevitably to a present-day truth, I could hardly presume the political outcome was more predetermined. In a way, this was my repayment for the debt I owed science, to its empiricism and its logic. Making this argument stick, therefore, de-pended on finding the proper balance of similarity and difference between the there-and-then and the here-and-now. That was what made eighteenth-cen-tury France so attractive as a historical subject; for the sort of problem I had chosen, it seemed to have just the right Panglossian distance. I certainly spent more time studying eighteenth-century France than I ever intended.

But you know what (else) they say about grad school: it's all about sub-limation.

By the time the book came out, the Cold War was over, and I had tenure. It is hard, even at this short distance, to recall just how unexpected that was. Tenure too. Certainly my father never thought the Cold War would end. It would appear that every geopolitical arrangement generates its own aura of permanence. But the logic of mutually assured destruction had seemed to guarantee the kind of permanence only Armageddon can confer. Besides, the Cold War was too useful to give up: too useful for the politicians, the arms merchants, the scientists. Instead, unexpectedly, the Russians gave up.

In retrospect, of course, it is obvious that . . . I would become an academic.

My father was very pleased I got tenure. This at least made sense to him. He even offered me his used Volvo station wagon, sober-gray of course. And I even accepted it. This somehow clinched a reconciliation long in the works. No doubt my lovely Aussie wife and our baby daughter played a role. But I never could bear to run the seat warmers. That was too comfortable for comfort.

Not for a moment did I regret the passing of the Cold War. I had never had much patience for the idea that the Soviet Union represented an "alternative" to American hegemony. But it did mean rethinking my work. The debate had turned from the problems of a divided world to those of a homogeneous globe. Did the supremacy of market logic promise political liberation or the eradication of local particularity? I became interested in the way markets were historical constructs, the result of institutions nourished by state power and scientific authority. In the Revolutionary debate over the metric system, I saw an example of how science had been used to create the seemingly neutral standards that would underpin a national and global market. It seemed ironic that this innovation had taken place in France, where the complaints against globalization were now most vocal and where the call to eradicate local differences (patois, customary practice) had been so fierce during the French Revolution. I published an article to that effect.

Then in 1999–2000 I received a grant to spend a sabbatical year in France and brought my family with me. We found an apartment not far from the Panthéon—that other French center and the site of Delambre's Parisian observation signal. We placed my seven-year-old daughter in the local public school (no École Bilingue for her). Everything would seem set for me to start pedaling down the meridian.

Except that my grant was to work on a quite different project, a comparative study of the forensic sciences in France and America since the seventeenth century. In it, I planned to examine identification techniques from handwriting analysis to DNA typing. How has the use of scientific expertise been differently shaped by the Anglo-American and French legal systems? How have these techniques shaped our notion of the self? I spent considerable time that year researching that project (grant officers, take note), but I decided that it would be fun, in-between stints in the archives, to ride my bike down the French meridian on the trail of Delambre and Méchain.

❧

That evening in Bourges, writing in my journal, it dawned on me that Delambre, triangulating his way south toward Rodez, had surely realized that the entire expedition was a quixotic farce. He knew that the freshly promulgated "provisional meter"—a stand-in meter to be used while their mission was in progress—might just as readily serve as the permanent standard as the "true" ten-millionth of the quarter meridian he was laboring to extract from the earth. Yet he carried on, for no reason other than that he had agreed to complete the task and that his sense of honor obliged him to measure the world as accurately as he could. So there I was, in mid-trip, having outlined the argument of a book like a tale out of *Tristram Shandy:* the laborious means by which a universal truth had been unexpectedly extracted from the particular features of the world. But there was still something missing, the punch line: the two discoveries that confirmed how pointless the entire expedition had been ... and how unexpectedly transformative. First came Delambre and Méchain's discovery—made possible by the superfluous precision of their labor—that the earth's curvature did not just flatten at the poles but was sufficiently irregular that each meridian was distinct; in short, that our globe was buckled, bent, and warped, and could never serve as the basis for a universal standard of measurement, simultaneously invalidating the core premise of their expedition and constituting a stunning new piece of evidence that the earth had been created *over time,* from contingent processes. And second followed the realization—again prompted by their obsession with precision—that investigators of nature needed some way to distinguish in their data between the lumpiness possibly due to nature and the lumpiness due to the inevitable errors that crept into any scientific observations, thereby inspiring the development of the least square law, which became the foundation of all statistical science.

That's what comes from getting a research grant: You can never quite anticipate what you'll find. . . . So what had I found?

I had found that outside the major cities, the roads of France, except for the *autoroutes,* remained largely where Cassini had marked them down. I had found that, of the hundred-odd churches the surveyors had used as observation towers (it being my penance to visit them all), the vast majority still stood, albeit now mostly empty of parishioners. I had found that many of the surveyors' hilltop sites had been transformed into modern telecommunication relays, while global measurements were now taken by satellites. I had found that local markets still prospered, although the products now came from farther afield (Asia, Africa), with transactions in metric units and prices marked in both francs and soon-to-come euros, for which the metric system had paved the way. And I had found that I admired Delambre and Méchain.

I had set out to write a book "against" science—still on the lookout for the adolescent "Ah-ha!" thrill of unmasking—and had found myself unexpectedly in sympathy with the two men sent out on this quixotic expedition. I liked and admired Delambre: his lack of pretension, his classical learning, his cosmopolitan grace, his capacity for physical and mental work, his scrupulousness in both science and friendship, and his blend of political flexibility and intellectual integrity. A ragman's son, nearly blinded by smallpox as a child, he had risen to become perpetual secretary of the Academy of Science. And when he learned, after Méchain's death, of Méchain's erroneous data, he had published the "shameful" record without impugning his former colleague. Then he became the first major historian of science.

And I had even come, against all odds, to sympathize with Méchain, an impossibly fastidious man: melancholic, obsessive, jealous, full of *orgueil* (like pride, only more French). Yet I found it impossible not to empathize with his self-lacerating discovery that he had made a mistake—and his secret, futile attempt to correct an error that didn't even matter.

Seen in this quixotic light, I liked science. I even liked my father.

The *course d'âne* was just getting underway in Morlac when I arrived in the late afternoon. For his signal in Morlac, Delambre had hoped to use the belfry of the same twelfth-century church Cassini III had used before him. He had found it in ruins. During the previous year—the year of the Terror—the forty-foot belfry had fallen to the "hammer of the revolutionaries." Delambre offered to split the costs of rebuilding it with the villagers. This they refused to do. So he instead proposed erecting a cheap eighteen-foot wooden pyramid, the cost of which he would split and which would also keep the congregants dry when the rains came. They spurned this offer too. So, somewhat peeved, he cut a deal with a local lumber merchant who would build the tower at a reduced fee in exchange for the reclaimed timbers once his observations were done. Delambre took his measurements and moved on. But a month later, when the merchant arrived to remove the lumber, the villagers balked. A trial ensued, and five years later the church tower was still standing.

Two hundred years later, the belfry looked to be in good shape, and the locals were celebrating the Feast of the Assumption with a donkey race in an open field just west of town: eleven contestants trying to coax their carts three times around the perimeter. The winner (and only finisher) was an ardent young peasant with a droopy blond moustache, rolled-up sleeves, and a battered hat who stood in his cart like Ben-Hur, hollering at his donkey and lashing her to victory. He grinned on the podium as if this were the most euphoric day of his life. Afterwards, eight couples dressed in local costumes danced a folkloric dance to mournful music. When they were done, the loudspeakers reverted to Europop. A group of teenagers with cell phones (with uplinks by satellite) were hanging about the market filled with products from local farms plus goods from across the globe: textiles from Asia, wicker from South America, carved doodads from Africa, and cheap plastic from all over. It was a French village at the end of the millennium, both typical and particular, the there-and-then having become the here-and-now.

❧

I never appreciated working on France as much as when I stopped. As I write this essay I am completing a history of the lie detector, an offshoot of my project on the history of the forensic sciences. (I would explain, but that's another autobiography entirely.) The lie detector is a device unique to twentieth-century America, invented in my childhood hometown of Berkeley and first used extensively in Chicago, the city I currently call home. This proximity to my subject makes me uncomfortable. It's not that I worry about introducing biases—I have no expectation that history can ever be free of subjective influences—but I do worry that my biases will be parochial, based on unacknowledged intuitions, garnered from comic strips and the pabulum doled out in the press. There is also the problem of historical craft. I am accustomed to controlling the distance between my text and the period under discussion. When the subject matter is eighteenth-century France and I am writing in late twentieth-century English, I can occasionally slip into an older English diction or startle the reader with a deliberate anachronism, like "military-industrial-research triangle." Now I find myself fighting to keep the past from collapsing into the present. In this, my study of eighteenth-century France has been a great help. In part because of the training it provided in self-distancing. But also in part because the arguments surrounding the use of the lie detector have close parallels in the Old Regime arguments against the use of judicial torture—just as they do with arguments surrounding the current use of torture in American detention centers in Iraq and around the world.

So it's not about France. Except when it isn't.

CHAPTER 15

Pilgrim's Progress:
From Suburban Canada to Paris
(VIA MONTREAL, TOKYO, AND TEHRAN)

Clare Haru Crowston

Why France? The short answer is Blame Canada. Or, more precisely, blame Madame Boucher, my second-grade French teacher, and her ingenious reward system: a paper ticket for each correct answer; a gold star in exchange for five tickets. *"Bonjour, Madame," "Puis-je vous aider?" "Je voudrais une pomme."* Greeting customers, shopping for wax apples and bananas; my affinity for the French language and my future interest in material culture were predetermined by the lure of colored tickets and shiny stars. Growing up in the suburbs of Toronto in the 1970s, French-language classes were a federal requirement. No one acquired real spoken proficiency from these lessons, but several years of grammar, vocabulary, and *dictées* inevitably have an impact. I had an affinity for French and continued to study the language beyond the mandatory period. On top of that, my parents required that even summer camp be a learning experience, so I attended camp in the Laurentians north of Montreal. The counselors professed to speak only French and obliged me to put my school lessons to the test.

My Canadian childhood meant that French was my official second language from the age of seven on. Although I did not learn to speak French very well in school, it has been part of my life for almost as long as I can remember. Canada's colonial past also meant that France figured elsewhere in our curriculum, in ways that it does not in the United States. Hearing about Jacques Cartier from Mr. McLean (who thrillingly looked like a *voyageur* to my eleven-year-old eyes) or studying Quebec's Quiet Revolution, we learned that France

had played a key role in our country's history and that the colonial legacy remained of utmost importance in its current affairs. Without thinking about
it—and without ever visiting the country—France became a natural reference point, albeit more historical than contemporary.

This affinity, however, came with a price. Through childhood and adolescence, I took several years of Japanese lessons without acquiring more than the
rudiments of my mother's native tongue. In high school, I similarly failed to
master German or Latin, which I found outrageously difficult after French,
whose grammatical lessons had been absorbed so many years earlier. Farsi, my
husband's native language, remains for me at a level sufficient only to eaves-
drop on simple telephone conversations. Not only have I not learned these languages—despite compelling personal reasons to do so—I have never even
summoned the will to try very hard. It is as though my mind is convinced that
it has room for only one foreign language, that becoming proficient in another
language will inevitably mean losing the intimacy I worked so hard to attain
with French. Fragments of each language lie dormant and emerge unpre-
dictably. Strung together, I know enough of all these different languages to
muddle through, if I ever encounter a Japanese-German-Farsi speaker who
knows no English or French.

The story so far tells how I got to the French language, but getting to France
and French history was another matter. While all Anglophone Canadians are
required to study French, relations among English Canada, Quebec, and
France are complicated and ambiguous. The French I learned at school—and
later on at McGill University in Montreal—was metropolitan French, and the
accent we strove for was Parisian. With the exception of my professor at
McGill, none of my teachers was French. They ranged from the Québécois
Madame Boucher, to the Franco–Prince Edward Islander M. Gallant, to Anglophone Canadians of varying accent and proficiency. References to Quebec
or the French spoken there were absent, as far as memory serves. In high
school, we read Camus and Ionesco, not Gilles Archambault or Anne Hébert
(I had to Google Québécois authors for that line, since none came immediately
to mind). In my advanced French class at McGill, we began to learn some
French-Canadian French, with vocabulary lessons devoted to local slang and
fill-in-the-blank lyric sheets from Robert Charlebois and Gilles Vigneault.
McGill itself is an Anglophone institution, despite a 25 percent Francophone
enrollment. One could easily attend classes at McGill for four years without
speaking more than a few phrases in French.

My attraction to the French language, and my schooling in it, therefore did
not entail a strong relationship to Quebec. Although we all studied "French,"
my fellow students and I remained profoundly ignorant of Quebec's cultural

and linguistic heritage, even while living and studying in the province itself. This did not mean, however, that we learned anything significant about France. French was something you learned with the notion that it was good for you, good for the country (these were the years of Trudeau-style federalism and growing separatism in Quebec), and good for your career prospects. I studied the language for twelve years without aspiring to go to France or become an expert about the country. France had a particular kind of resonance in our understanding of what it meant to be Canadian, but this was a historical and abstract sense rather than a concrete tie to the actual place.

The first step toward France was the result of encounters with new teachers. At McGill, I chose a double major in English literature and European history. My highest aspiration, formed in the first few weeks of a compulsory class on literary theory, was to become a literary critic. It was 1983 and our professor was fresh from a Ph.D. at Yale under the renowned critic Harold Bloom. The way he talked about the "sublime" and the heady bewilderment of his introduction to Foucault sparked a desire to follow him to the theoretical heights. This dream was crushed when I received a C on my first writing assignment. I bitterly concluded that literary theory was for geniuses and that I had better stick to something safer, where dutiful plodding could achieve what my lack of brilliance could not. History was the obvious alternative.

At this point, two years into a three-year B.A. program, I encountered Professor John Hellman. His course on modern European cultural history introduced us to the idea that history could be as much about ideas and culture as people and events. When he talked about *mentalités,* or collective mentalities, and insisted on the historical significance of graveyards, emotions, and bodies, a new vision of history opened before me. He was a deeply inspiring teacher who showed me that history professors write and publish books. He was also the first passionate Francophile I encountered, and his love of France shone through the ostensibly European course material (a bias I have not resisted in my own teaching). I did not realize it at the time, but through him I became acquainted with the achievements of the famed *Annales* school of social and cultural history, and I was deeply impressed.

To that point, my university education had been desultory. Released from the intimacy of a small lab school, I was adrift at McGill. I did a minimum of work, and my professors rewarded my lackluster performance with their own indifference. John Hellman invited me to the weekly salon he held at his house; in my final year, he invited me to join his graduate seminar. These were deliciously terrifying experiences. My father was a professor, in fact a dean for almost thirty years, so I was familiar with the all-too-human nature of academics. Nonetheless, being invited to a professor's house to talk about ideas with grownups was a new experience. Attending a graduate seminar, where I could not nurse my hangover quietly in the back but would be expected to participate and perform at a new level, was another giant step. When the Princeton historian Natalie Zemon Davis visited campus, our assignment was to attend the lecture and write a critical review. Almost twenty years later, I still remember the outlines of her talk (from her work on the gift) and how moved I was by this introduction to the world of ideas. Finding that I could understand her points and come up with some kind of critique was a key moment of intellectual empowerment.

It was John Hellman who encouraged me to apply to graduate school in history and who guided me toward the programs to which I applied. At this point, however, a fateful irony took place. Given my mediocre first-year grades, my GPA was not particularly impressive. Professor Hellman came up with a devious plan to circumvent this problem. Do not apply to study modern Europe, he told me, the competition is too fierce and you won't get in. Apply instead for early modern Europe, where there is less competition and you'll have a much better shot. Once you get there, no one will care what you do and you can switch fields. I dutifully filled in the applications and tried my best to come up with a personal statement reflecting my interest in a period I had never studied beyond an introductory survey of Western Civilization.

Cornell University alone fell for my ruse, and even they were skeptical. I was the last student admitted in an overly large class. During my visit to the department that spring, the director of graduate studies was polite but discouraging. When the new class arrived that fall, we learned how chagrined the department was by our numbers. I sensed the underlying resentment that I had actually shown up. This was not a conducive climate for a change in my primary field. Moreover, when I encountered my putative advisor in early modern France, Steven Kaplan, I was taken so firmly on board that I did not dare to mention my *real* intellectual interests. Thus, my bluff was called and a budding twentieth-century intellectual historian became an early modernist.

At Cornell, I encountered the second *force majeure* in my intellectual development. In addition to shaping my mind in ways to which I cannot do justice here, Steven Kaplan imposed upon me a new relationship to France. He is well known in the profession as a Francophile's Francophile, a historian almost unparalleled in his intimate knowledge of France, his mastery of the language, and his love of the country. He made it clear from our first meeting that his students had to share this engagement with France. Our first meeting was in fact conducted in French: "*Alors, vous parlez français?*" "*Oui, au Canada nous sommes obligés d'étudier le français à l'école.*" "*Ça? Ce n'est pas du français.*" Despite this dismissal, my previous French studies served me well at Cornell.

That I could read the language at a high level helped justify my place in the large first-year class.

Under Steven Kaplan's guidance, I quickly developed a new and intense relationship with France. Going there, it became clear, was a top priority. In our first meeting, Professor Kaplan explained that I must visit France in the summer following my first year in the doctoral program and every subsequent summer. He also told me that to complete a dissertation with him I must spend at least two years undertaking archival research in France. Far from being disconcerted by this demand, I was pleased at having been assigned to go to Paris and then to return there as often as possible for as long as possible. (This still seems to me an incredibly good deal. Why wouldn't everyone want to be a French historian?) Potential financial impediments to carrying out his orders were dismissed. Staying home was not an option.

✝

In the summer of 1989, at the age of twenty-one, I embarked on my first trip to France, armed with a letter of introduction to the Bibliothèque nationale presenting me as a junior scholar with a potential dissertation topic. I had never been to Europe before, and my arrival at Charles de Gaulle was a revelation. After the all-night transatlantic flight I debarked from the airplane into a new world. What struck me as I emerged from the police control to wait for my luggage was the strangeness and difference of the entire environment. It was like an instant hit of a hallucinogenic drug: the heightened sensation of reality as each sense was bombarded with new impressions—a total body experience. The smell of Charles de Gaulle is unmistakable (disinfectant, tobacco, recycled air) and to this day remains the first sign that I have arrived in France. The sights were also brand-new and surprising: police with machine guns and dogs patrolling the airport; people lighting up in the baggage area under the "no smoking" signs; crowds of people waiting for their luggage, people who were clearly different in all sorts of ways: language, clothing, haircut, body shape, gesture, attitude. On the cab ride into Paris through the strengthening morning sun, I began to assimilate this new world and, in broken conversation with the driver, to find out how I could function in it.

I have flown into Charles de Gaulle perhaps thirty times since then, and I still experience the feeling of entering an entirely different environment. Leaving the plane, I look forward to the now-familiar shock and the rediscovery of the sights and smells I left behind. On that first trip, I fell hard for France. This passion has determined my professional and personal life and kept me coming back again and again. I spent that first summer in Paris doing some library work for Steve Kaplan and conducting research on what would become my dissertation topic, on seamstresses and their guilds in eighteenth-century France. I returned the next summer for my *"tour de France,"* a research trip that took me to Caen, Rouen, Bordeaux, Marseilles, and Lyons in six weeks of lonely, impoverished, and back-breaking travel with my laptop and worldly belongings gathered into a huge knapsack (yes, with a Canadian maple leaf attached). I was back in Paris in January 1991 to conduct research for my dissertation. I planned to stay for the obligatory two years but ended up staying until 1996, when I took up my current position at Urbana-Champaign. Having had the good fortune to fall in love in Paris and to lure my husband to Urbana, obligatory visits to in-laws and archives meant that, until the birth of my twin boys, we returned to Paris several times a year.

This repetition-compulsion raises the question of what I loved so much about France. Why did I not only fall in love with France but also become a complete French wannabe, so much so that I spent my first six months in the archives pretending to be French and resolutely ignoring the American scholars drinking coffee beside me in the foyer? I loved France in part because of that whole body experience. The apprehension of a completely different world made me want to know it and learn to act in it. I derived particular pleasure from my growing awareness of an elaborate system of etiquette—cultural knowledge—that was "natural" for French people and that I could learn, slowly and painfully but progressively. (This was often expressed to me in negative terms in the great French phrase: *"ça ne se fait pas."*) One marvelous introduction to these codes occurred when I visited a Franco-American friend in southwestern France and participated in the annual grape harvest, known as the *vendanges,* where my weak back (and spirit) earned the ridicule of my colleagues. The meals served for the hired pickers would have satisfied anyone's fantasy of the rustic French *terroir.* After an early morning breakfast of pâtés and cheeses consumed standing up in the kitchen, a long table was set for the huge midday meal. Hands and family sat down together, with the farmer at the head of the table. Each dish was served as an individual course, passed down the table, eaten, and then replaced. I had the usual problem learning to pace myself when I mistook the peas for a main course and tried to fill myself. The apogee of the meal came early for me, when the radishes were sent around and with a single gesture everyone seated at the table—young, old, male, female, worker, owner—took out a pocketknife and began peeling the radishes. I had no pocketknife; I did not know what to do with the butter that accompanied the radishes; I was baffled—and in heaven. This was culture, and like any ethnographer I wanted to immerse myself in it and crack its codes.

My mother left Japan in part to get away from a culture of rigid expectations and rules. I ended up fascinated and attracted by cultural codes and etiquettes. It may have something to do with a residual Japanese-ness that she passed on to us. More likely, it is the product of growing up half-Japanese, feeling slightly alienated from the dominant culture without having any real access to my mother's culture of origin. This outsider feeling drove me to study and interact with a foreign culture and then marry into yet another culture. It also gave me a predilection for the more formal culture of France compared to the United States. There is a thread between my attempts to understand French culture of the eighteenth century and my attempts to understand contemporary France. To the outsider that I am, many of the central values and ways of being remain similar. To experience the one is to better understand the other. I do not have an elaborate theoretical or historiographical apparatus to defend this feeling, but I am convinced that my understanding of contemporary France has helped immensely in my attempts to understand France in the past.

One aspect of French culture in particular impressed me: the emphasis on collective bonds and behavior. One of my first French friends, Emmanuelle, worked at the Bibliothèque nationale, and we often met for coffee breaks. I loved seeing her, but I was constantly baffled by the etiquette of drinking coffee with a friend in France. She found the each-pays-for-herself model—my standard North American approach to the matter—distasteful. That was not an enjoyable way for friends to drink coffee together. There was only one alternative—one buying for the other—but I seemed incapable of achieving it with the proper grace. I was always forgetting that she had paid last and then remembering at the last minute and announcing it was my turn, an announcement that she clearly found as distasteful as the American model we had abandoned. I gathered that we were supposed to spontaneously buy coffees for each other, not on a strictly alternating basis (which was as calculated and as lacking in sincerity as the pay-your-own-way model) but according to an affectionate whimsy that would over time work out to a rough and comradely equality. I did embrace the principle and its assumptions about sincerity, spontaneity, and the lack of calculation involved in true friendship. I was simply unable to perform it correctly.

My failure at this simple act of friendship revealed a lot about my Americanized take on human interactions. I contrasted Emmanuelle's ethos with the elaborate calculations surrounding any shared meal in the United States: I did not drink wine, you had a coffee, I had a starter but no main course, you a main course but no salad. When I came back from France and briefly tried to implement my new coffee etiquette, my friends and colleagues were so nonplussed that I quickly abandoned the experiment. It had nothing to do with affluence or background. True, Emmanuelle was the daughter of a Communist Party organizer, but I had the same difficulties going out for sushi with my friend Catherine, daughter of a French navy officer. The problem lay, I think, in an American discomfort with being in someone's debt, with being implicated in an unspoken, open-ended relationship in which someone else might be silently waiting for you to reciprocate. In short, everything Natalie Davis taught me in 1983 about the gift and the use of gifts to forge social relations was exactly what disturbed my American friends. Freedom, individuality, and transparency versus fraternity, mutuality, and unspoken bonds; I wasn't very skilled at practicing the second triad, but I was attracted by the generosity and the human values they represented.

This aspect of French culture was linked to the value placed on the social good in France. Sharing coffee was a personal version of a larger political principle: everyone should have a minimum of material security and dignity: everyone, likewise, is diminished by abandoning that goal. I had to acknowledge that the French were far from achieving this nirvana, but I admired the shared commitment to maintaining social bonds, the self-conscious opposition to an individualistic, market-driven culture. For me, the most joyous expression of this principle occurred in 1995 during the general strikes set off by the railway workers, who were protesting a raise in their retirement age. Most Parisians supported the strikes despite having to walk three hours to work. The atmosphere of carnival and solidarity during those days moved me deeply. Many observers believe, I know, that this dedication to the social welfare net dooms France to economic stagnation and that the country must adapt to modern capitalism or wither away. I do not know if this platitude of globalization is true, but I am sympathetic with the principles that resist it and seek another path. The coffee culture I encountered every day showed me that the values of community remained widespread despite the encroachment of American-style liberalism.

The gift relation's acceptance of ambiguity and complexity likewise struck me as related to the inherently grownup nature of French culture. As everyone knows, the French are not shocked by nudity or coarse language; they accept that people will do bad things, cheat, have sex, take their clothes off. The famous cynicism of the Gallic shrug is an acknowledgement of the *vie compliquée* that so many people lead. Part of this is an acceptance that conflict is an inevitable part of human relations. People will go on strike; it will be disagreeable and inconvenient for many; and yet, if this is the only way to defend one's rights, so be it. This grownup culture is one of self-restraint. Every time I drive to a strip mall in Urbana to load up the car with big cheap plastic things,

I think about the differences between America and France in terms of living space, notions of convenience, and attitudes to consumption. I know from experience that it is much easier to have three small children with a parking lot, super-stores, a minivan, and a backyard (which is why many French people want and use those things too). But I also admire people who know how to live in smaller spaces, without cars, with small refrigerators, and fewer but nicer things. Overall, I relish the French sense of dignity. At its worst those traits fall into the pomposity and stiffness ridiculed by detractors, but I would take those failings any day over the firestorm unleashed by Janet Jackson's nipple.

Part of my fondness for the "adultness" of French culture no doubt stems from the fact that I became a grownup in France. I lived there, with occasional trips home, from the age of twenty-two to twenty-eight. I learned during those years that comfort was not necessarily the supreme value of daily life. In America, I had accepted the dogma that comfort was natural and thus inherently superior. It was a shock to discover that many intelligent women routinely accepted discomfort (in shoes, deprived appetites, underwire bras, and so on) for appearances' sake and that I could not only learn how to do so but enjoy it too. I learned to wax and never shave, to eat steak and green beans rather than pasta, and to hold dinner parties with the best ingredients I could afford. I got my first great haircut in France, and it was as empowering as any other experience of my life.

Although this may sound like a step backward for an enlightened feminist, I do not really believe that it diminishes me as a woman to have absorbed these practices of femininity (whether I practice them daily in Urbana is another question). Moreover, the lessons I learned about being a woman in contemporary France helped me understand women's lives in the eighteenth century. The subject of my dissertation, after all, was seamstresses and their contribution to the intertwined cultures of appearances and femininity. Experiencing these cultures in my own body—in whatever attenuated and evolved form— was probably as important an apprenticeship as the one I undertook in the archives.

As my linguistic skills improved, I realized that I could be a different person in French. In English, I am as adverse to confrontation as one might expect from a Japanese-Canadian. Steve Kaplan used to exhort me to look people in the eyes when speaking to them. In French, I get into public arguments, I answer back to shopkeepers, and I use an expanded vocabulary to talk about emotions I would never admit to in English. One reason I enjoy speaking French is that I love the person I can become in French. After several years in France, I began to combine the words with the right gestures: the *"bof"* with the shrugged shoulders and pursed lips; the raised eyebrows, head cocked forward, and rotating wrist at the temple to accompany "*ça va pas?*" Having the right body movements and expressions enabled me to feel the emotions and attitudes that they conveyed. I was learning to be French from the outside in.

Much as I struggled to learn French, to learn about France and, at some level, to become French, my relationship to France is, in some ways, not really about the French. First, my "France" is limited almost entirely to Paris. Apart from short provincial research trips and regular vacations in the south of France, the Hexagon for me is essentially Paris. Moreover, my desire to be in France has as much to do with the other cultures I experience there as it does with the native one. When I arrive in Paris, the first place I head to is not a little bistro but the Opéra neighborhood and the most authentic bowl of ramen noodles I have found outside of Japan. That is the meal I crave when I think of Paris. My second favorite Parisian meal is the rice and Persian stew at my in-laws' house, where you will find the best *tadig* (crispy rice crust) in the world. Before I shacked up in the tony seventh *arrondissement,* my Parisian neighborhood was working-class Belleville, which combines a new China-town with an older North African Jewish and Muslim population. My multi-cultural experience of France reflects the realities of the country's urban life, and I am glad to have been part of it.

Along those lines, one of the central questions for me these days is not so much "why France?" but "what France?" Like others, I am taking stock of the American historical profession's current fascination for transnational and global history. My department, like so many, has been seized by enthusiasm for these topics. Our graduate students' dissertations address themes in transnational, global, or postcolonial history, just as in my day they tended to speak to gender, class, or labor history (usually all three). I have tried to edu-cate myself. In the last few years I have joined a faculty seminar on globaliza-tion, co-taught a course on "Universal History and its Discontents" with a South-Asianist colleague, and founded a reading group on "Pre-Modern Global History." I am very sympathetic with the move to view history from non-European perspectives and to uncover the ways Europe was shaped by its colonies, but I have yet to work through what this means for my own research and writing. How this will shape my current book—on credit, fashion, and sex in eighteenth-century France—remains to be seen. Will I need to visit new archives and acquaint myself with new techniques, new historiographies, even new languages?

These questions challenge my Francophilia by asking me to reconsider what is French. Studying French history always felt different to me than studying Germany or Britain. For German historians of any period, the hor-rendous Nazi era forces a certain distancing from their object of study. My friends in British history—to judge from their stories—experienced life in modern Britain as dismal and were often motivated in their study of Britain by anti-imperialist politics. For French historians, this relationship has more often been characterized by love and desire than a wish to explain or judge. We experience France, I think, as a seduction of the mind and senses; we wish to identify with it and abandon our American selves. It will be a loss to give that up and to reposition myself as a historian of a more complex and equivocal identity. My slowness to do so—shared by many of my colleagues, I suspect—reflects and reinforces France's own difficulties in confronting the legacies of colonialism and, until recently, World War II. While American historians of contemporary France have been speaking out more on these issues, it is probably time for those of us who work in earlier periods to reassess French identity and our own identification with it. I am not sure what that entails, but it strikes me as the next step toward growing up in and with France. I am looking forward to seeing what my own children—products of a love affair between a Japanese-Canadian-American woman and an Iranian-French man—will make of this and what new perspectives they will bring to their inevitable love of France and the French.

CHAPTER 16

✺ Between Douai and the U.S.A

Todd Shepard

It was during my first flight across the Atlantic that I abandoned all allegiance
to the Republican Party. It was 1985, and I was on the way to spend my junior
year of high school as an exchange student in France. The trip from suburban
Rochester, New York, had already been eventful, starting at the airport with
an early morning sighting of the rap group the Fat Boys, then my first ever
bird's eye view of New York City—my first actual visit would have to wait
until college—and finally meeting the other sixteen- to nineteen-year olds
who would soon spread out among host families across France. In midflight,
after taking out my contact lenses, I realized that I had not brought my glasses,
which meant I could barely see. I also, however, could not sleep, and so I began a long conversation with a girl from Portland about politics, Ronald Reagan, Nicaragua, El Salvador, abortion, the environment. I think it started with
a comic book she showed me, one wickedly critical of our president. As we
talked, I began to realize that it wasn't just that I disagreed with Reagan's policies on all of these questions: they indicated a specific way of seeing the world.
I began to think that I didn't share his vision, and something else clicked into
place as well: there were other ways of understanding the world. My previous
admiration for Reagan turned, with adolescent zeal, into dislike. During the
school year that followed, I was lucky enough to have many similar revelations, all of which followed the simple plotline that things were not as I had
presumed and that there were other ways to think about them. Indeed, I remember the brief and intense year of my French youth as the crucible in which

I changed from boy to man. Perhaps this is why I have found that studying the history of late twentieth-century France and its empire allows me to understand better questions that matter to me, whether about the United States, France, or life in general.

Before I became an exchange student, France was not a topic I thought much about, although I do have childhood memories of reading many Babar books and maybe even having the Madeleine series read to me. My parents had never been there, or anywhere in Europe for that matter. I now know that my father's parents loved France, something I was not aware of then. My father, who had quit college to join the army and then went to work for our town's highway department, kept a protective distance from his rather Waspy family, gently mocking their lack of Middle American mannerisms. He referred to his older sister as "Ay-dl," rather than Adèle, for example. I grew up in a suburban subdivision of nearly identical ranch and raised-ranch houses. We spent vacations either camping with my maternal grandparents in St. Petersburg, Florida, or around the string of major amusement parks that interrupted the long drive down from upstate New York to the Gulf Coast. Television played a far greater role than books, museums, or films, although my mother, who was a teacher, encouraged my love of reading. My literary interests were squarely focused on adventure and, slightly later, science fiction novels, a training in generic convention that prepared me better, I suspect, to become a historian than a literary scholar.

By the time I reached high school, I was a fine student and a loner, decent at French, particularly strong in "social studies," not so excited about math or science. I had the enormous benefit of attending an excellent public high school. Due to a promotion with a residency requirement, my father had moved us from the most racially diverse of the middle- to lower middle-class suburbs that surrounded Rochester to the richest suburb. This meant moving all of two hundred yards and also that neighbors whom we'd known for years jokingly began to call my dad the "Earl of Pittsford." I can't judge the qualitative differences in the education I enjoyed and that which my former classmates from the other side of Townline Road received. I do know, however, that the difference in possibilities those schools offered us was enormous. In my new school, we were all going to college, preferably a private one. To realize that plan, every element of upper middle-class life was made available to us: a top-ranked soccer team seemed among the most important, although the college-level courses, the guidance counselors, the funds for student activities, and the great teachers surely helped as well. Instead of sports or other extracurricular activities I mainly did my own thing, although I was very interested in politics and in the world as a place where the United States and its leaders faced many challenges.

My understanding of politics seems to me to exemplify a certain mid-1980s Middle America, an autobiographical reference that I have often constructively compared to France or remembered with stunned bemusement since the early 1990s when hearing fellow academics discuss the "political correctness" that supposedly controls our country. Nearly everyone around my family voted Republican. Many were "Reagan Democrats"; some, in my father's family and among the people I met in high school, were well-off and voted with their pocketbooks; many others were suspicious of New York City and its liberal elites, a feeling particularly prevalent in upstate New York. My parents voted Republican, too, although not consistently. My dad had taken from his family background and his work experience a deep distrust of unions and welfare programs. Over time, however, this was joined with a usually muted, although occasionally ironic, resentment of the very well-off townspeople he served, who constantly subjected him and his colleagues to a thinly veiled disdain for the manual work they did. I came to some awareness of what was going on in the world in the 1970s, when I watched Richard Nixon fly away in disgrace from the White House and clips of fighting in Vietnam on the television. What most caught my attention were the hostages in Iran and, far more directly, the oil crisis.

It was really in the early 1980s that I started to think in political terms, however. I saw what was going on as an exciting renaissance in American self-assuredness. It was morning again in America! I adored Ronald Reagan, was proud to be an American, and thrilled at the flag-waving that had marked the 1980 Winter Olympics and characterized the renewed Republican Party. At the same time, the anti-abortion crusade didn't make sense to me, and a report I did on the Nicaraguan situation made me mighty skeptical about U.S. policy there. Still, what made me a Reaganite was more than my upbringing: it was my intense attachment to a certain form of identification as an American and to very visible unifying signs of that identity.

Along with my understanding of politics, it was my relationship to religion that my encounter with France most changed. From the age of twelve on, as I began the usual intense contemplation of what death meant to me, I did a fair amount of Bible reading and participated actively in our church youth group. My religious enthusiasm was suitably mainstream (we were Episcopalians) but sustained enough that I planned on becoming a minister. In suburban Rochester, Christianity was fairly omnipresent but in the background. It provided nursery schools and softball leagues, organized Sunday plans, and, at least in my neighborhood, allowed children to sort themselves into groups, although I wouldn't say that the differences among Catholics, Methodists, and Lutherans seemed that great to us. I had encountered more aggressive versions of religious faith, however, at the first summer camp I ever attended, at age ten. Unbeknownst to my parents, Camp Li-Lo-Li (Life-Love-Light) was run by evangelical Christians. At the end of my time there I took the opportunity to proclaim that I was born-again during a campfire meeting, right after someone explained how the star Wormwood would soon crash into the Earth. But that I had forgotten to bring my glasses stunted my enthusiasm. Not being able to focus made it difficult to get caught up in the films the organizers showed us about the coming Rapture or to participate in the nightly campwide competition to identify the Bible passages flashed on a large screen. Had I won the competition (and a ride on a hot-air balloon), perhaps my faith would have withstood later challenges.

Although I highlight my engagement with religion and politics, my desire to go abroad coalesced against a background of teenage boredom rather than deep reflection. What sparked it was meeting the two exchange students, Anna from Sweden, and Anja from West Germany, who spent a year with our next-door neighbors and attended high school in my old town. Anna, in particular, not only shared my enthusiasm for new wave and "alternative" music but brought news from across the sea of all sorts of groups I had never heard of. She was a DJ at a local noncommercial radio station, taking full advantage of the opportunities she never would have had at home. The only thing I knew about Sweden was that, because of socialism, they only had seven colors of paint to choose from, information my friend Mark had learned from the "elders" at the Mormon temple his family attended. Anna let me know that this was a ridiculous claim, but she was far more interested in discussions of pop culture than in political debates or explanations of social democracy.

My friendship with Anna and Anja was the first clear indication that being interested in something a bit out of the mainstream, in this case music, could create bonds with other people. It was also an incitation to do what they had done, and go abroad. Since I had taken four years of French, I applied to go to France, but I was told that there were no spots left, so I chose Sweden. I had already sent a French version of the required letter to my eventual host family, however, and apparently it was better than most. It contained the key information that I did not like seafood, although I had decided I would show how open-minded I was by not including the other foods I couldn't stand. My file was sent along to France, rather than Sweden, and I was mighty pleased. I began to read up on different parts of the country and could not decide if I would prefer to stay with a family along the Riviera or in Paris, although the country seemed to have natural wonders galore. When I received a letter from my future host family, I learned that they lived just outside of Douai, which I had never heard of, but, as the map made clear, was far from the Mediterranean, the mountains, and Paris and, I learned, was blessed with constant cloudy weather. In early August 1985, I left home for my first trip to any foreign country besides Canada.

🕸

My first weeks in France were spent at a small *château* in the Loire Valley, which served as the dormitory and classrooms for our orientation session. Our teachers introduced us to French food, cognac, and the local region. The current events lesson that shocked us the most concerned the rise to prominence of Jean-Marie Le Pen and his Front National (FN). The FN had emerged as a force to be reckoned with in 1984, during the mayoral election in Dreux and in the subsequent European parliamentary elections. It seemed obvious to all of us that this party was racist, similar to the type of racism that we Americans talked about so much and claimed to reject, and maybe worse. As we wandered the countryside one day, a group of us ripped down a poster with Le Pen's image. Our instructors, a group of twentysomethings with a unisex look that mixed long hair and odd-looking eyeglasses (and an amazing ability to dance like 1950s rock and rollers), cheered us on. All of my new friends seemed to come from liberal Democratic families, and on more than one occasion we talked about "what was wrong with America," meaning Reagan and his supporters. I was a quick study. Our discussions focused mainly, however, on the surrounding area. Located between Blois and Amboise, the site was magnificent, both naturally and, of course, because of the *châteaux*. We visited François I's castle, Leonardo da Vinci's workshop, and the cave homes, some still occupied, that had been built into chalk cliffs along the Loire. The strangest trip was an overnight visit to a Buddhist monastery located, of course, in a *château*. Meditation hurt, and it involved getting hit with large sticks. It was an idyllic two weeks.

My arrival in Douai was the real beginning of my encounter with France. There were no Americans, I was taken in by a family I knew little about, and I found myself in an environment that, far from the Loire Valley, was heavily industrialized. As would quickly become clear to me, the area around Douai actually was more postindustrial, since I arrived just a year after the major local mine had shut down, part of a series of closings that began in 1982 and led eventually to the closure of all local mines. Douai had been, until then, the capital of France's northern coal-mining zone, and signs of this were everywhere.

This heritage was what charmed me about Douai and the much-maligned North of France. As Martin, Jeannette, and their daughters Sheila and San-drine (names of my French host families have been changed) drove me to their home in the adjoining suburb, my shock at learning that Sin-le-Noble had a Communist mayor was matched by my amazement at the endless rows of identical brick houses, the *corons* that mining companies had built for their employees, the regular presence of large slag heaps, and the very odd look of the water towers. I found it all very beautiful. After a small party with a ba-roquely decorated chocolate cake, my memory of the evening that followed involves television. We saw *Top 50,* a music video show on the cable channel Canal+, followed by a documentary entitled *Renaud in the Land of the Sovi-ets,* which followed a well-known French singer and Communist Party mem-ber on his visit to a festival in Moscow, and finally what the girls announced to me was a "pornographic" film. It was on a regular public television station, so I guess there was some female nudity. Although the music videos allowed us to bond, the last two programs, in retrospect, were a far better prediction of the months to come. Renaud, whose fairly nasal voice and folk-singer ways at first led me to think that he was to Bob Dylan as Johnny Hallyday is to Elvis Presley, quickly became a favorite of mine. He was deeply political, his lyrics were beautifully written, and several of his songs were about the Nord (he was from nearby Lille) and the so-called *ch'timis* who lived and worked there. His music still evokes the highly romanticized image I have of that region and its working-class culture.

Living with a host family, of course, was different than anything I had known before. The father was a kindergarten teacher. He took care of the shopping, the cooking, and much of the housework as well, a reversal of my family's more *Leave It to Beaver* household, which did not trouble me. The mother was a nurse, and from her I learned that in France, doctors (and nurses) did make house calls. I was impressed. She was constantly on the run, from patient to patient, from pharmacy to clinic. Martin was of Polish descent, as his grandfather had come to France to work in the mines, while Jeannette, as she later proudly told me, was "one hundred percent French." They seemed to me younger and hipper than my parents, they ate well, with lots of *sauce béchamel,* and they became the first people I ever despised. More important, they became the first people I knew who hated me.

I'll reduce the reasons to politics: they loved Jean-Marie Le Pen and the FN. They were generally right-wing and remained marginally Gaullist, fans of Paris mayor and neo-Gaullist party leader Jacques Chirac. They also had a statuette of Napoleon. What drew them to Le Pen, however, was racism, which I had never encountered at this level before. My first weekend there (before going upstairs to watch Renaud and the film), I had a long discussion about colonialism with Martin. I had made some surely uninformed comment about the French colonial empire in Africa, and I was wholly unprepared for the ringing defense of empire that followed. For many minutes I remained convinced that my poor French was at the heart of our misunderstanding. Yet when he responded to a criticism I made by insisting that it was not racist to recognize that people from Africa were naturally lazy and that people from North Africa could not help being thieves and liars, I opted to slide out of the argument, to agree to disagree. Over the next several months, I was treated to more and more examples of the same mindset. Martin would explain how the mothers of his pupils who were of North African origin were so pleased to finally have their children under the authority of his firm hand, even as he mocked their accents and their origins. "Arabs" were the people he and his wife really disliked, Algerians in particular. Douai had a significant number of *Maghrébins,* so they had ample opportunity to express their disdain. Blacks, who had such a central role in my own limited understanding of racism's targets, came off slightly better in their descriptions. They claimed that they were not anti-Semitic, that they would be proud to have one of their daughters marry a Jew. Given their Polish family name, the anti-immigrant aspect of their positions seemed strange to me. It dawned on me, however, that Jeannette did not dislike Martin's father because of his leftist politics: she wanted to make sure that her daughters were only exposed to things French, and Martin's family was too Polish. (It only became clear to me why they had welcomed me, a foreigner, into their home when they dragged me to see the unrecognized film gem *Rambo II: La Mission*—the dubbed version of *Rambo: First Blood*—in which Sylvester Stallone embodied the type of American bonhomie abroad that they had expected I would bring.) What I realized as well, thanks to their hatred of me, was how their racism was structured.

It was over the Christmas holidays that I finally asked my parents to get me out of there, shortly before the Kossoczaks asked the program to remove me. I called right after Jeannette had sought to disrupt my first attempt to ski by trying to run me down. Still convinced that I understood French as poorly as I spoke it, she announced at dinner that she was only rude to people on the slopes if they tried to hurt her family. Jeannette and Martin's anger that I had beaten them to the punch was outdone only by their consternation that I wanted to stay in France. Over the next several weeks, as we waited for the organization to find a new host family, they repeated how they hated me because they knew that I hated France and was out to hurt their family. This was where my first days in their home assumed such importance. The key moment seemed to be my second day there, which was also the first day of the new school year, during which I had recounted to my host sisters' friends that we had watched a "pornographic" film. As I remember it, everyone laughed, including Sheila and Sandrine. Months later, their parents brandished the story as clear proof that I was hell-bent on attacking their family. It turned out that everything I had done or said was not just wrong but an effort to demean them. When I had remarked that it was strange for me to see French rather than American flags, they remembered an intentional insult to France. When I had offered them a jar of peanut butter, which I had read didn't exist in France, they took it as a jibe at French cuisine. Every comparison I had made between my life in the United States and my new life in France was taken as an implicit criticism of France and of them. It would be a while before I learned what binary thinking was and how it demands hierarchies. My encounter with the Kossoczak family, however, offered me an early lesson in how it worked. Things could not be different: difference could only mean "one bad, one good"; when it concerned identity, the group you belonged to determined how you thought.

Living in Douai, however, offered me many more immediate and more pleasant chances to grow up and think differently. This was particularly the case with religion. I felt very little complicity with my two host sisters, yet I will never forget the shock I felt when Sheila responded to some comment I made invoking Jesus with a dismissive "There is no God." Like my experience on the flight from JFK to Charles de Gaulle, I was confronted with a certainty that I had never encountered. I think that I stopped believing right then, since her comment just made so much sense to me. Even today, whenever I try to explain to French friends the level of religiosity that characterizes so much of the United States, or wonder how my best students in Oklahoma could be so sure that nobody believes in Darwin anymore, I think back to how foreign, in the sense of truly strange, it was for me at sixteen to hear an affirmation so distinct from what I knew. To complete my lesson in a certain French approach to religion, Sheila's parents once explained to me, on the way to a baptism, that they found it rather annoying that they couldn't attend the local Catholic Church—not because they were atheists, but because it had been taken over by "communist" priests. I was secretly pleased. While the French Communist Party and its leader, Georges Marchais, never tempted me, the other key insight I got from my time in Douai concerned class. If I continue to find that American understandings of race and racism are very useful in thinking about late twentieth-century French history, I know that the attention to class that I began to develop while living in the collapsing economy of the close-knit Nord shapes my view of America. The effects of the mine closings were obvious, although little discussed. The giant public high school I attended, for example, was filled with kids from throughout the region, most of whom were not so well off, with many from immigrant backgrounds, and unemployment was a regular part of their family situation. Beyond the raw data I saw all around me, it was teachers who channeled my perception of how class mattered, especially my history teacher (reputed to be a Communist). This cast the lack of opportunity on the side of Townline Road I had left behind and the incredible school facilities in Pittsford in a new light.

The other obvious difference from my American high school was that learning was the only thing that took place in my *lycée,* with no extracurricular activities. Even the gym classes took place off school grounds. I was impressed that the school, located in a working-class milieu, not only encouraged my academic interests but also conveyed how much they were connected to a larger vision of culture. I was placed in the same "literary track" (*première A2*) as my host sister. Although my math and science skills never recovered (if in the Third Republic, history was the most important discipline taught in secondary schools, in the late Fifth Republic math skills determined your place, and everyone in A2 was presumed to be very weak in math), I enjoyed the classes in French literature and French history enormously. They were taught in such a different style, and taken much more seriously, than I was accustomed to. I was moved when the principal walked in to announce to us his great joy that Claude Simon, a writer unknown to me, had won the Nobel Prize in Literature.

In mid-January 1986, I left Douai to stay with another family, the Lantelmes, who lived in the small village of Pélussin, in the département of the Loire, right above the Rhône River. Pélussin, which was perched on the slopes of the highest mountain in the *Massif Central,* and its surrounding area were stunning. Robert Lantelme had retired there with his somewhat younger wife, Miriam, and their two children Laurent, age fifteen, and Stéphanie, age twelve. Robert was unlike anyone I had ever met. He was larger than life and quickly became (and remained) my idol. He had been born in a very poor family in Lyons, which he had left in order to flee from the "draft" of young men the collaborationist government at Vichy had sent to work in Germany during World War II. Robert was very proud to have been in the *maquis,* although he never claimed that his resistance had entailed much more than hiding out. After the war, he had joined the French Army and served in what were still the French colonies of Côte d'Ivoire and Sénégal. When he returned, he began a career that culminated with the ownership of one of the largest art galleries in Lyons. He had become quite rich. What most impressed me, though, were his radicalism and his attachment to culture. He was a committed Socialist, proud that the first "people's" theater in France had been founded near

Lyons and eager to get into political fights with his wife's relatives, all of them, he told me, so "*bourgeois.*" Robert could be described as an "autodidact," who had little formal education but read everything he could and still tried to get his hands on more. As the French use it, the term carries a smirking disdain, clear in books like Jean-Paul Sartre's *Nausea* or Marc Fumaroli's *Cultural State,* so I prefer to identify him with the more laudatory American term "self-made man." It was Robert who introduced me to his favorite novel, John Steinbeck's *Grapes of Wrath,* and who encouraged my love of *la chanson française,* from Edith Piaf to the more contemporary Renaud and Serge Gainsbourg. Robert admired Gainsbourg's daring and willingness to shock as much as his talent. He taught me how to drink wine, particularly the Côte Rôtie that was cultivated in the nearby valley, and the family's large garden and chicken pen, along with cheeses from the local goat herders, provided the basics for Miriam's cooking. To please them, I even agreed to eat a seafood dish. I loved it.

Under Robert's tutelage, I became an ardent supporter of the Mitterrand government, which had been in power for five years and, in the spring of 1986, was confronted with legislative elections. With friends I plastered posters warning "*Au secours, la droite revient!*" ("Help! The Right is Coming Back!") and read up on the Left's accomplishments. On the radio show that I co-hosted, we mainly played music (our theme song was the Dream Syndicate's "Life in a Northern Town") but reminded our listeners that the Left had made independent radio stations possible. I watched the young prime minister Laurent Fabius, whom the Kossoczaks had despised, savage Jacques Chirac in a televised debate. With the Lantelmes, I was relieved that the Socialists, despite losing, didn't do so poorly. This was in large part due to the introduction of proportional voting, a change that also allowed numerous representatives of the FN to enter the National Assembly. I, however, was sure that Mitterrand's strategy would marginalize the FN and allow him to dominate the right-wing parliament with which he now had to "cohabitate." The second belief turned out to be correct. To this day I remain fascinated with François Mitterrand, despite his responsibility for a number of horrible things (his role in allowing the Rwandan genocide to take place, most particularly). Although most of my French friends see him as the great betrayer of the Left and left-wing values, he was my introduction to the possibility of a left-wing government. I was amazed at the policies his governments had tried to put into place, even those he later abandoned, which were so alien to the faith in the markets that dominated discussion in the United States at the time and even more so now. Mostly, I admit, I liked that he knew how to win, how to beat the Right.

I have returned regularly to France since that high school year. I spent a sophomore semester of college in Paris, where I took classes that, among other things, introduced me to cinema as an art form, Nietzsche and Sartre, structuralist linguistics, and May 1968, which apparently had changed the lives of all my professors. Having lived through the defeat of Dukakis, I was pleased that Mitterrand had crushed Chirac to win a second term. When I got back to the States, however, I thought far more about poststructuralism, cultural studies, and post-identity politics. By junior year, I had become active in ACT UP/ NY and the newly formed group Queer Nation. I planned to go to graduate school in American history, to explore the role of class in constructions of sexual and gender identities—or something like that. I was told that, given my background, I might make a stronger case for acceptance in French history. So I decided to come up with a French topic and quickly realized both that I would rather spend my research time in France than anywhere in the United States and that my new topic, on the Algerian war as a "French revolution," allowed me to address all of the questions about identity, difference, and universalism that had made me want to pursue my studies in the first place. It took slightly longer to see the obvious: how closely the project was tied to the experiences I had gone through and the people I had met during my high school years.

My memories of my first year in France are my compass for how unexpected information, intense discussion, and encounters with people who are different can change how one thinks and can also do the opposite: confirm reassuring presumptions. This double-edged lesson, above all, anchors my love of history as method, how I read archival documents and use theoretical and historiographical writings as prods to remain wide-eyed rather than dead certain. It was, of course, American examples and scholarship that sparked my research on how race, gender, and sexuality shaped government institutions and public debates in late twentieth-century France. In my attention to such questions as how the French responded to the Algerian Revolution by defining Algerians out of the nation, debates among American academics and activists about the limits of identity politics as well as the effects of racial thinking helped me conceptualize what was at stake. My work has allowed me to think through key similarities between France and the United States, similarities to which most French scholars pay little attention: for instance, parallels between the ways that certain differences (homosexuality after 1945, Algerian "Muslims" in 1962) find their way into law. With other developments, however, French history reveals ways of doing and imagining that, for me, are essential to distinguish from lessons drawn from American history. This includes the more nuanced roles that race plays over time in French institutions but also the different possibilities and limits that universalist ideologies (republicanism most especially) have offered certain types of people in both countries, whether workers, women, racial "others," or queers. These dual concerns drew my attention to the important fact that all Algerians did have full French citizenship rights between 1958 and 1962, before the French Republic took them away; the surprising realization that France had "affirmative action"–style policies before the United States (policies that later disappeared); or the ways that questions of homosexuality and understandings of masculinity became intertwined with debates about race in postcolonial France.

At this point in my life, with one book done, I no longer feel like my work simply responds to what shocked me at the Kossoczak's or even the inspiration I drew from Robert Lantelme's dinnertime dissertations. More recent conversations and discoveries now structure the questions I ask. It is no surprise to me, however, that among the relationships that I still find most meaningful—of love, friendship, or intellectual and political camaraderie—many began in France. I do not believe that this is just because Paris is so beautiful or because good wine and food make conviviality easy. My transatlantic journeys convince me that the questions that French-American encounters raise remain compelling to think about as well as resistant to easy answers. They are fine grounds on which to pursue deep personal connections as well as engaged scholarship.

Afterword

Roger Chartier
(translated by Arthur Goldhammer)

The question that Laura Lee Downs and Stéphane Gerson put to the sixteen American and Canadian historians who contributed to this volume was a terribly simple one: "Why France?" Nothing could be easier, it might seem, than to explain how a foreign country became the focal point of a scholar's research and thus a place to visit often and in which to reside for extended periods of time. A simple question, then, but a supremely difficult one to answer. Illustrious predecessors in the genre had bequeathed powerful images: on the one hand, nostalgia for a France that no longer exists—a country that was only yesterday the France of the 1950s, of Inspector Maigret's investigations, of Marcel Carné's films, of the songs of Prévert and Kosma; on the other hand, the enduring mythology of the American in Paris, the frequenter of cafés and smoker of Gauloises or Gitanes, who becomes a genuine intellectual by fleeing the prevailing conformity back home. Wisely, our authors kept these facile clichés at arm's length. To write as they have written, they had to sift through countless memories and experiences, hopes and heartbreaks.

My country does not emerge from their stories unscathed. Its functionaries are merciless, its citizens often surly and arrogant, its provinces boring, its capital unfriendly. The French historical profession comes off better, on the whole: of the various guilds encountered, it is not the worst. It is worth noting, however, that three of the essays mention no French historian, while eight mention the names of no more than four attentive and helpful French colleagues. Only those historians who knew France in the 1950s tell of a more generous welcome and cite more than fifteen names. As Norbert Elias wrote of his months of exile in Paris in 1933 and 1934: "I loved France, I loved Paris, and that is why I was so sad to see that no Frenchman invited me to visit his home. This is something they do not do." Reading the stories of the American and Canadian historians collected in this volume, one has the clear sense that, but for a few exceptions, this bad habit persists virtually unchanged to this day.

With this in mind, it is easy to understand why a number of these writers strenuously reject the identity of "professional Francophile" and profess an ambivalent, neurotic relationship with France and the French—a relationship more given to criticism than to passionate enthusiasm. It would clearly be false to the spirit of this book to suggest that the answer to the question "Why France?" is, "Because the French are odious and the country is detestable." Declarations of love are not lacking, and in some cases it is love at first sight; more often, though, it is a love that was slow to develop and matured with time, in the course of agreeable and enthralling discoveries of places, customs, and people that, all things considered, were not without a certain charm. Few, however, emulate Richard Cobb in claiming to have forged a second identity in France, and those who do are apt to judge their second homeland as harshly as their first.

Another pitfall that awaited our contributors was "the autobiographical illusion," that is, the assumption that what were in fact contingent choices were somehow necessary and that what was in fact a shared experience was somehow irreducibly individual. It is not easy for what has been called "ego history" to incorporate the collective dimension of experience; biographical narrative has little use for life's randomness. Rationalization of choices and first-person narration are implicit in the exercise. Fortunately, however, some of these writers chose the more arduous path of attempting an objective account, even to the point of refusing to write in the first person, while others (including some from the first group) attributed their decision to work on French history to pure chance, to their knowledge of French, or to the impossibility of choosing some other country, rather than to any irrepressible Francophilia. Even when the choice is explained after the fact by a need to satisfy some desire for history or to recover a severed or hidden family past, it is not the real or supposed identity of France that is at issue.

Even in this respect, however, we must take care not to exaggerate. In the context of the war in Vietnam (mentioned in half the essays), the student revolts of 1968, the assassinations of Martin Luther King and Robert Kennedy, a certain idea of France as a nation of revolution and resistance retained its force as a possible alternative. Seven of the sixteen contributors to this volume made their first trip to France between 1968 and 1970, and though not all of them were moved by memories of the taking of the Bastille in 1789, the Commune of Paris in 1871, the "Front populaire" in 1936, or the Liberation of Paris in 1945, some crossed the Atlantic in the hope of discovering the fatherland of "the rights of man." Disillusionment came later.

Part of the disappointment came from the feeling that French historians did not acknowledge or were perhaps even unaware of the work of their American colleagues, a source of sadness and bitterness. It is difficult for me to judge whether this perception is accurate or not. During the 1960s and 1970s, the period of my apprenticeship in the profession, my teachers (Daniel Roche at the École Normale Supérieure de Saint-Cloud and Denis Richet at the Sorbonne and later the École des Hautes Études en Sciences Sociales) were always interested in, and showed respect for, books and articles published by American and other non-French historians, who were often warmly received whenever they came to Paris. I tried to follow their example in my own courses, seminars, research projects, and reviews. As can be seen from the generally quite favorable reception afforded to the work of any number of the contributors to this volume, my attitude was far from unusual. Nevertheless, it is plausible that some French historians, whether out of neglect or arrogance, presented the image of a profession not well versed in foreign languages and keen to defend its turf, including its archives and its nation's past, against foreign interlopers. It is therefore difficult to offer any overall judgment of the way in which American works about France were read (if they were read). To do so would require a careful evaluation of the reviews published not only in scholarly journals but also in newspapers and weekly magazines as well as attention to offers of visiting professorships, course syllabi, and bibliographies. Whatever the results of such an investigation might be, however, the fact remains that wounds inflicted early in the careers of certain scholars would remain indelible.

The lure of the *Annales* school is less apparent than one might have imagined. To be sure, seven authors explicitly allude to their reading, often enthusiastic, of Lucien Febvre, Marc Bloch, and Fernand Braudel, but one contributor proclaims his immunity to such influence, and the others (particularly the youngest) ignore the "*école*" and its masters. The perfect balance between those who chose areas of research favored by the *Annales* (economic history, social history, cultural history) and those who preferred areas less familiar to the several generations of (real or supposed) "*Annalistes*" shows clearly that there was a real connection (but one whose importance should not be exaggerated) between those historians who chose France and the most visible school of French historiography. Much the same can be said about chronological preferences. Half of the contributors chose to specialize in what the

French call "contemporary history," that is, the nineteenth and twentieth centuries, while the other half chose periods more thoroughly explored by the medieval and early modern historians of the *Annales*. One might object that this sample of sixteen historians is not representative and that such a rudimentary statistical evaluation, a pale reminder of the heyday of serial history, is not to be taken seriously. Granted. But imagining in my mind other groups of sixteen, chosen with a similar concern for a balance between generations, I come to a similar conclusion. Compared with the history of France as written by French historians, the history of France as written by American historians is more focused on the least ancient past.

More striking still is the interest shown, and not only by the youngest of these writers, in a France that the vast majority of French historians until recently neglected or ignored. More than half of the essays deal with the multicultural France stemming from immigration. This theme appears in a variety of ways: in memories of encounters with everyday racism, in the anxious or bitter discovery that the fatherland of the rights of man was not welcoming to all, and in the focus of research, be it the colonial past, present-day tensions in various communities, or the limitations and failures of the secular and obligatory Republic. Today, of course, we are well aware that without the contribution of American and Canadian historians of France, the history of Vichy would not be what it is. Several of the essays collected here demonstrate that from their vantage point, which combined intimacy with distance, it became possible to see realities that we French could not or would not recognize.

We also find, in several of the contributions, harsh (or perhaps, depending on one's point of view, lucid) judgments of another lost France: the France that exported "French Theory," with its intellectual fashions, "master thinkers," and great historians. The most Francophile of our writers are not the least eager to paint a picture of decline and to describe the new provincialism of a France that has ignored the "linguistic turn," "gender," "queer theory," and "agency." The very absence of satisfactory French translations for any of these terms is a clear indication of French blindness when it comes to the latest transatlantic fashions. I am not in the best position to judge the accuracy of this diagnosis. It is nevertheless an important indicator of a changed attitude toward the country chosen as an object of study—a change fraught with disenchantment, criticism, and nostalgia.

Several of the contributors accordingly seek to relate their interest in the history of France to some larger intellectual project. For some, the French case serves as a laboratory for studying problems that are in no way specifically French. For others, the history of France is to be seen in a European context. And for still others, recent interest in postcolonial history means that French identity must be seen in the perspective of a global history. Breaking down the traditional frameworks of French history (that of the nation-state and that of the regional monograph) in this way has without a doubt yielded great intellectual benefits, but it is not without danger for the future of French history in American universities. The editors of this volume are not the only ones to ask, "Why France?" Department chairs and deans in defining new teaching positions are asking it. There is no question that in recent years their answers have tended to favor other kinds of history or other ways of dividing history than those based on national divisions.

Some may deplore this development, but I am inclined to share the hopes of several of the contributors, who see it as an opportunity to reconsider specific features of France's history and experience in a broader geographical or thematic context. In recent years, it seems to me, this broadened perspective has superseded the implicit or explicit comparison between the two republics born at the end of the eighteenth century. To be sure, the parallel between France and the United States is a recurrent theme in this volume, invoked both to explain why a particular writer chose to study French history and to understand why categories (such as race) that seem obvious in the American context have been ignored not only by French historians but, more generally, in the representations that the French themselves make of their history and society. It is not given to everyone to be Tocqueville, however, and the contributors are properly cautious in making comparisons. Some are passionate about French politics, others seem indifferent to it, but more than a few allude to the tensions between the two countries, or at any rate their governments, in recent years. In its resistance to the new empire, France retains some of the values that justified the decision of some to make it a focus of research twenty or thirty years ago.

I know nearly all of the contributors to this volume personally, and some have long been friends of mine, so I hope that this brief commentary on their texts does not leave the impression that I found in them nothing but a record of disappointments and anxieties born of their deep knowledge of my fellow Frenchmen and French historians. In these autobiographical fragments there are splendid and moving passages on the loveliness of the French countryside, on the *art de vivre* in French provincial towns, and on the pleasures of a summer night in Paris after a long day in the archives or the Bibliothèque nationale. More impressive still are the memories of camaraderie, not only among expatriate American historians, who constitute a warm and mutually supportive community, but also with ordinary Frenchmen and historians (the population of France being divided between these two categories) which has led to long and faithful friendships. Hence there is no reason to give up hope in France. Yet among the things I enjoyed in these essays were the lack of patience with French national arrogance, the reminder that the world is much vaster than the small "hexagonal" excrescence on the European land mass, and the scathing description of a France that is no longer the traditional France of Richard Cobb but rather a country in which men and women who have come from various parts of the world with their own memories and their own culture live side by side and yet have no direct contact with one another. Thus not all the images in the mirror held up to the French reader are pleasant ones. But is not sincerity the first duty of a friend?

Notes

INTRODUCTION

1. See Edward Berenson and Nancy L. Green, "Quand l'Oncle Sam ausculte l'Hexagone: Les historiens américains et l'histoire de la France," *Vingtième siècle* 88 (October–December 2005): 121–31.

2. Jan Goldstein, "The Future of French History in the United States: Unapocalyptic Thoughts for the New Millennium," *French Historical Studies* 24, no. 1 (Winter 2001): 3–4. On the statistics above, see François Lagarde, "La France et les Français aux Etats-Unis," *France-Amérique,* April 30–May 6, 2005; on French immigration to America, see Ronald Creagh, *Nos cousins d'Amérique: Histoire des Français aux Etats-Unis* (Paris: Payot, 1988); on this "anomalous" American interest in French history, see Jeremy D. Popkin, "The American Historian of France and the 'Other,'" in *Objectivity and its Other,* ed. Wolfgang Natter, Theodore R. Schatzki, and John Paul Jones (New York: Guilford Press, 1995), 96.

3. Ralph Waldo Emerson, "The Conduct of Life" (1860), in his *Essays and Lectures* (New York: Library of America, 1983), 1023.

4. For this argument, see Frank Costigliola, *France and the United States: The Cold Alliance since World War II* (New York: Twayne Publishers, 1992). See also André Siegfried, *Les Etats-Unis d'aujourd'hui* (Paris: A. Colin, 1927), 313, cited in Jean-Baptiste Duroselle, *France and the United States: From the Beginnings to the Present Day,* trans. Derek Coltman (Chicago: University of Chicago Press, 1978), 245–46.

5. Harvey Levenstein, *We'll Always Have Paris: American Tourists in France Since 1930* (Chicago: University of Chicago Press, 2004), 280. See, for instance, Thomas Friedman, "Our War With France," *New York Times,* September 18, 2003; John J. Miller and Mark Molesky, *Our Oldest Enemy: A History of America's Disastrous Relationship with France* (New York: Doubleday, 2004); Kenneth Timmerman, *The French Betrayal of America* (New York: Crown, 2004); and Harlow Giles Unger, *The French War against America: How a Trusted Ally Betrayed Washington and the Founding Fathers* (Hoboken, NJ: Wiley, 2005).

6. Duroselle, *France and the United States,* 25.

7. On gender history, for instance, see Rebecca Rogers, "Rencontres, appropriations et zones d'ombre: les étapes d'un dialogue franco-américain sur l'histoire des femmes et du genre," *Revue d'Histoire des Sciences Humaines* 11 (December 2004): 101–26. See also *Libération,* July 6, 2005.

8. One could make an argument for the inclusion of other American scholars in this collection—literary critics, for instance. We decided to focus on one discipline (our own) in order to preserve the book's coherence and delineate a particular kind of relationship with France.

9. Richard Kuisel, "American Historians in Search of France: Perceptions and Misperceptions," *French Historical Studies* 19, no. 2 (Fall 1995): 307–19; R. R. Palmer, "A Century of French History in America," *French Historical Studies* 14, no. 2 (Autumn 1985): 160–75; Popkin, "The American Historian of France," cited above, and "Made in USA," *Revue d'histoire moderne et contemporaine* 40, no. 2 (April–June 1993): 303–20.

10. See, for instance, Steven Englund, "Note critique: Lieux de mémoire en débat," Politix 26 (June 1994): 168; and Natalie Zemon Davis, *L'histoire tout feu tout flamme: Entretiens avec Denis Crouzet* (Paris: Albin Michel, 2004).

11. All contributors are accomplished scholars and many teach in elite universities, but this book is not designed to be a pantheon. Likewise, a majority are Caucasian, of middle-class origin, and politically liberal—which is true of the profession as a whole. We did not, of course, inquire about class or politics prior to inviting contributors. We define American historians as citizens or long-term residents of the United States or Canada who obtained their doctorate from a North American university. See David H. Pinkney, "American Historians on the European Past," *American Historical Review* 86, no. 1 (February 1981): 1.

12. See Susan A. Crane's rich "Historical Subjectivity: A Review Essay," *Journal of Modern History* 78, no. 3 (June 2006): 434–56.

13. J. H. Hexter, *Reappraisals in History: New Views on History and Society in Early Modern Europe* (London: Longmans, 1961), 13, cited in John Higham, *History* (Englewood Cliffs, NJ: Prentice-Hall, 1965), 136; and Lewis P. Curtis Jr., *The Historian's Workshop: Original Essays by Sixteen Historians* (New York: Knopf, 1970), xiv–xv. On the autobiographical tradition among historians, see Luisa Passerini and Alexander C. T. Geppert, "European Ego-Histoires: Historiography and the Self, 1970–2000," introduction to *Historein* 3 (2001), 8–13. On historians' misgivings about self-revelation, see Pierre Nora, "L'ego-histoire est-elle possible?" in the same issue of *Historein,* 23; and Popkin, *History, Historians, and Autobiography* (Chicago: University of Chicago Press, 2005), 62–64. For autobiographical reflections by French literary critics, see for instance Alice Kaplan, *French Lessons: A Memoir* (Chicago: University of Chicago Press, 1993) and Nancy K. Miller, *But Enough about Me: Why We Read Other People's Lives* (New York: Columbia University Press, 2002).

14. Pivotal books include Hayden White, *Metahistory: The Historical Imagination in Nineteenth-Century Europe* (Baltimore: Johns Hopkins University Press, 1973); Michel de Certeau, *The Writing of History,* trans. Tom Conley (New York: Columbia University Press, 1988); and Pierre Nora, ed., *Essais d'ego-histoire* (Paris: Gallimard, 1987). On these trends, see Nora, "L'ego-histoire est-elle possible?," 20–22 ; Philippe Carrard, "History as a Kind of Writing: Michel de Certeau and the Poetics of Historiography," *South Atlantic Quarterly* 100, no. 2 (Spring 2001): 477; and, more broadly, Deborah H. Holdstein and David Bleich, eds., *Personal Effects: The Social Character of Scholarly Writing* (Logan: Utah State University Press, 2001). On the historian as author, see Olivier Dumoulin, *Le rôle social de l'historien: de la chaire au prétoire* (Paris: Albin Michel, 2003), 318–26.

15. Jeffrey Rubin-Dorsky and Shelley Fisher Fishkin, "Reconfiguring Jewish Identity in the Academy," in their collection *People of the Book: Thirty Scholars Reflect on their Jewish Identity* (Madison: University of Wisconsin Press, 1996), 8. See also Peter Alter, ed., *Out of the Third Reich: Refugee Historians in Post-War Britain* (London: I. B. Tauris, 1998); Eileen Boris and

Nupur Chaudhuri, eds., *Voices of Women Historians: The Personal, the Political, the Professional* (Bloomington: Indiana University Press, 1999); Paul A. Cimbala and Robert F. Himmelberg, eds., *Historians and Race: Autobiography and the Writing of History* (Bloomington: Indiana University Press, 1996); and C. L. Barney Dews and Carolyn Leste Law, eds., *This Fine Place So Far From Home: Voices of Academics from the Working Class* (Philadelphia: Temple University Press, 1995). See also, for instance, *Journal of American History* 89, no. 1 (June 2002), special issue on "Self and Subject"; and Roger Adelson, ed., *Speaking of History: Conversations with Historians* (East Lansing: Michigan State University Press, 1997).

16. There are few works of this kind. Samuel H. Baron and Cathy A. Frierson's *Adventures in Russian Historical Research: Reminiscences of American Scholars from the Cold War to the Present* (Armonk, NY: M. E. Sharpe, 2003) focuses on research experiences, whereas John B. Boles, ed., *Autobiographical Reflections on Southern Religious History* (Athens: University of Georgia Press, 2001) is concerned with historical vocations. In 1999, the journal *French Cultural Studies* devoted a special issue to the "personal voices" of British specialists in French Studies: Brian Rigby, ed., "Personal Voices: Personal Experiences," *French Cultural Studies*, vol. 10, part 3 (1999).

17. On this specifically American divide, see François Cusset, *French Theory: Foucault, Derrida, Deleuze & Cie et les mutations de la vie intellectuelle aux Etats-Unis* (Paris: La Découverte, 2003), 44–46. See, however, Crane Brinton, *The Americans and the French* (Cambridge, MA: Harvard University Press, 1968) or David A. Bell's recent contributions to *The New Republic*. On the American historian and the public, see Ian Tyrrell, *Historians in Public: The Practice of American History, 1890–1970* (Chicago: University of Chicago Press, 2005).

18. See the critique in Pierre Bourdieu, "L'illusion biographique," *Actes de la recherche en sciences sociales* 62–63 (1986): 69–72.

19. Historians have been making similar predictions for at least twenty-five years: see Pinkney, "American Historians on the European Past," 19.

20. These two paragraphs rest on Henry Blumenthal, *American and French Culture, 1800–1900: Interchanges in Art, Science, Literature, and Society* (Baton Rouge: Louisiana State University Press, 1975); James Buzard, *The Beaten Track: European Tourism, Literature, and the Ways to Culture, 1800–1918* (Oxford: Clarendon Press, 1993); William L. Chew III, "Life Before Fodor and Frommer: Americans in Paris from Thomas Jefferson to John Quincy Adams," *French History* 18, no. 1 (March 2004): 25–49 and, as editor, *National Stereotypes in Perspective: Americans in France, Frenchmen in America* (Amsterdam: Rodopi, 2001); Duroselle, *France and the United States;* Adam Gopnik, ed., *Americans in Paris: A Literary Anthology* (New York: Library of America, 2004); Nancy L. Green, "The Comparative Gaze: Travelers in France Before the Era of Mass Tourism," *French Historical Studies* 25, no. 3 (Summer 2002): 423–40; Levenstein, *Seductive Journey: American Tourists in France from Jefferson to the Jazz Age* (Chicago: University of Chicago Press, 1998) and *We'll Always Have Paris;* and Cushing Strout, *The American Image of the Old World* (New York: Harper and Row, 1963).

21. Guillaume de Bertier de Sauvigny, *La France et les Français vus par les voyageurs américains, 1814–1848,* 2 vols. (Paris: Flammarion, 1982–85); and Douglas C. Ridgley et al., *Home Study Course for European Travel* (Worcester, MA: Clark University, 193?). See also François Chaubet, "L'Alliance française ou la diplomatie de la langue (1883–1914)," *Revue historique* 632 (October 2004): 763–85; John L. Harvey, "The Common Adventure of Mankind: Academic Internationalism and Western Historical Practice from Versailles to Potsdam," Ph.D. diss., Pennsylvania State University, 2003; Whitney Walton, "Internationalism and the Junior Year Abroad: American Students in France in the 1920s and 1930s," *Diplomatic History* 29, no. 2 (April 2005): 255–78; and Robert Young, *Marketing Marianne: French Propaganda in America, 1900–1940* (New Brunswick, NJ: Rutgers University Press, 2004).

22. Saul Bellow, "My Paris," in *The Sophisticated Traveler. Beloved Cities: Europe,* ed. A. M.

Rosenthal and Arthur Gelb (New York: Penguin, 1985), 169; and Julia Child with Alex Prud'homme, *My Life in France* (New York: Knopf, 2006).

23. Thomas Jefferson, *Autobiography*, and Jefferson to Anne Willing Bingham, May 11, 1788, in *Writings*, ed. Merril D. Peterson (New York: Library of America, 1984), 922–23; and Anne C. Loveland, *Emblem of Liberty: The Image of Lafayette in the American Mind* (Baton Rouge: Louisiana State University Press, 1971), 89–93. On the allure of the French and French culture in Antebellum America, see Howard Mumford Jones, *America and French Culture, 1750–1848* (Chapel Hill: University of North Carolina Press, 1927); on France as arbiter of style, see Joan DeJean, *The Essence of Style: How the French Invented High Fashion, Fine Food, Chic Cafés, Style, Sophistication, and Glamour* (New York: Free Press, 2005).

24. Strout, *The American Image*, 29. See also Daniel J. Boorstin, *America and the Image of Europe: Reflections on American Thought* (Cleveland: World Publishing, 1960); and Stacey Schiff, "Found in Translation," *New York Times*, May 29, 2005.

25. Hart Crane, postcard to Samuel Loveman, January 23, 1929, quoted in Gopnik, ed. *Americans in Paris*, 335. The literature is vast: see, for instance, Petrine Archer-Straw, *Negrophilia: Avant-Garde Paris and Black Culture in the 1920s* (New York: Thames and Hudson, 2000); Donald Pizer, *American Expatriate Writing and the Paris Moment* (Baton Rouge: Louisiana State University Press, 1996); Christopher Sawyer-Lauçanno, *The Continual Pilgrimage: American Writers in Paris, 1944–1960* (San Francisco: City Lights, 1992); Tyler Stovall, *Paris Noir: African Americans in the City of Light* (New York: Houghton Mifflin, 1986); and William W. Stowe, *Going Abroad: European Travel in Nineteenth-Century American Culture* (Princeton: Princeton University Press, 1994).

26. Edith Wharton, *French Ways and Their Meaning* (1919; repr. Woodstock, VT: Countryman Press, 1997), 9; on Wharton and France, see Katherine Joslin and Alan Price, eds., *Wretched Exotic: Essays on Edith Wharton in Europe* (New York: Peter Lang, 1993). American progressives also traveled to Europe in search of models of urban planning or municipal government, but France was a secondary destination: see Daniel T. Rodgers, *Atlantic Crossings: Social Politics in a Progressive Age* (Cambridge, MA: Belknap, 1998); and Pierre-Yves Saunier, "Les voyages municipaux américains en Europe, 1900–1940. Une piste d'histoire transnationale," *Jarhbuch für Europäische Verwaltungsgeschichte* 15 (2003): 267–88. On European travel and American self-definition around 1900, see Christopher Endy, "Travel and World Power: Americans in Europe, 1890–1917," *Diplomatic History* 22, no. 4 (Fall 1998): 565–94. Consider also the more sanguine appraisals in Wanda M. Corn, *The Great American Thing: Modern Art and National Identity, 1915–1935* (Berkeley: University of California Press, 2000); and Mark Rennella and Whitney Walton, "Planned Serendipity: American Travelers and the Transatlantic Voyage in the Nineteenth and Twentieth Centuries," *Journal of Social History* 38, no. 4 (Winter 2004): 372–73.

27. This discussion rests on Leonard Krieger, "European History in America," *History*, ed. Higham, 233–311; William H. McNeill, "Modern European History," in Michael Kammen, ed., *The Past Before Us: Contemporary Historical Writing in the United States* (Ithaca, NY: Cornell University Press, 1980), 95–112; Palmer, "A Century of French History"; Popkin, "'Made in USA'"; and Fritz Stern, "German History in America, 1884–1984," *Central European History* 19, no. 2 (June 1986): 131–63.

28. Charles Homer Haskins, "European History and American Scholarship," *American Historical Review* 28, no. 2 (January 1923): 226; and Paul Gerbod, "L'enseignement de la langue française aux Etats-Unis (1900–1950)," *Revue historique* 576 (October–December 1990): 387–406. On historians and Germany, see Jurgen Herbst, *The German Historical School in American Scholarship: A Study in the Transfer of Culture* (Ithaca, NY: Cornell University Press, 1965); and Hartmut Lehmann and James J. Sheehan, eds., *An Interrupted Past: German-Speaking Refugee Historians in the United States after 1933* (Cambridge: Cambridge University Press, 1991). On the

Western Civilization course, see Gilbert Allardyce, "The Rise and Fall of the Western Civilization Course," *American Historical Review* 87, no. 3 (June 1982): 695–725; Agnès Bouchet-Sala, "The General Education Course at Stanford University (1935–1998): From Transmitting Substances to Structuring Metasubstance," *La Revue LISA/LISA e-journal 2,* no. 1 (2004): 140–53 (available at www.unicaen.fr/mrsh/lisa/publications/002/02j_bouchet.pdf); Sylvia Federici, "The God That Never Failed: The Origins and Crises of Western Civilization," in Federici, ed., *Enduring Western Civilization: The Construction of the Concept of Western Civilization and Its 'Others'* (Westport, CT: Praeger, 1995), 63–89; and Daniel A. Segal, "'Western Civ' and the Staging of History in American Higher Education," *American Historical Review* 105, no. 3 (June 2000): 770–805.

29. Robert A. McCaughey, *International Studies and Academic Enterprise: A Chapter in the Enclosure of American Learning* (New York: Columbia University Press, 1984); Randall Bennet Woods, "Fulbright Internationalism," *Annals of the American Academy of Political and Social Science* 491 (May 1987): 22–35; and Peter Novick, *That Noble Dream: The "Objectivity Question" and the American Historical Profession* (Cambridge: Cambridge University Press, 1988).

30. Henri Peyre, *History in Modern Culture* (New York: French Embassy, 1950), 9. Peyre was an expatriate Frenchman. The French History Society's founding members included the publisher Alfred A. Knopf, the director of the Metropolitan Museum of Art, and several French embassy officials, but it apparently did not last very long.

31. Thomas J. Schaeper, "French History as Written on Both Sides of the Atlantic: A Comparative Analysis," *French Historical Studies* 17, no. 1 (Spring 1991): 235–36; Berenson and Green, "The Society for French Historical Studies: The Early Years," *French Historical Studies* 28, no. 4 (Fall 2005): 579–600; Pinkney, "American Historians on the European Past"; and Popkin, "The American Historian of France."

32. Bellow, "My Paris," 175–76. On the progress of American consumerism in postwar Europe, see Victoria de Grazia, *Irresistible Empire: America's Advance through Twentieth-Century Europe* (Cambridge, MA: Belknap, 2005).

33. See Tony Judt, *Postwar: A History of Europe since 1945* (New York: Penguin Press, 2005).

34. Kaplan, *French Lessons,* 207.

35. Ibid., 132.

36. Richard Cobb, "Experiences of an Anglo-French Historian," in his *A Second Identity: Essays on France and French History* (London and New York: Oxford University Press, 1969), 18, 50.

37. Goldstein, "The Future of French History," 4.

38. While it would be risky to generalize from such a small sample, one cannot help but notice that the women's essays seem more attuned to this particular conflict.

39. Carolyn Walker Bynum, "The Last Eurocentric Generation," *Perspectives* 34, no. 2 (February 1996): 3–4. The authors thank Jerry Seigel for pointing out this reference

40. See Bertram M. Gordon, "The Decline of a Cultural Icon: France in American Perspective," *French Historical Studies* 22, no. 4 (Autumn 1999): 625–51.

41. Gayle K. Brunelle, professor of history, California State University at Fullerton, posting on H-France listserv, October 2005.

Contributors

KEN ALDER is Professor of History at Northwestern University, where he is the Milton H. Wilson Professor in the Humanities and directs the program in Science in Human Culture. He is the author of *Engineering the Revolution: Arms and Enlightenment in France, 1763–1815* (Princeton University Press, 1997) and *The Measure of All Things: The Seven-Year Odyssey and Hidden Error that Transformed the World* (Free Press, 2002), translated into French as *Mesurer le monde, 1792–1799: l'incroyable histoire de l'invention du mètre* (Flammarion, 2005).

JOHN W. BALDWIN is the Charles Homer Haskins Professor of History Emeritus at the Johns Hopkins University in Baltimore, Maryland. His most recent publications include *The Language of Sex: Five Voices from Northern France around 1200* (University of Chicago Press, 1994), *Aristocratic Life in Medieval France: The Romances of Jean Renart and Gerbert de Montreuil, 1190–1230* (Johns Hopkins University Press, 2000), and *Paris, 1200* (Aubier-Flammarion, 2006).

EDWARD BERENSON is Professor of History and Director of the Institute of French Studies at New York University. He is the author of *Populist Religion and Left-Wing Politics in France, 1830–1852* (Princeton University Press, 1984) and *The Trial of Madame Caillaux* (University of California Press, 1992). He is currently writing a book on the reception of empire, 1870–1914, to be published by the University of California Press.

HERRICK CHAPMAN is Associate Professor of History and French Studies at New York University. He is the author of *State Capitalism and Working-Class Radicalism in the French Aircraft Industry* (University of California Press, 1991) and coeditor of several books, including *Race in France: Interdisciplinary Perspectives on the Politics of Difference* (Berghahn, 2004). He is also the editor of the interdisciplinary journal *French Politics, Culture, and Society.*

ROGER CHARTIER is Directeur d'études at the École des Hautes Études en Sciences Sociales (Paris) and Annenberg Visiting Professor at the University of Pennsylvania. His books include *The Cultural Origins of the French Revolution* (Duke University Press, 1991), *The Order of Books* (Stanford University Press, 1994), *Forms and Meaning* (University of Pennsylvania Press, 1995), and *On the Edge of the Cliff: History, Language, Practices* (Johns Hopkins University Press, 1997).

CLARE HARU CROWSTON is Associate Professor of History at the University of Illinois at Urbana-Champaign. Her areas of interest include the history of women and gender, work, material culture, and consumption. She is the author of *Fabricating Women: The Seamstresses of Old Regime France, 1675–1791* (Duke University Press, 2001). Her current projects include a study of credit, fashion, and sex in eighteenth-century France and a joint study of apprenticeship in France from the seventeenth to the nineteenth century.

BARBARA B. DIEFENDORF is Professor of History at Boston University. She is the author of *Paris City Councillors: The Politics of Patrimony* (Princeton University Press, 1983), *Beneath the Cross: Catholics and Huguenots in Sixteenth-Century Paris* (Oxford University Press, 1991), and *From Penitence to Charity: Pious Women and the Catholic Reformation in Paris* (Oxford University Press, 2004).

LAURA LEE DOWNS is Directeur d'études at the Centre de Recherches Historiques, École des Hautes Études en Sciences Sociales (Paris). She is the author of *Manufacturing Inequality: Gender Division in the French and British Metalworking Industries, 1914–1939* (Cornell University Press, 1995), *Childhood in the Promised Land: Working-Class Movements and the Colonies de Vacances in France, 1880–1960* (Duke University Press, 2002), and *Writing Gender History* (Hodder Arnold, 2004).

STÉPHANE GERSON is Associate Professor of French and French Studies at New York University. He has written *The Pride of Place: Local Memories and Political Culture in Nineteenth-Century France* (Cornell University Press, 2003) and guest-edited a special issue of *French Politics, Culture, and Society* on "Alain Corbin and the Writing of History" (2004).

JAN GOLDSTEIN is Norman and Edna Freehling Professor of History at the University of Chicago and an editor of the *Journal of Modern History*. Her books include *Console and Classify: The French Psychiatric Profession in the Nineteenth Century* (Cambridge University Press, 1987; University of Chicago Press, 2001), *Foucault and the Writing of History* (Routledge, 1994), and *The Post-Revolutionary Self: Politics and Psyche in France, 1750–1850* (Harvard University Press, 2005).

LYNN HUNT is Eugen Weber Professor of Modern European History at UCLA. She is the author of *Politics, Culture, and Class in the French Revolution* (University of California Press, 1984, 2004) and *The Family Romance of the French Revolution* (University of California Press, 1992) and editor with Jacques Revel of *Histories: French Constructions of the Past* (New Press, 1995). She was President of the American Historical Association in 2002.

STEVEN LAURENCE KAPLAN is Goldwin Smith Professor of European History at Cornell University. He also teaches French social history each spring semester at the Université de Versailles-Saint-Quentin. Among his most recent writings are *La Fin des corporations* (Fayard, 2001), *Le Retour du bon pain: une histoire contemporaine du pain, de ses techniques et de ses hommes* (Perrin, 2002), *Cherchez le pain: Le Guide des meilleures boulangeries de Paris* (Plon, 2004), and editor with Philippe Minard of *La France, Malade du corporatisme?* (Belin, 2004).

THOMAS KSELMAN is Professor of History at the University of Notre Dame. He is the author of *Miracles and Prophecies in Nineteenth-Century France* (Rutgers University Press, 1983) and *Death and the Afterlife in Modern France* (Princeton University Press, 1993).

HERMAN LEBOVICS is Professor of History at Stony Brook University. For many years, he chaired the New York Area French History Seminar. His books include *True France: The Wars over Cultural Identity, 1900–1945* (Cornell University Press, 1992), *Mona Lisa's Escort: André Malraux and the Reinvention of French Culture* (Cornell University Press, 1999), *Bringing the Empire Back Home: France in the Global Age* (Duke University Press, 2004), and *Imperialism and the Corruption of Democracies* (Duke University Press, 2006).

ROBERT O. PAXTON is Professor Emeritus of History at Columbia University. His books include *Vichy France: Old Guard and New Order, 1940–1944,* second ed. (Columbia University Press, 2001), *French Peasant Fascism: Henry Dorgères's Greenshirts and the Crises of French Agriculture, 1929–1939* (Oxford University Press, 1997), and *The Anatomy of Fascism* (Knopf, 2004).

TODD SHEPARD is Assistant Professor of History at Temple University. He recently published *The Invention of Decolonization: The Algerian War and the Remaking of France* (Cornell University Press, 2006). He is currently writing a book on "integration" in France (1956–1962).

LEONARD V. SMITH is Frederick B. Artz Professor of History at Oberlin College. He is the author of *Between Mutiny and Obedience: The Case of the French Fifth Infantry Division during World War I* (Princeton University Press, 1994), coauthor of *France and the Great War, 1914–1918* (Cambridge University Press, 2003), and author of *The Embattled Self: French Soldiers' Testimonies of the Great War* (Cornell University Press, forthcoming in 2007).

GABRIELLE M. SPIEGEL is Krieger-Eisenhower Professor of History at the Johns Hopkins University, where she also serves as Chair of the Department of History and Acting Dean of Faculty. She is the author of *The Chronicle Tradition of Saint-Denis: A Survey* (Classical Folia, 1978), *Romancing the Past: The Rise of Vernacular Prose Historiography in Thirteenth-Century France* (University of California Press, 1993), and *The Past as Text: The Theory and Practice of Medieval Historiography* (Johns Hopkins University Press, 1997). She recently edited *Practicing History: New Directions in Historical Writing after the Linguistic Turn* (Routledge, 2005).

TYLER STOVALL is Professor of History at the University of California, Berkeley. He is the author of *The Rise of the Paris Red Belt* (University of California Press, 1990) and *Paris Noir: African Americans in the City of Light* (Houghton Mifflin, 1996). Most recently, he and Georges Van Den Abbeele edited *French Civilization and its Discontents: Nationalism, Colonialism, and Race* (Rowman and Littlefield, 2003).